Public Sector
Entrepreneurship

Public Sector Entrepreneurship

U.S. Technology and Innovation Policy

DENNIS PATRICK LEYDEN

and

ALBERT N. LINK

OXFORD
UNIVERSITY PRESS

OXFORD
UNIVERSITY PRESS

Oxford University Press is a department of the University of
Oxford. It furthers the University's objective of excellence in research,
scholarship, and education by publishing worldwide.

Oxford   New York
Auckland   Cape Town   Dar es Salaam   Hong Kong   Karachi
Kuala Lumpur   Madrid   Melbourne   Mexico City   Nairobi
New Delhi   Shanghai   Taipei   Toronto

With offices in
Argentina   Austria   Brazil   Chile   Czech Republic   France   Greece
Guatemala   Hungary   Italy   Japan   Poland   Portugal   Singapore
South Korea   Switzerland   Thailand   Turkey   Ukraine   Vietnam

Oxford is a registered trademark of Oxford University Press
in the UK and certain other countries.

Published in the United States of America by
Oxford University Press
198 Madison Avenue, New York, NY 10016

Library of Congress Cataloging-in-Publication Data
Leyden, Dennis Patrick.
Public sector entrepreneurship : U.S. technology and innovation policy / Dennis Patrick Leyden,
Albert N. Link.
pages cm
Includes bibliographical references and index.
ISBN 978–0–19–931385–3 (alk. paper)
1. Public-private sector cooperation.   2. Entrepreneurship—United States.
3. Public administration—United States.   4. Technology and state—United States.
5. Technological innovations—Government policy—United States.   I. Link, Albert N.
II. Title.
HD3872.U6L49 2015
338.973—dc23
2014024786

1 3 5 7 9 8 6 4 2
Printed in the United States of America
on acid-free paper

for Peggy; for Carol

CONTENTS

ACKNOWLEDGMENTS

This book represents the evolution of our thought about entrepreneurial dimensions of government's role in technology and innovation policy. As we note in the first chapter, our journey along this path could be dated to the publication of our joint effort in 1992: *Government's Role in Innovation*. Since then, our colleagues at the University of North Carolina at Greensboro, along with our virtual colleagues at other institutions, have encouraged us to continue to develop related themes and have offered helpful guidance for which we are greatly appreciative. Toward that end, we have benefited from and remain thankful for comments and suggestions from the many scholars with whom we presented our ideas at conferences sponsored by the Organization for Economic Co-Operation and Development (OECD), the Asia-Pacific Economic Cooperation (APEC), the United Nations, and the U.S. National Academies.

We are especially pleased to thank attendees of a number of conferences for their insight on public sector entrepreneurship. These conferences include the 2010 joint conference in Helsinki sponsored by the United Nations Economic Commission for Europe (UNECE) and the Ministries of Employment and the Economy and Foreign Affairs of Finland; the 2010 annual conference of the American Association for the Advancement of Science (AAAS) in Washington, DC; the 2013 UNECE conference on innovation in the public sector in Geneva; and, most recently, the 2014 conference on entrepreneurship, employment dynamics, and productivity at the OECD.

Terry Vaughn, former economics editor at Oxford University Press, and Scott Parris, the current economics editor at Oxford, have been very supportive through the writing and preparation of this book. For that we are very grateful.

Lastly, our wives, Peggy and Carol, have embraced this project through their continued love and patience, and for that they have our heartfelt thanks.

ABOUT THE AUTHORS

Dennis Patrick Leyden is an associate professor of economics at the University of North Carolina at Greensboro (UNCG). He received his B.A. in economics with high honors from the University of Virginia, and his M.S. and Ph.D. from Carnegie Mellon University. He has been a member of the economics faculty at UNCG since 1984.

Professor Leyden's current research focuses on entrepreneurship in both the public and private sector, and on the role and behavior of universities in furthering such entrepreneurial activity and its impact on innovation and economic development. In addition to prior work on R&D policy, he has conducted research on bureaucratic, legislative, and court behavior in the context of public education funding. His books include *Adequacy, Accountability, and the Future of Public Education Funding* (Springer, 2005) and *Government's Role in Innovation* (Kluwer, 1992).

Recent conferences at which he has spoken include *Universities, Innovation, and Territory* (University of Barcelona, Barcelona, Spain), *Science and Technology Research in a Knowledge-based Economy* (University of Torino, Torino, Italy), *Academic Policy and the Knowledge Theory of Entrepreneurship* (University of Augsburg, Augsburg, Germany), and *Policies for Innovation and Knowledge-based Development in the 21st Century: Innovation in the Public Sector* (Team of Specialists on Innovation and Competitiveness Policies, UNECE, Geneva, Switzerland).

Albert N. Link is a professor of economics at the University of North Carolina at Greensboro (UNCG). He received, with honors, a B.S. in mathematics from the University of Richmond and a Ph.D. in economics from Tulane University. After receiving his Ph.D., he joined the economics faculty at Auburn University, where he remained until joining the economics faculty at UNCG in 1982.

Professor Link's research focuses on entrepreneurship, technology and innovation policy, the economics of R&D, and policy/program evaluation. He is currently the editor-in-chief of the *Journal of Technology Transfer*. Among his more than 40 books, some of the more recent ones are *Handbook for University Technology Transfer* (University of Chicago Press, 2014), *Bending the Arc of Innovation: Public Support of R&D in Small, Entrepreneurial Firms* (Palgrave Macmillan, 2013), *Valuing an Entrepreneurial Enterprise* (Oxford University Press, 2012), *Public Goods, Public Gains* (Oxford University Press, 2011), *Employment Growth from Public Support of Innovation in Small Firms* (W.E. Upjohn Institute for Employment Research, 2011), and *Government as Entrepreneur* (Oxford University Press, 2009). His other research consists of more than 130 peer-reviewed journal articles and book chapters, as well as numerous government reports. His scholarship has appeared in such journals as the *American Economic Review*, the *Journal of Political Economy*, the *Review of Economics and Statistics, Economica*, and *Research Policy*.

Professor Link was a member of the National Research Council's research team that formulated a survey instrument and analyzed the survey findings for its evaluation of the Small Business Innovation Research (SBIR) program. Professor Link subsequently testified before Congress in April 2011 on the economic benefits associated with the SBIR program.

Among other accomplishments, Professor Link was tapped by the State Department in 2007 to serve as the U.S. representative to the UNECE in Geneva (2007–2012).

Public Sector Entrepreneurship

1

Introduction

Two roads diverged in a wood, and I—I took the one less traveled
by, and that has made all the difference.
                                                    —Robert Frost

About the Title of This Book

The phrase *public sector entrepreneurship* has had increasing currency in recent
years, but even a cursory look at its uses suggests that it often means quite
different things to different people, so much so that it is a reasonable question
whether the idea of public sector entrepreneurship has any meaning at
all. However, despite the wide variety of usages by scholars from other disciplines,
we argue that *public sector entrepreneurship* can be defined precisely in a
manner that is both consistent with a more than three-centuries-old literature
on entrepreneurship and, more importantly, a useful construct for analyzing
public sector policies and behaviors.

Consider, then, three questions: What is meant by the term *public sector*?
What is meant by the term *entrepreneurship*? And what is the relationship
between the public sector and entrepreneurship?

Although this book focuses on federal government policies, the term *public
sector* and the concepts that we develop are applicable to all levels of government:
federal, state, and local. Our focus is on the federal government because
that is where the most significant public policy examples of public sector entrepreneurship
have taken place.

We use the term *entrepreneurship* to describe activities by those in the public
sector that roughly align with what it is that a private sector entrepreneur does.
However, such a definition of the term *entrepreneurship* is tautological; it necessitates
that we be more specific about the relevant characteristics of an entrepreneur.
In Chapters 2 and 3 we do elaborate on entrepreneurship; for now,
consider an entrepreneur one who perceives an opportunity heretofore unexploited
and who acts on that opportunity. Thus, entrepreneurship involves perception
and action,[1] and perception and action imply that entrepreneurship

needs to be understood as a dynamic functional concept instead of a static or descriptive one. Entrepreneurship is best understood in terms of a time dimension rather than in terms of individual characteristics.

What then of the relationship between the public sector and entrepreneurship? Even with these introductory definitions of the terms *public sector* and *entrepreneurship*, some dissonance may remain about the relationship between the topics of the public sector and entrepreneurship because of the long history of thinking about entrepreneurship in purely private sector terms.[2]

Certainly, it is true that those scholars who have contributed to the intellectual history of who the entrepreneur is and what he or she (hereafter, he) does have focused on the entrepreneur in a private sector market environment. Those markets operate through the laws of supply and demand, and economic actors within markets—entrepreneurs in particular—are viewed as responding to explicit and implicit prices in an effort to maximize profits, the result being that the entrepreneur plays a significant role in determining both positively and normatively the outcomes of those private sector markets.

Given that intellectual history and the fact that public sector actors rarely, if ever, operate primarily within a private sector market environment or have the possibility of earning personal profit through the activities that they pursue,[3] it would appear that there is little room for the notion of entrepreneurship within a public sector context. However, such a view confuses the specific context in which the entrepreneur operates with the fundamental characteristics of the entrepreneur, namely opportunity recognition and the pursuit of those opportunities. While the specific nature of the opportunities as well as the motivation of the public sector may, and in all likelihood will, differ, public sector actors recognize opportunities and pursue them when they perceive such pursuits to be beneficial and when they are not constrained by the public sector environment in which they function.[4] Furthermore, public sector agents respond to more than incentives signaled by the market.

All of this is not to argue that public sector actors never engage in private sector market activity or that they do not influence market activity directly or indirectly. Indeed today, one of the objects of public policy from an economic perspective is growth and development. However, as we illustrate in this chapter's appendix with a simple example, not all public sector policies that are intent on influencing market activity are entrepreneurial. What makes them entrepreneurial is that they are associated with the recognition and exploitation of opportunities heretofore not exploited, and hence they are associated with the special type of risk that is associated with the unknown (i.e., with uncertainty).

Throughout this book we illustrate our conceptualization of public sector entrepreneurship using examples from U.S. technology and innovation policy. This particular policy focus is not by chance. Technology policy—policy to enhance the application of new knowledge, learned through science, to some known problem—and innovation policy—policy to enhance the commercialization of a technology—are the academic basis of what we have researched for decades, and thus it is familiar ground.[5] But more to the point, technology and innovation policy is arguably a quintessential example of public sector entrepreneurship.

Technology and innovation policies transcend the policy agendas of all industrialized nations because technology and innovation are the drivers of economic growth and development. While the examples that we discuss are based on the technology and innovation policy history of the United States, they are relevant to other nations. All nations will be addressing various issues of economic growth and development in the decades ahead (and some might even say that the issues to be addressed are long overdue). And, as we discuss in the chapters that follow, many of these issues will drive, at least in part, future technology and innovation policies. It will then be incumbent on public sector leaders to think entrepreneurially as they formulate initiatives to meet these demands.

The remainder of this book explores public sector entrepreneurship as a lens through which to view economic public policies that, like most entrepreneurial actions, alter the status quo and bring about change and efficiency. Our more formal definition of *public sector entrepreneurship* is given below.

Ideally, we would like to present in parallel in the following chapters one technology or innovation policy that is entrepreneurial and another that is not. Then—again ideally—we would like to illustrate that the entrepreneurial policy is more efficient and effective than the non-entrepreneurial policy, thus making the case that it is important for the public sector to act entrepreneurially when it comes to the promulgation of policy. However, this is not the format of the chapters that follow, and we doubt that such a counterfactual experiment is even possible within the realm of technology and innovation policy because each policy has a dynamic and often unique character. Rather, what is in the chapters that follow is the development of the concept of public sector entrepreneurship. We illustrate that construct in terms of well-motivated, yet selectively chosen, technology and innovation policies, and we explore empirically how, as a group, these polices have been effective in stimulating the U.S. economy.

A Road That Has Been Traveled

We are not the first to think about public sector entrepreneurship. Other scholars have laid an intellectual path for us to follow, although we follow it from an economic perspective.

The intellectual history of public sector entrepreneurship is clearly an out-growth of a more general literature on entrepreneurship that goes back three centuries. Chapter 2 describes the details of that literature, but for the purposes of better understanding the more recent literature on public sector entrepreneurship, it helps to start with a brief summary of the more general entrepreneurship literature.

Entrepreneur has meant different things to different authors. Some (Adam Smith, 1723–1790, the earliest proponent of this view) emphasized the entrepreneur as a capitalist, that is, someone who provides financial capital. Others—the list is long but it includes such notable writers as François Quesnay (1694–1774), Amasa Walker (1799–1875), John Stuart Mill (1806–1873), Léon Walras (1834–1910), and Carl Menger (1840–1921)—emphasized the entrepreneur as some type of decision-maker (e.g., owner, manager, employer, or contractor) in an enterprise. Others emphasized the social role of the entrepreneur: an industrial leader (Jean-Baptiste Say, 1767–1832), an allocator of resources among alternative uses (T. W. Schultz, 1902–1998), or even an arbitrageur (Israel Kirzner, 1930–).

Yet, for all these different views, the two that dominate the literature are those of the entrepreneur as innovator and as risk-taker. Richard Cantillon (1680–1734), who was the first writer to use the word *entrepreneur* in the modern sense in his *Essai* (1755), characterized the entrepreneur as the central figure in the private sector marketplace. The entrepreneur for Cantillon was the intermediary who, through creativity and a willingness to assume risk, guided the production process to assure that demands in the marketplace were satisfied. Abbé Nicolas Baudeau (1730–1792) and later Jeremy Bentham (1748–1832) picked up on Cantillon's argument, refining and emphasizing the role of the entrepreneur as an innovator. But it was Joseph Schumpeter (1883–1950) who, in our opinion, has been most influential in characterizing the entrepreneur as an innovator. Part of this influence is no doubt due to historical and geographical accident—he studied and taught in Austria, Germany, Japan, and the United States. But part of that influence is also due to his ability to frame his view of the entrepreneur as innovator within a broader macroeconomic theory of economic growth, famously known as "creative destruction."

While Schumpeter emphasized the role of the entrepreneur as innovator, and indeed elevated it to the primary role, he rejected the notion that risk-taking was also a characteristic. For him, risk-taking—along with many of the other roles noted above—was not essential to the character of the entrepreneur. Entrepreneurs might engage in these other activities, but all except the role of innovator could be delegated to others. It is because of Schumpeter's forceful arguments that the dominant view today is of the entrepreneur as innovator, not necessarily as risk-taker.

But the argument that risk-taking is equally important had other propo-
nents. The most notable early proponent was J. H. von Thünen (1785–1850),
who first combined the risk-taking argument of Cantillon with the innovation
arguments of Baudeau and Bentham and then developed a theory of entrepreneurial profits consistent with the notion of the entrepreneur as innovator
and risk-taker. It was Frank Knight (1885–1972), however, after the influence of Schumpeter had been felt, who revived the notion of the entrepreneur as risk-taker and reintegrated it with the notion of the entrepreneur as
innovator. Key to that revival and integration was distinguishing two types of
risk—those that are insurable and those that are not. Insurable risks, which
Knight called *risk*, are those for which possible outcomes and probabilities are
known. Uninsurable risks, which Knight called *uncertainty*, are those for which
possible outcomes are not fully known or for which probabilities are not known.
Simple risk, Knight argued, was no problem for private sector markets. It could
be priced like any other good and hence dealt with efficiently. But the risk due
to uncertainty could not be priced like any other good, and therefore those who
would bear it, whom Knight called *entrepreneurs*, were those who were willing
to make a leap of faith, that is, to make decisions without complete knowledge,
either certain or with simple risk, about the circumstance. And it was therefore
the entrepreneur who bore for good or for bad the returns for such exposure.

What then are examples of these two types of risk? Simple risks are those
risks that come from investment and business activities for which there is a
long and known track record or for which one can logically calculate the outcomes and probabilities. Thus, investment in a broad portfolio of stocks is an
example of simple risk, as is betting on the role of dice. Risks due to uncertainty however cannot be objectively assessed. For Knight, the best example of
such was that of innovation, the hallmark of the Schumpeterian entrepreneur.
By definition, innovation is about doing something never done before, that has
no prior track record, and whose impact cannot be deduced logically. Thus, the
entrepreneur is fundamentally an innovator, but to be an innovator means to
be willing to bear the risk that comes from uncertainty.

The concept of *public sector entrepreneurship*, while clearly grounded on
the more general notion of entrepreneurship, is of more recent vintage.[6] The
first mention of the notion seems to have arisen almost simultaneously in
the economics literature and the public administration and political science
literatures in the mid-1960s with a brief mention by Wagner (1966) and a
more methodical treatment by Ostrom (1964). For Wagner, a public sector
entrepreneur was simply someone who supplied collective benefits for political profit (he made no reference to Schumpeter's very similar notion). The
public sector entrepreneur, as Wagner characterized him, operated through
the expenditure and service mechanisms of government—what we call direct
public sector entrepreneurship—rather than by altering the private sector

market environment to induce desirable behaviors on the part of private sector entrepreneurs—what we call indirect public sector entrepreneurship. There is no recognition of the subtleties raised by Schumpeter and Knight, among others, as discussed in Chapter 2, regarding innovation or risk, be it simple risk or uncertainty. Ostrom, in contrast, has a richer notion of public sector entrepreneurship, arguing that it is fundamentally about innovation. But while Wagner was quite specific about motivations (i.e., political profit), Ostrom was agnostic. Like Wagner, however, Ostrom did not consider the role played by risk.

In the subsequent economics literature, as summarized in Table 1.1, little came of these initial analyses.[7] What was written tended to follow Wagner's view that the public sector entrepreneur was self-serving (Casson 2003, Holcombe 2002, Shockley et al. 2006, Schnellenbach 2007), a view that is consistent with the neoclassical economics assumption of utility maximization. But a utility-maximizing individual is not necessarily motivated by personal aggrandizement, and it should be noted that Hughes (1991) and Link and Link (2009) suggested motivations more closely tied to the putative economic purpose of government. For all these authors, with the exception of Link and Link, the public sector entrepreneur worked within the normal mechanism of government as Wagner had characterized—direct public sector entrepreneurship. The possibility of indirect public sector entrepreneurship policy was not considered. Link and Link are the only authors who suggested that public sector entrepreneurship can also operate indirectly by altering the private sector market environment in which the private sector entrepreneur operated. All of these writers, with the exception of Casson, at least implicitly argued that public sector entrepreneurs are like their private sector counterparts—innovators, as Schumpeter had maintained. But none of them, with the exception of Link and Link, either recognized the distinction between ordinary risks and the risks associated with uncertainty or argued that the willingness to bear the risks associated with uncertainty is a fundamental characteristic of the public sector entrepreneur. And none of the authors explored the process of innovation itself or attempted to characterize the underlying process or production function of innovation. Innovation was essentially an exogenous presence ready to arise spontaneously and seemingly costlessly under the right circumstances.

The public administration and political science literatures, in contrast to the economics literature, have made more use of the concept of public sector entrepreneurship, though much of that has been with only passing mention of the idea rather than explicit examination of the concept. For those who have explored the concept explicitly, there is little sense of a convergence of views. As Table 1.1 summarizes, what the public sector has been considered to be has varied considerably. For some (Jones 1978, Ramamurti 1986, Schneider

Table 1.1 **Who Is a Public Sector Entrepreneur?**

Author(s)	The public sector entrepreneur is a person who . . .	Motivation	Innovation	Uncertainty	Networks	Direct	Indirect
ECONOMICS LITERATURE							
Wagner 1966	supplies collective benefits for political profit.	Political profit	No	No	No	Yes	No
Casson 1982, 2003	specializes in making judgmental decisions about the coordination of scarce resources.	Career advancement	No	No	No	Yes	No
Hughes 1991	is a bureaucrat who makes discretionary decisions.	Bureaucratic mission	Yes	No	No	Yes	No
Holcombe 2002	observes and acts on a political profit opportunity.	Political profit	Yes	No	No	Yes	No
Shockley et al. 2006	is "alert to, and acts on, potential political profit opportunities."	Political profit	Yes	No	No	Yes	No
Schnellenbach 2007	promotes non-incremental changes in political paradigms.	Personal utility	Yes	No	No	Yes	No
Link and Link 2009	takes innovative actions in the face of risk.	Innovation and economic growth	Yes	Yes	No	Yes	Yes

(continued)

Table 1.1 **(Continued)**

Author(s)	The public sector entrepreneur is a person who...	Motivation	Innovation	Uncertainty	Networks	Direct	Indirect
MANAGEMENT LITERATURE							
Boyett 1997	is in the public sector and has the ability to spot and exploit market opportunities.	Idiosyncratic, perhaps influenced by higher ups	No	No	No	Yes	No
Morris and Jones 1999	creates value for citizens by combining resources to exploit social opportunities.	Power, achievement	Yes	No	No	Yes	No
Sadler 2000	identifies and exploits value-enhancing opportunities through innovations in uncertain environments.	Non-monetary objectives	Yes	No	No	Yes	No
Zerbinati and Soutaris 2005	discovers and exploits rewarding opportunities without control of required resources.	Non-monetary career enhancements	Yes	No	No	Yes	No
Klein et al. 2009, 2011	experiments with resource combinations to achieve social objectives.	Personal benefit	Yes	Yes	No	Yes	Yes

Source	Description	Motivation					
Zampetakis and Moustakis 2010	is a civil servant who generate and use innovative resource combinations to create value.	To create social value	Yes	No	No	Yes	No
Padt and Luloff 2011	is competitive, enterprising, customer driven, anticipatory, market oriented, and catalytic.	Mission Driven	No	No	No	Yes	No
Hisrich and Al-Dabbagh 2012	initiates "change by adapting, innovating and assuming risk" with a focus on the organization and not the self.	Personal power and achievement	Yes	No	No	Yes	No
PUBLIC ADMINISTRATION/POLITICAL SCIENCE LITERATURE							
Ostrom 1964, 2005	produces public goods via creation of new, innovative non-market organizations in changing environments.	Diverse interests (social benefit, personal respect, income, etc.)	Yes	No	No	Yes	No
Jones 1978	maximizes net return through rational analysis with complete information.	Personal profit	No	No	No	No	No
Kingdon 1984	attempts to control public policy from outside or inside the government.	Personal utility, altruism, ideology, etc.	No	No	No	Yes	No

(continued)

Table 1.1 (Continued)

Author(s)	The public sector entrepreneur is a person who…	Motivation	Innovation	Uncertainty	Networks	Direct	Indirect
Ramamurti 1986	"undertakes purposeful activity to initiate, maintain, or aggrandize … public sector organizations."	Achievement and power	Yes	No	No	Yes	No
Kirchheimer 1989	starts and manages new organizations, produces new services, applies innovative strategies, and is willing to bear risk.	N/a	Yes	No	No	Yes	No
Bellone and Goerl 1992	seeks new revenue sources for economic development and to create more private sector entrepreneurs.	Responsible administration consistent with democratic values	Yes	No	No	Yes	Yes
Osborne and Gaebler 1992	uses resources in new ways to maximize productivity and effectiveness.	Mission driven	Yes	No	No	Yes	No
Roberts 1992, 1999	generates an innovative idea, designs a plan to bring that idea to fruition, and implements that plan.	N/a	Yes	No	No	Yes	No

Source	Description	Outcome				
Schneider and Teske 1992, Schneider et al., 1995	acts in the political arena for political profit.	Political profit, reputation, satisfaction, financial return	Yes	No	Yes	Yes
Moon 1999	enhances customer satisfaction, reduces red tape, or engages in risk-taking.	Greater efficiency	Yes	No	Yes	No
Oakerson and Parks 1988	has the ability and freedom to exercise initiative.	Satisfy citizen demand	No	No	Yes	No
Bernier and Hafsi 2007	builds a public organization or increases its ability to deliver services of value.	Social and political goals	Yes	No	Yes	No

and Teske 1992, Schneider et al. 1995), the public sector entrepreneur was, as Wagner had argued initially, interested solely in personal aggrandizement through the manipulation of the political or the institutional apparatus of government. For others (Bellone and Goerl 1992, Osborne and Gaebler 1992, Moon 1999, Oakerson and Parks 1988, Bernier and Hafsi 2007), the public sector entrepreneur was a manager dedicated to fulfilling the mission of his public organization through improved efficiency and greater responsiveness to social needs. Though there appears to be no connection, the similarity here to the older entrepreneurship literature and the works of Mill, Walras, and Schultz is interesting. However, Kingdon (1984) viewed the notion of the public sector entrepreneur more broadly, as anyone in or out of government who sought to control public policy through the use of resources and effort. And still others, such as Kirchheimer (1989) and Roberts (1992, 1999), focused less on motivation, choosing to focus instead simply on behavior (similar to Schumpeter's view of the entrepreneur as innovator). That is not to say, however, that the other scholars did not recognize innovation at least implicitly: Ramamurti et al., Osborne and Gaebler, Schneider and Teske, Schneider et al., Moon, and Bernier and Hafsi certainly did. But like the economics literature, these have no exploration of the process of innovation; it is exogenous, seemingly arising spontaneously and costlessly.

With regard to the form of public sector entrepreneurship, most of the authors in the public administration and political science literatures—like most of their counterparts in the economics literature—only recognized direct public sector entrepreneurship as an option. The exceptions (Bellone and Goerl 1992, Schneider and Teske 1992, Schneider et al.1995), however, are instructive. Bellone and Goerl argued that there may be incentives for indirect public sector entrepreneurship because of the greater latitude that such activity affords in terms of entrepreneurial autonomy and accountability. Interestingly, Terry (1993, p. 394), in an otherwise critical response to Bellone and Goerl's main point that public sector entrepreneurship can and ought to be in line with the democratic values inherent in responsible government administration, provides forceful arguments in support of that conclusion: direct public sector entrepreneurship, because of its "heavy reliance on domination and coercion, a preference for revolutionary change (regardless of circumstances), and a disrespect for tradition," is inherently and unavoidably in conflict with the democratic values essential for responsible government administration. Schneider and Teske hinted, and Schneider et al. provided specific evidence that indirect public sector entrepreneurship is a relatively common occurrence at the local governmental level.[8]

Finally, with respect to risk, only two authors (Kirchheimer, Moon) include risk as a fundamental characteristic of the public sector entrepreneur. But neither distinguished simple risk from the risk due to uncertainty, and a careful reading of their works indicates that the risk they had in mind was simple, or insurable, risk, not the risk due to uncertainty.

Before moving on, it is important to note that there is also an important management literature on public sector entrepreneurship. Though of more recent origin than the economics, public administration, and political science literatures—the first reference we have is from 1997—it has been relatively active since then. As in the other literatures, writers in the management literature split on whether the public sector entrepreneur is motivated by personal gain (Morris and Jones 1999, Sadler 2000, Zerbinati and Souitaris 2005, Klein et al. 2009 and 2011, Hisrich and Al-Dabbagh 2013) or reasons attached to increasing social value and fulfilling an organizational mission (Boyett 1997, Zampetakis and Moustakis 2010, Padt and Luloff 2011). While all the literatures generally include innovation as a characteristic of the public sector entrepreneur, the management literature emphasizes the role of innovation and the exploitation of opportunities more distinctly than the other literatures; only Boyett and Padt and Luloff did not. But the management literature is like the others in its understanding of the process of innovation as exogenous and seemingly spontaneous and costless.

The same parallel with the other literatures exists with respect to the distinction between direct and indirect public sector entrepreneurship. With two exceptions, all of the management literature authors have focused solely on direct public sector entrepreneurship. The two exceptions are the Klein et al. (2009, 2011) working papers that argued more forcefully than any other author in this review that public sector entrepreneurship is fundamentally about altering the "the institutional environment or the rules of the game (constitutions, laws, norms, property rights and regulatory systems)" within which private sector entrepreneurs operate (Klein et al. 2009, p. 17). Thus, for Klein et al., public sector entrepreneurship is fundamentally indirect. Likewise, Klein et al. are the only authors other than Link and Link to explicitly recognize Knight's distinction between ordinary risk and the risk due to uncertainty, and to clearly associate public sector entrepreneurship with the willingness to bear uncertainty.

Defining Public Sector Entrepreneurship

In summary, then, the extant literature on public sector entrepreneurship generally—though not universally—associates innovation and the direct use of the mechanisms of governmental institutions with the public sector entrepreneur. However, while there are a few authors who have recognized at least the presence of indirect public sector entrepreneurial behavior and the role that Knightian uncertainty plays in that behavior, the vast majority recognized neither. And no author has explored the process of innovation itself. It has therefore been implicitly treated as an exogenous process that arises spontaneously and costlessly under particular circumstances.

It is our view that public sector entrepreneurship is a variant of the more general notion of entrepreneurship, which, in a private sector setting, has been the subject of study for three centuries. What makes public sector entrepreneurship different is not its fundamental modus operandi but rather its observable behaviors that are due, as one might expect, to the different institutional environment in which it operates.[9] Thus, the public sector entrepreneur, like his private sector counterpart, seeks to identify and exploit heretofore unexploited opportunities, and this means that the public sector entrepreneur engages in a process of innovation whose outcome is uncertain. In contrast to the private sector, the public sector innovation process focuses on government policies of one form or another. Those policies may be directed toward a variety of ends ranging from purely personal aggrandizement to a desire to improve the common weal, and those policies can take either a direct form (i.e., manifest in the creation or control of government bureaus for the purpose of producing goods or services) or an indirect form (i.e., changes in private sector rules of the game through changes in laws, regulations, etc.) that attempt to induce primarily private sector behavior toward the desired end.[10] Although public sector entrepreneurship may manifest itself in direct or indirect form, we are persuaded by the argument in Klein et al. (2009) that there are significant institutional and cultural impediments to personal aggrandizement as well as to the use of direct forms of public sector entrepreneurial policy. As a result, public sector entrepreneurship will tend to be manifested indirectly through changes in laws and regulations. In an economic context, such goals will focus broadly on economic growth and prosperity by transforming a status-quo economic environment into one that is more conducive to economic units engaging in creative activities in the face of uncertainty. While the ability to engage in such creative activities can be affected by a range of policies, the dominant method by which public sector entrepreneurship can improve that transformation today is by increasing the effectiveness of social networks, that is, by increasing the heterogeneity of experiential ties among economic units and the ability of those same economic units to exploit (i.e., to learn from) such diversity.[11]

Thus, stated more succinctly, public sector entrepreneurship refers to innovative public policy initiatives that generate greater economic prosperity by transforming a status-quo economic environment into one that is more conducive to economic units engaging in creative activities in the face of uncertainty. Through policy initiatives that are characterized by public sector entrepreneurship, there will be more development of new technology and hence more innovation throughout the economy.

The Evolution of Our Ideas

The ideas and concepts that we present in this book have, like most ideas, evolved over time. Looking back—and retrospection is never perfect—the seeds for the concept of public sector entrepreneurship may have come from our initial research on government's role in innovation in general, and in public-private partnerships in particular (Leyden and Link 1992). But certainly, our ideas began to crystallize as a result of a change in direction by the U.S. Office of Technology Policy (1996a, 1996b) with regard to the role and structure of classified public-private partnerships in the United States.

In an influential report, *Effective Partnering: A Report to Congress on Federal Technology Partnerships*, the Office of Technology Policy took the position that U.S. public-private partnerships have evolved from a relationship wherein the government is merely a customer of private research to a relationship wherein the government is a partner in research. In other words, the Office of Technology Policy's taxonomy stressed the evolution of the public role in technology-based partnerships.

> By the late 1980s, a new paradigm of technology policy had developed. In contrast to the enhanced spin-off programs—enhancements that made it easier for the private sector to commercialize the results of mission R&D—the government developed new public/private partnerships to develop and deploy advanced technologies. ... [T]hese new programs ... incorporate features that reflect increased influence from the private sector over project selection, management, and intellectual property ownership. Along with increased input, private sector partners also absorb a greater share of the costs, in some cases paying over half of the project cost.
>
> The new paradigm has several advantages for both government and the private sector. By treating the private sector as a partner in federal programs, government agencies can better incorporate feedback and focus programs. Moreover, the *private sector as partner* [emphasis added] approach allows the government to measure whether the programs are ultimately meeting their goals: increasing research efficiencies and effectiveness and developing and deploying new technologies. (Office of Technology Policy 1996a, pp. 33–34)

Figure 1.1 draws from the Office of Technology Policy report, and it is a clear illustration of the office's new approach.

Over time we built on this idea as we developed a framework of our own for classifying public-private partnerships (Link 1999), and we operationalized that framework empirically through our earlier study of U.S. federal

Federal government as customer
for industry programs

Industry as partner in joint
government - industry programs

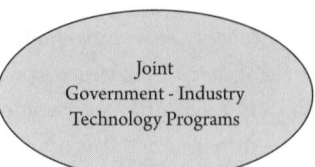

- Conformance with government specifications
  and regulations
- Success of agency mission

- Development of commerical technology that also meets
  government needs
- Innovation, commercialization, economic growth
- Leadership, competitiveness, jobs

Figure 1.1 A New Paradigm for Public-Private Partnerships.

Source: Office of Technology Policy 1996a, p. 34.

laboratories as research partners (Leyden and Link 1999). Our framework to define the public-private partnership is illustrated in Table 1.2. The first column of the table describes the nature and scope of public sector involvement in a public-private partnership. Public sector involvement can be indirect or direct. If direct, there is then an explicit allocation of financial resources, infrastructural resources, and research resources. The second and third columns in the table relate to the economic objective of the partnership. Of course, with any innovation-related activity there are spillovers of knowledge, and thus economic objectives are multidimensional. For purposes of illustration, a single overriding economic objective is assumed in our framework. Broadly, the objective is to leverage private sector research and development (R&D) investments (e.g., the R&E tax credit discussed in Chapter 7) or to leverage public sector R&D (e.g., the Small Business Innovation Research program discussed in Chapter 8).

Most recently, we took a first step toward establishing the nexus between government and entrepreneurship in *Government as Entrepreneur*. Thinking of government in terms of agencies, offices, and infrastructures, we wrote (Link and Link 2009, p. 17): "Government acts as entrepreneur in the provision of technology infrastructure when its involvement is both innovative and characterized by entrepreneurial risk (i.e., uncertainty)."

This point of view of government as entrepreneur draws directly from the intellectual thought of scholars, most notably Cantillon and Knight, who assumed that an entrepreneur is one who assumes the risk associated with uncertainty—entrepreneurial risk—and those, most notably Schumpeter, who assumed that an entrepreneur is one who innovates and applies new techniques. In other words, in terms of the static model in Figure 1.2, government either assumes entrepreneurial risk or it does not, and it is either innovative in its development and application of relevant actions (i.e., agencies, offices,

Table 1.2 **A Framework of Public-Private Partnerships**

Public sector Involvement	Leverage Public Sector R&D	Leverage Private Sector R&D
Indirect	...	...
Direct		
Financial resources	...	...
Infrastructural resources	...	...
Research resources	...	...

	No Entrepreneurial Risk	Assumes Entrepreneurial Risk
Not Innovative	A	B
Innovative	C	D: Government as Entrepreneur

Figure 1.2 A Static Representation of Government as Entrepreneur

or infrastructures) or it is not. When government does both as represented in cell D, it is—within this static framework—entrepreneurial. Cell A in the figure represents government that is neither innovative in the development of a relevant action nor willing to assume entrepreneurial risk. In a broad sense, cell A characterizes much of current macroeconomic policy in the United States.[12] Cell B represents a government that is willing to assume entrepreneurial risk in pursuing the status quo, and cell C represents a government that is unwilling to assume entrepreneurial risk in developing and implementing an innovative action.[13]

From a myopic point of view, this book could be thought of as a sequel to *Government as Entrepreneur*, but this book more accurately represents a new approach for thinking about public policies, technology, and innovation policies in particular.[14] The dimension of newness comes from the fact that our arguments here draw from a formal model of entrepreneurship that is based on economic concepts and principles.

Our model, developed and discussed in Chapter 3, leads to an expanded definition of public sector entrepreneurship, especially as it relates to technology and innovation policy. Our model is thus the cornerstone of our ability to formalize the concept of public sector entrepreneurship. We see public sector entrepreneurship manifested primarily indirectly, referring to policy initiatives that generate greater economic prosperity by transforming a status-quo economic environment into one that is more conducive to economic units engaging in creative activities in the face of uncertainty. Given the current state of public policies and the private sector entrepreneurial environment, public sector entrepreneurship affects that transformation primarily by increasing the effectiveness of social networks, that is, by increasing the heterogeneity of experiential ties among economic units and the ability of those same economic units to exploit (i.e., to learn from) such diversity. This conclusion follows directly from our model of the innovation production process, which until now has not been part of the discussion in the various private and public sector entrepreneurial literatures. And through policy initiatives that are characterized by public sector entrepreneurship, there will be more development of new technology and hence more innovation throughout the economy.

The Remaining Chapters

Before describing the remaining chapters in this book, it is useful to first emphasize what this book is not about. It is not about entrepreneurs engaging in direct public sector activities.

The notion of entrepreneurs in the public sector of the United States recently gained renewed visibility during the 2008–2009 Great Recession. During that period of slowdown—perhaps more so than in other recent periods of time—entrepreneurship was heralded as a fundamental activity to revive the U.S. economy. For example, President Barack Obama released *A Strategy for American Innovation: Driving towards Sustainable Growth and Quality Jobs* in which he states, "Entrepreneurship has played, and will continue to play, an essential role in generating innovation and stimulating economic growth" (Executive Office of the President 2009, p. 16).

Perhaps not so surprisingly, this strategic approach to economic growth was followed by the president's Startup America initiative, designed to accelerate high-growth entrepreneurship throughout the nation:

> Entrepreneurs embody the promise of America: the idea that if you have a good idea [i.e., *perception*] and are willing to work hard and see it through [i.e., *action*], you can succeed in this country. And in fulfilling this promise, entrepreneurs also play a critical role in expanding our economy and creating jobs. [15]

Based on the belief that the benefits generated by entrepreneurs in the private sector could be generated as well in the public sector, Congressman Honda introduced the Entrepreneur-in-Residence Act (H.R. 6119) on July 12, 2012:

> The mission of the program shall be to (1) provide for better outreach by the Federal Government to the private sector; (2) strengthen

coordination and interaction between the Federal Government and the private sector on issues relevant to entrepreneurs and business concerns; and (3) make Federal programs simpler, quicker, and more efficient, and more responsive to the needs of business concerns and entrepreneurs ... by appointing entrepreneurs-in-residence.

Thus, entrepreneurs in government might facilitate a model for routine public sector activities—not for the design and execution of policies—intended to make the government more efficient and more aligned with the ways that businesses operate. However, not all acts to make government efficient can be characterized as entrepreneurial. And in any event, as potentially useful as H.R. 6119 might be, it is not the same as government acting entrepreneurially in how it structures and implements public policies toward the private sector entrepreneur. As we have discussed, there are reasons to believe that such direct public sector entrepreneurial behavior has significant institutional and cultural constraints that limit its ability to function.

While we have written extensively about the private sector entrepreneur and what he does from the perspective of intellectual thought, we would be remiss if we did not summarize those ideas in greater detail so as to place our theoretical model of public sector entrepreneurship within the extant literature on that topic. We do this in Chapter 2. Then, in Chapter 3, we present our theoretical model of public sector entrepreneurship. This model is the foundation for how we have defined public sector entrepreneurship and how we have related that concept to U.S. technology and innovation policy. We also compare and contrast our economic approach to public sector entrepreneurship to the scholarly views of others as summarized in Table 1.1.

Chapter 4 sets the stage for the six technology and innovation policies that we use to illustrate our concept of public sector entrepreneurship. The technology and innovation policies that we consider are summarized in Table 1.3.

Chapters 5 through 10 are formatted similarly. Each begins with a statement and interpretation of the seminal technology or innovation policy under consideration, followed by a discussion of how and why this policy is an example of public sector entrepreneurship, and finally by a concluding section on the economic impact of the policy.

Chapter 5 begins by examining the Bayh-Dole Act of 1980 and the connection between that act and proof of concept centers (PoCCs). We argue that PoCCs serve to enhance the experiential ties of faculty entrepreneurs as they attempt to commercialize a technology through their university technology transfer office.

Chapter 6 analyzes the Stevenson-Wydler Act of 1980. This gives us an opportunity to segue into a discussion of the current state of the U.S. manufacturing sector. We offer a model of a manufacturing firm's strategic behavior

Table 1.3 **Technology and Innovation Polices Considered in Subsequent Chapters**

Chapter	Policy	Intended Economic Impact
5	University and Small Business Patent Procedure Act of 1980 (known as the Bayh-Dole Act of 1980)	Technology transfer primarily from universities to the private sector
6	Stevenson-Wydler Technology Innovation Act of 1980 (known at the Stevenson-Wydler Act of 1980)	Technology transfer primarily from federal laboratories to the private sector
7	Economic Recovery Tax Act (ERTA) of 1981 (relevant section known as the R&E Tax Credit of 1981)	Tax credit to eligible private sector firms to increase their R&E investments
8	Small Business Innovation Development Act of 1982	Financial support to small firms to conduct targeted R&D
9	National Cooperative Research Act of 1984	Incentivize cooperative R&D among firms
10	Omnibus Trade and Competitiveness Act of 1988	Subsidize R&D cooperation among firms engaged in research related to generic technologies

and suggest areas in which public sector entrepreneurship can enhance the effectiveness of social networks emanating from federal laboratories. Here we draw a parallel between our concept of public sector entrepreneurship and purposeful knowledge supply chains.

We then examine the R&E Tax Credit Act of 1981 in Chapter 7 and the Small Business Innovation Development Act of 1982 in Chapter 8, before turning to the National Cooperative Research Act of 1984 in Chapter 9. Chapter 9 affords us the opportunity to discuss in depth the role of universities as research partners. This analysis is prompted by the fact that several of the technology and innovation policies discussed in Chapter 9, as well as previous chapters, focus on universities as an effective extension of the networks of the policy-affected economic unit(s). We then turn to our final illustration of various public sector entrepreneurial efforts by examining the Omnibus Trade and Competitiveness Act of 1988 in Chapter 10.

The final arguments of this book begin in Chapter 11, which summarizes the previous six chapters by comparing them to what might be viewed as a, if not the most, important building block for U.S. technology and innovation policy, namely Vannevar Bush's (1945) *Science—the Endless Frontier*. We argue in this chapter that Bush's writings and ideas were a precursor for thinking about public sector entrepreneurship.

Chapter 12 concludes our discussion. There we reprise our definition of public sector entrepreneurship and why we believe that this construct is of economic importance. We also provide exploratory empirical support for the supposition that the entrepreneurial technology and innovation policies discussed in the previous chapters have been effective in stimulating the U.S. economy.

Appendix: Public Sector Economic Growth Policies

When we, economists by training, think about public policy and the public sector, we think about macroeconomic initiatives designed to stimulate economic growth. Traditionally, such policies broadly fall within two categories: demand management policies and supply management policies.

Consider the aggregate supply and demand model in Figure A1.1 The vertical axis measures the inflation rate associated with an index of the aggregate level of prices; the horizontal axis measures an index of aggregate economic output.

The aggregate demand (AgD) schedule reflects the aggregate demand for all goods and services. Central banks informally or formally target an inflation rate that they believe is in the best interests of the nation's economy. Hence, if we suppose that we start with inflation at the desired level, a fall in the inflation

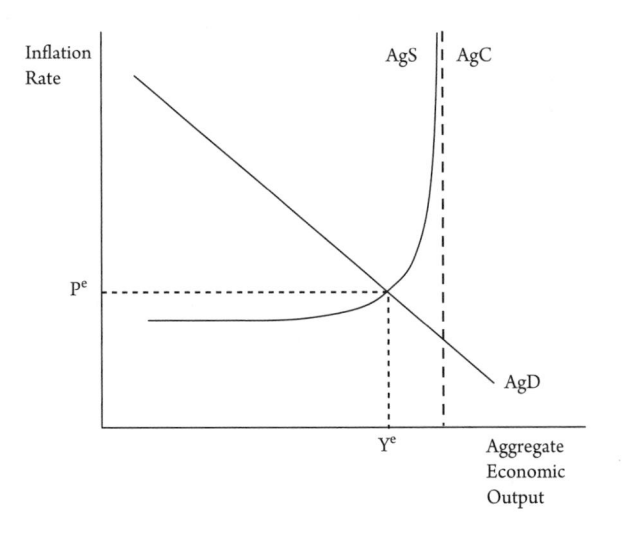

Figure A1.1 Aggregate Supply (AgS) and Demand (AgD) Model

rate will result, all else held constant, in the central bank increasing the rate of growth in the money supply to push the inflation rate back to its desired level. This in turn reduces interest rates, and so induces economic agents (i.e., consumers, producers, and government) to invest and to consume more. Thus, aggregate output increases. Likewise, if the inflation rate rises above the desire level, the central bank will take action to bring it back to the desired level, and that will in turn reduce aggregate output. In short, an initial fall in inflation will result in an increase in the aggregate demand for goods and services; an initial rise in inflation will result in a decrease in the aggregate demand for goods and services.

The aggregate supply (AgS) schedule reflects the aggregate supply of all goods and services. While workers and businesses may eventually perceive the actual inflation rate, in the short term that is a more difficult task, particularly for workers. When inflation initially rises, all else held constant, workers' monetary wages will rise. But because of the short-term problem of perceiving what is happening elsewhere in the economy, workers will tend to perceive this as an increase in the purchasing power of their wages (i.e., the workers' real wage), and hence they will increase their work effort. Firms, however, by being more in tune to the overall economy, can be expected to perceive better the fact that only the monetary wage and not the real wage of workers has increased. As a result, they are glad to increase production in the face of a greater supply of labor. Hence, the higher inflation rate will, at least in the short run, be associated with more goods and services being produced. Of course, the same process works in reverse, so that a lower inflation rate results in a reduced level of aggregate supply.

There are limits to the ability of a nation to produce more as a result of higher inflation. Some of this limitation is due to workers eventually figuring out the impact of inflation on their real wage.[16] But in even in the short run, when workers still misperceive circumstances, the ability of aggregate output to expand with higher inflation is constrained because of the fixed technology that exists at any point in time and because of the finite amount of resources that are within the command of the nation. This aggregate capacity (AgC), represented in Figure A1.1 by the vertical line AgC, is fundamentally a technological construct and indicates the absolute maximum level of output that could possibly be produced by the economy at any given point in time. Hence, at any given point in time, while a higher inflation rate will result in a greater level of aggregate supply, that higher level of aggregate supply can never surpass the nation's aggregate capacity to produce. And so, as we entertain higher and higher inflation rates at a given point in time, the associated increase in the level of aggregate supply will gradually diminish so that the AgS schedule becomes asymptotic to the AgC line. Because the actual level of economic activity and the inflation rate are the result of both aggregate demand and aggregate supply forces, the intersection of AgS and AgD represents the current level of economic activity in the economy and the current inflation rate. Moreover, because as a practical matter a nation never reaches its aggregate capacity of output, full employment is associated with a region of aggregate output somewhat less than the theoretical maximum productive capacity AgC. When aggregate output of the nation is below that full-employment level of aggregate output, we say the nation is in recession; when aggregate output of the nation is above the full-employment level of aggregate output, but of course still below the aggregate capacity of the nation, we say that the nation is in a boom.

Demand management policies are designed to shift the AgD schedule. For example, decreases in taxes, easing of interest rates (perhaps associated with an increase in the desired level of inflation), and increases in government expenditures shift the AgD schedule to the right, thus increasing aggregate economic activity as well as inflation.

Supply management policies shift the AgS schedule and the associated AgC line to the right. For example, policies that stimulate innovation indirectly through increased investments in research and development (R&D) or directly through incentives to purchase new technologies shift the AgS schedule to the right, thus increasing aggregate economic activity and decreasing inflation.

We do not view these forms of demand management policy and supply management policy as examples of public sector entrepreneurship because at present they are not characterized by innovation or the risk due to uncertainty. They are simply the application of economic tools that have a reasonably predictable impact on the economy. Notice, however, that before such tools were well understood and used, these would have been examples of public sector entrepreneurship. As Schumpeter (1934, p. 78) has observed: "Everyone is an entrepreneur only when he actually carries out new combinations, and loses that character as soon as he has built up his business, when he settles down to running it as other people run their businesses." This is as true for the public sector entrepreneur as it is for the private sector entrepreneur.

What then would be a macroeconomic example of public sector entrepreneurship? The experiment with quantitative easing by the U.S. Federal Reserve is a current and relevant example. Until the latest recession, quantitative easing had never been tried either in the United States or elsewhere in the world. While there were theoretical reasons to believe it might be effective, the degree to which that might be true was unknown as was the possibility that there be other, perhaps undesirable, consequences. It was thus an innovative policy taken in an uncertain environment.

Finally, it may be useful to observe why the focus in this appendix is on economic growth that correlates in the aggregate with shifts in the AgS and AgC curves to the right. A look at Figure A1.1 reveals that aggregate demand management policies, whether entrepreneurial or not, have limited ability to increase aggregate output because of the presence of the AgC curve which is unaffected by aggregate demand management policies. Thus, aggregate demand management policies—both fiscal and monetary policies—are useful for reducing inflation or helping pull an economy out of recession but are of no value for long-run economic growth. To affect long-run growth, one must shift the AgS and the AgC curves to the right; that is, one must engage in aggregate supply management policies. Some of these, as noted above, are well established and hence no longer considered examples of public sector entrepreneurship. Others however are not. This book is about the latter.

PART I

DEFINING PUBLIC SECTOR ENTREPRENEURSHIP

2

Entrepreneurship

Who in the world am I? Ah, that's the great puzzle!
—Lewis Carroll (*Alice*)

An Overview

Throughout intellectual history as we know it, the entrepreneur has worn many faces and played many roles. Table 2.1 lists those roles, along with the names of the scholars who are most clearly connected to those characterizations. As the length of the list of themes suggests, there has been and continues to be considerable dispute over the actual nature of the entrepreneur. Below we discuss in detail many of the themes associated with these roles, concentrating on the roles that our research has persuaded us are most central to the character of the entrepreneur—innovator and bearer of risk due to uncertainty. This discussion serves, too, as an introduction to our theoretical model of public sector entrepreneurship in Chapter 3.

Historical Perspectives About the Entrepreneur as Innovator

Clearly the most common characterization of the entrepreneur is as an innovator—an association made popular by Joseph Schumpeter. As Schumpeter's view has come to dominate the field of study of entrepreneurship by economics, management, and sociology scholars, the earlier history of the concept—particularly that part which linked entrepreneurship and risk-bearing—has unfortunately become increasingly obscured and forgotten. The taxonomy that we follow here to chronicle the changing views of the entrepreneur is to group theories of entrepreneurship as supply sided or demand sided.[1]

Table 2.1 **Themes About Who the Entrepreneur Is**

The Entrepreneur is...	Associated Scholar(s)
1. the person who assumes the risk associated with uncertainty	Richard Cantillon Frank Knight
2. the person who supplies financial capital	Adam Smith
3. an innovator	Richard Cantillon The Abbé Nicholas Baudeau Joseph Schumpeter
4. a decision-maker	Carl Menger
5. an industrial leader	Jean-Baptiste Say
6. a manager or superintendent	John Stuart Mill
7. an organizer and coordinator of economic resources	Léon Walras
8. the owner of an enterprise	François Quesnay
9. an employer of factors of production	Amasa Walker
10. a contractor	Jeremy Bentham
11. an arbitrageur	Israel Kirzner
12. an allocator of resources among alternative uses	T. W. Schultz

Supply-Side Theories of Entrepreneurship

A supply side theory of entrepreneurship is one that emphasizes the role of the entrepreneur in production and distribution of goods and services for which there is an independently determined demand. That is, given the demand for existing goods and services, a supply side approach to entrepreneurship would ask: What role does the entrepreneur play in the marketplace? This is the question on which many of the earliest inquiries into the subject of who the entrepreneur is and what he does focused on.[2]

The first significant writer to make frequent and distinct use of the term *entrepreneur* in a semblance of its modern form was Richard Cantillon (1680–1734), an 18th-century businessman and financier.[3] Cantillon's *Essai sur la nature du commerce en general* (Cantillon [1755] 1931) is a watershed in the history of entrepreneurship because it established the entrepreneur as a central figure in the marketplace. Cantillon established the entrepreneur as the intermediary between landowners and hirelings. Landowners established patterns of consumption in conformance with their individual tastes and preferences.

In turn, they relegated production of goods and services to entrepreneurs who embraced the risks associated with market judgments about production and distribution. Although Cantillon's entrepreneurs do not engage in the creative destruction of demand that Schumpeter described, they nevertheless innovate in ways befitting their intermediary status. For example, as they become aware that consumers are willing to pay a little extra in order to buy in small quantities rather than stockpile large quantities, they manage the circulation of goods accordingly.

Another way that Cantillon's entrepreneur can innovate is through arbitrage. An arbitrageur can create time and place utility by moving goods from low-valued use to high-valued use. Noting the opportunities for profit that existed between the countryside and Paris, Cantillon maintained that as long as entrepreneurs can cover their transportation costs, they "will buy at a low price the products of the villages and will transport them to the Capital to be sold there at a higher price" ([1755] 1931, p. 150–152). These two examples show that Cantillon's innovative entrepreneur works basically on the supply side of the market.

Another writer who developed a theory of entrepreneurship that anticipated future developments was the clergyman Abbé Nicolas Baudeau (1730–1792). A member of the French school of economists that has come to be known as the Physiocrats,[4] Baudeau believed in the primacy of agriculture. In depicting the agricultural entrepreneur as a risk-bearer, he echoed Cantillon. But Baudeau established, even more overtly than Cantillon, the concept of the entrepreneur as innovator, one who invents and applies new techniques or ideas in order to reduce his costs and thereby raise his profit.

Consider the nature of risk faced by the agricultural entrepreneur. The rent he pays to the landlord is the surplus of farm revenue over necessary costs of production, including some payment for his own services. For the tenant farmer, rent is a cost determined in advance of production. The Physiocrats favored stabilizing these costs as much as possible through long-term leases, while wage rates were usually fixed at or near subsistence levels. Thus, the farmer operating with a long-term lease not only faced certain fixed costs but also uncertain harvests and thus uncertain sales prices. Note the powerful suggestion that it is the role of the entrepreneur to devise legal/contractual/administrative arrangements that improve market efficiency or lower market risk.

In his analysis of entrepreneurship, Baudeau emphasized and explored the significance of ability. He underscored the importance of intelligence, the entrepreneur's ability to collect and process knowledge and information. Intelligence—knowledge and the ability to act on that knowledge, a point that is embedded in our own theory of entrepreneurship in Chapter 3—also gives the entrepreneur a measure of control so that he is not a mere pawn to the capitalist. Hence, Baudeau described the entrepreneur as an active agent:

> Such is the goal of the grand productive enterprises; first to increase the harvest by two, three, four, ten times if possible; secondly to reduce the amount of labor employed and so reduce costs by a half, a third, a fourth, or a tenth, whatever possible. ([1767] 1910, p. 46)

Baudeau's theory of entrepreneurship presupposes that economic events fall into two categories, those that are subject to human control and those that are not. To the extent that the entrepreneur confronts events under his control, his success depends upon knowledge and ability, which he may use in all manner of creative ways to try to reduce risk. To the extent that he confronts events beyond his control, however, he places himself at risk that is not likely to yield to innovative measures.

British classical economists paid little attention to the role of the entrepreneur in a market economy, choosing instead to elevate the capitalist to the top of the economic hierarchy. Jeremy Bentham (1748–1832), whose ties with France and its intellectual tradition were much stronger than those of his contemporaries, was an exception. Bentham agreed with the premise that the regime most favorable to the development of inventive faculties was that of economic liberalism. And, Bentham (1952) defended usurers and projectors as useful agents. Both helped to advance the cause of inventive genius, each in his own way. Bentham aptly pointed this out in his *Defence of Usury* (Bentham [1787] 2004), the first publication that brought him fame as an economist. Therein Bentham detailed how laws against usury limit the overall quantity of capital loaned and borrowed and how such laws keep foreign money away from domestic capital markets. Both effects tend to throttle the activities of successful entrepreneurs. Although Bentham used the customary term *projector*, he was quite precise in his definition of this term as any person who, in the pursuit of wealth, strikes out into any new channel, especially into any channel of invention. He argued that interest rate ceilings tend to discriminate against entrepreneurs of new projects, because such projects, by their novelty, are more risky than those already proven profitable by experience. Moreover, legal restrictions of this sort are powerless to distinguish bad projects from good ones.

In pleading the cause of the projectors, Bentham, the inventor of the Panopticon, was to some extent pleading his own case. Panopticon was the name Bentham gave to his idea of a model prison. The concept involved both an architectural and an institutional innovation. Bentham's ideal prison was circular. All the cells were arranged concentrically around a central pavilion, which contained an inspector, or at most a small number of inspectors. From his central position the inspector(s) could see at a glance everything that was going on, yet he was rendered invisible by a system of blinds. In this way, too, outside visitors could inspect the prisoners, as well as the prison's administration, without being seen. According to Bentham, this constant scrutiny would deprive the prisoners of the power, and even the will, to do evil. Bentham was never able to attract enough backers to make his model prison a reality, but his basic concept was tried in other countries. What is more pertinent about Bentham's plan of prison reform is the administrative innovation that he attached to it: the principle of contract management. This principle relies on the proper structuring of economic incentives and the dynamic activities of the entrepreneur to achieve the desired result of economic efficiency.

To Bentham, true reform would obtain in prisons only if the administrative plan simultaneously protected convicts against the harshness of their warders and society against the wastefulness of administrators. The choice, as he saw it, was between contract management and trust management. The differences have been summarized by Halévy:

> Contract-management is management by a man who treats with the government, and takes charge of the convicts at so much a head and applies their time and industry to his personal profit, as does a master with his apprentices. Trust-management is management by a single individual or by a committee, who keeps up the establishment at the public expense, and pay into the treasury the products of the convicts' work. (1955, p. 84)

In Bentham's judgment, trust management did not provide the proper junction of interest and duty on the part of the entrepreneur. Its success therefore depended on public interest as a motivating factor. Bentham, like his proclaimed mentor, Adam Smith, had much more confidence in individual self-interest as the spur to human action. The beauty of contract management was that it brought about an artificial identity of interests between the public on the one hand and the entrepreneur on the other. The entrepreneur in this case was an independent contractor who purchased, through competitive bid, the right to run the prison, thereby also acquiring title to whatever profits might be earned by the application of convict labor. Such an entrepreneur-manager could maximize his long-term gains by preserving the health and productivity of his worker-convicts. In this manner, public interest became entwined with private interest.

In 1787, Bentham completed the idea of contract management by a new administrative arrangement: he thought that life insurance offered an excellent means of joining the interest of one man to the preservation of a number of men. He therefore proposed that after consulting the appropriate mortality tables, the entrepreneur (e.g., prison manager) should be given a fixed sum of money for each convict due to die that year in prison, on condition that at the end of the year he must pay back the same sum for each convict who had actually died in prison. The difference would be profit for the entrepreneur, who would thereby have an economic incentive to lower the average mortality rate in his prison (Bentham [1838–1843] 1962, p. 53).

Aside from the fact that Bentham was virtually alone among British classical economists in his repeated emphasis on the entrepreneur as an agent of economic progress, it is noteworthy that his administrative arrangement of contract management recast the entrepreneur in the position of government contractor, that is, a franchisee who undertakes financial risk in order to obtain an uncertain profit. Bentham also explicitly tied his notion of entrepreneur-contractor to the act of innovation. He defended contract management as the proper form of prison administration on the ground that it is a progressive innovation and should therefore be rewarded accordingly, no less than an inventor is rewarded for his invention (Bentham [1838–1843] 1962, p. 47).

J. H. von Thünen (1785–1850) is best known in the history of economics for his contributions to location theory, but in the second volume of *The Isolated State* (1960) he set forth an explanation of profit that clearly distinguished the function and reward of the entrepreneur from that of the capitalist. Thünen identified entrepreneurial gain as profit minus (1) interest on invested capital, (2) insurance against business losses, and (3) the wages of management. For Thünen, this residual is a return to entrepreneurial risk. Entrepreneur risk is uninsurable: "There exists no insurance company that will cover all and every risk connected with a business. A part of the risk must always be accepted by the entrepreneur" (Thünen 1960, p. 246).

Contemporary economics relies on the concept of opportunity costs to measure entrepreneurial risk (Kanbur 1980). Thünen seems to have had the same argument in mind when he wrote:

> He who has enough means to pay to get some knowledge and education for public service has a choice to become either a civil servant or, if equally suited for both kinds of jobs, to become an industrial entrepreneur. If he takes the first job, he is guaranteed subsistence for life; if he chooses the latter, an unfortunate economic situation may take all his property, and then his fate becomes that of a worker for daily wages. Under such unequal expectations for the future what could motivate him to become an entrepreneur if the probability of gain were not much greater than that of loss? (1960, p. 247)

Thünen clearly appreciated the difference between management and entrepreneurship. He maintained that the effort of an entrepreneur working on his own account was different from that of a paid substitute (i.e., a manager), even if each has the same knowledge and ability. The entrepreneur takes on the anxiety and agitation that accompanies his business gamble; he spends many sleepless nights preoccupied with the single thought of how to avoid catastrophe, whereas the paid substitute, if he has worked well during the day and finds himself tired in the evening, can sleep soundly, secure in the knowledge of having performed his duty. Anyone who has nursed along a new enterprise knows precisely of what Thünen speaks.

What is especially interesting about Thünen's treatment is how he turned the discussion from the trials of the entrepreneur into a kind of crucible theory of the development of entrepreneurial talent. The sleepless nights of the entrepreneur are not unproductive; it is then that the entrepreneur makes his plans and arrives at solutions for avoiding business failure. Adversity in the business world thereby becomes a training ground for the entrepreneur. As Thünen put it:

> Necessity is the mother of invention; and so the entrepreneur through his troubles will become an inventor and explorer in his field. So, as the invention of a new and useful machine rightly gets the surplus which its application provides in comparison with an older machine, and this surplus is the compensation for his invention, in the same way what the entrepreneur brings about by greater mental effort in comparison with the paid manager is compensation for his industry, diligence, and ingenuity. (1960, p. 248)

What makes this a significant step forward in the theory of entrepreneurship is the fact that Thünen successfully joined the separate strands of entrepreneurial theory that, on the one hand, characterized the entrepreneur as risk-bearer (e.g., Cantillon), and, on the other hand, portrayed him as innovator (e.g., Baudeau and Bentham). Economic analysis having come this far by 1850, we may well question whether Schumpeter took a step backward in the next century by excluding risk-bearing from the nature of entrepreneurship, confining its meaning to innovative activity.

Thünen was quite explicit about the fact that there are two elements in entrepreneurial income: a return to entrepreneurial risk and a return to ingenuity. Labeling the sum of these two as business profit, Thünen established a cleavage between the respective roles of capitalist and entrepreneur:

> Capital will give results, and is in the strict sense of the term capital, only if used productively; on the degree of this usefulness depends the rate of interest at which we lend capital. Productive use presupposes an industrial enterprise and an entrepreneur. The enterprise gives the entrepreneur a net yield after compensating for all expenses and costs. This net yield has two parts, business profits and capital use. (1960, p. 249)

Demand-Side Theories of Entrepreneurship

A demand-side theory of entrepreneurship is one that emphasizes the role of the entrepreneur in changing the nature of demand for existing goods and services by introducing new goods and services or new combinations of existing goods and services. Such theories address the question of the entrepreneur's role in the marketplace, given the pattern of supply for existing goods and services.[5]

Economic thought in the late nineteenth and early twentieth centuries developed differently in Germany than it did in England, or throughout the rest of Europe. This was due in part to the influence of the German Historical School. The historicists believed that in order to understand man's economic behavior and the institutions that constrain it, economics must describe human motives and behavioral tendencies in psychologically realistic terms. Gustave Schmoller (1838–1917) represented the second generation of German historicists. He amassed mountains of historical data in order to analyze actual economic behavior. From his examination of these data he discovered a unique factor central to all economic activity—the enterprising spirit, the *Unternehmer*, or entrepreneur. Schmoller's entrepreneur was a creative organizer and manager whose role was innovation and the initiation of new projects (Zrinyi 1962). He combined factors of production to yield either new products or new methods of production. Schmoller's entrepreneur possessed imagination and daring. More significantly, Schmoller began to direct attention to the role of the entrepreneur on the demand side of economic activity.

Schmoller's ideas were extended by third-generation German historicists Werner Sombart (1863–1941) and Max Weber (1864–1920). Sombart introduced a new leader who animates the entire economic system by creative innovations. This entrepreneur combined the powers of organization described by Schmoller with a personality and ability to elicit maximum productivity from individuals engaged in the productive process. Whether a financier, manufacturer, or trader, Sombart's entrepreneur was a profit maximizer.

The German historicists characterized the entrepreneurial process as a breaking away from the old methods of production and a creation of new ones. This disequilibrating process was particularly emphasized by Weber. He sought to explain how a social system, as compared to an individual enterprise, could evolve from one stable form, perhaps under an authoritarian structure, to another type of system. Historically, he identified such changes with a charismatic leader, or entrepreneur-like person (Carlin 1956).

As if to heighten the dynamic nature of his entrepreneurial construct, Weber began his analysis of change with a stationary state situation:[6]

> We may ... visualize an economic process which merely reproduces
> itself at constant rates; a given population, not changing in either

numbers or age distribution. ... The tasks (wants) of households are given and do not change. The ways of production and usances of commerce are optimal from the standpoint of the firm's interest and with respect to existing horizons and possibilities, hence do not change either, unless some datum changes or some chance event intrudes upon this world. (1930, p. 67)

In such a stationary society there is nothing that requires the activity traditionally associated with the entrepreneur. Weber declared: "No other than ordinary routine work has to be done in this stationary society either by workmen or managers" (1930, p. 67). Yet, inevitably, change does occur. Weber described a likely scenario:

Now at some time this leisureliness was suddenly destroyed, and often entirely without any essential change in form of organization. ... What happened was, on the contrary, often no more than this: Some young men from one of the putting-out families went out into the country, carefully chose weavers from his employ, greatly increased the rigor of his supervision of their work, and thus turned them from peasants into laborers ... he would begin to change his marketing methods ... he began to introduce the principle of low prices and large turnover. There was repeated what everywhere and always is the result of such a process of rationalization: those who would not follow suit had to go out of business. The idyllic state collapsed under the pressure of a bitter competitive struggle. (1930, p. 68)

Competition, in other words, is driven by an entrepreneur type. The critical characteristics of Weber's successful entrepreneur are his religious imperatives, which make up what is called the "Protestant ethic." Consequently, in the final analysis, Weber's theory of social and economic change is as much sociology as economics.

Joseph Schumpeter (1883–1950) was schooled by the Austrian economists of the Vienna Circle but was heavily influenced by Weber. He set out to develop a theory of economic development in which the entrepreneur plays a central role. By applying new combinations of factors of production, Schumpeter's entrepreneur becomes the motive force of economic change. He is thereby responsible for the rise and decay of capitalism. The talented few who carry out innovations by devising new technologies, discovering new products and developing new markets account for the short and long cycles of economic life. Schumpeter saw economic development as a dynamic process, a disturbing of the status quo. He viewed economic development not as a mere adjunct to the central body of orthodox economic theory but as the basis for reinterpreting a vital process that had been crowded out of mainstream economic analysis by the static, general equilibrium approach. The entrepreneur is a key figure for Schumpeter because, quite simply, he is the *persona causa* of economic development.

Schumpeter combined ideas from many earlier writers, but the demand-side emphasis that marked the Germanic tradition dominated his treatment of entrepreneurship. His entrepreneur is a disequilibrating force. For Schumpeter, the concept of equilibrium that prevailed in 20th-century economics served as a mere point of departure. The phrase he coined to describe this equilibrium state was "the circular flow of economic life." In this state, economic life proceeds routinely on the basis of past experience; there are no forces evident for any change of the status quo. Schumpeter described the nature of production and distribution in the circular flow in the following way:

> In every period only products which were produced in the previous period are consumed, and ... only products which will be consumed in the following period are produced. Therefore workers and landlords always exchange their productive services for present consumption goods only, whether the former are employed directly or only indirectly in the production of consumption goods. There is no necessity for them to exchange their services of labor and land for future goods or for promises of future consumption goods or to apply for any advances of present consumption goods. It is simply a matter of exchange, and not of credit transactions. The element of time plays no part. All products are only products and nothing more. For the individual firm it is a matter of complete indifference whether it produces means of production or consumption goods. In both cases the product is paid for immediately and at its full value. (1934, pp. 42–43)

Within this system, the production function is invariant, although factor substitution is possible within the limits of known technological horizons. The only real function that must be performed in this state is

> that of combining the two original factors of production, and this function is performed in every period mechanically as it were, of its own accord, without requiring a personal element distinguishable from superintendence and similar things. (Schumpeter 1934, p. 45)

In this artificial situation, the entrepreneur is a nonentity. "If we choose to call the manager or owner of a business 'entrepreneur,'" wrote Schumpeter, then he would be an entrepreneur "without special function and without income of a special kind" (1934, pp. 45–46).

For Schumpeter, the circular flow is a mere foil. The relevant problem, he wrote in *Capitalism, Socialism and Democracy* (1950), is not how capitalism administers existing structures but how it creates and destroys them. This process—what Schumpeter called "creative destruction"—is the essence of economic development. In other words, development is a disturbance of the circular flow. It occurs in industrial and commercial life, not in consumption. It is a process defined by the carrying out of new combinations in production. It is accomplished by the entrepreneur.

Schumpeter reduced his theory to three elemental and corresponding pairs of opposites: (1) the circular flow (i.e., tendency toward equilibrium) on the one hand versus a change in economic routine or data on the other, (2) statics versus dynamics, and (3) entrepreneurship versus management. The first pair consists of two real processes; the second, two theoretical apparatuses; the third, two distinct types of conduct. The theory maintained that the essential function of the entrepreneur is distinct from that of capitalist, landowner, laborer, or inventor. According to Schumpeter, the entrepreneur may be any and all of these things, but if he is, it is by coincidence rather than by nature of function. Nor is the entrepreneurial function, in principle, connected with the possession of wealth, even though Schumpeter held that "the accidental fact of the possession of wealth constitutes a practical advantage" (1934, p. 101). Moreover, entrepreneurs do not form a social class, in the technical sense, although in a capitalist society they come to be esteemed for their ability.

Schumpeter admitted that the essential function of the entrepreneur is almost always mingled with other functions, such as management. But management, he asserted, does not elicit the truly distinctive role of the entrepreneur: "The function of superintendence in itself, constitutes no essential economic distinction" (1934, p. 20). The function of making decisions is another matter, however. In Schumpeter's theory, the dynamic entrepreneur is the person who innovates, who makes new combinations in production.

Schumpeter described innovation in several ways. Initially he spelled out the kinds of new combinations that underlie economic development. They encompass the following: (1) creation of a new good or new quality of good, (2) creation of a new method of production, (3) the opening of a new market, (4) the capture of a new source of supply, and (5) a new organization of industry (e.g., creation or destruction of a monopoly). Over time, of course, the force of these new combinations dissipates, as the new becomes part of the old (i.e., the circular flow). But this does not change the essence of the entrepreneurial function. According to Schumpeter, "everyone is an entrepreneur only when he actually carries out new combinations, and loses that character as soon as he has built up his business, when he settles down to running it as other people run their businesses" (1934, p. 78).

Alternatively, Schumpeter defined innovation by means of the production function. The production function "describes the way in which quantity of product varies if quantities of factors vary. If, instead of quantities of factors, we vary the form of the function, we have an innovation" (1939, p. 62).

Mere cost-reducing adaptations of knowledge lead only to new supply schedules of existing goods, so true innovation must involve a new commodity, or one of higher quality. However, Schumpeter recognized that the knowledge supporting the innovation need not be new. On the contrary, it may be existing knowledge that has not been utilized before. According to Schumpeter,

> There never has been anytime when the store of scientific knowledge has yielded all it could in the way of industrial improvement, and, on the other hand, it is not the knowledge that matters, but the successful solution of the task *sui generis* of putting an untried method into practice—there may be, and often is, no scientific novelty involved at all, and even if it be involved, this does not make any difference to the nature of the process. (1928, p. 378)

In Schumpeter's theory, successful innovation requires an act of will, not of intellect. It therefore depends on leadership rather than intelligence, and, as noted above, it should not be confused with invention. On this last point, Schumpeter was explicit:

> To carry any improvement into effect is a task entirely different from the inventing of it, and a task, moreover, requiring entirely different kinds of aptitudes. Although entrepreneurs of course may be inventors just as they may be capitalists, they are inventors not by nature of their function but by coincidence and vice versa. Besides, the innovations which it is the function of entrepreneurs to carry out need not necessarily be any inventions at all. (1934, pp. 88–89)

The leadership that constitutes innovation in the Schumpeterian system is disparate, not homogeneous. An aptitude for leadership stems in part from the use of knowledge, and knowledge has aspects of a public good. People of action who perceive and react to knowledge do so in various ways; each internalizes the public good in potentially a different way. The leader distances himself from the manager by virtue of his aptitude. According to Schumpeter, different aptitudes for the routine work of static management result merely in differential success at what all managers do, whereas different leadership aptitudes mean that "some are able to undertake uncertainties incident to what has not been done before; [indeed] ... to overcome these difficulties incident to change of practice is the function of the entrepreneur" (1928, p. 380).

Schumpeter's influence on the theory of economic development has been enormous, in part because of the simplicity and power of his theory, and in part because that theory extends rather than replaces many ideas from earlier writers. The simplicity and power of Schumpeter's theory is summed up in his own words: "The carrying out of new combinations we call 'enterprise'; the individual whose function it is to carry them out we call 'entrepreneurs'" (Schumpeter 1934, p. 74).[7]

Thus, through the force and clarity of his argument, Schumpeter is generally credited with establishing the entrepreneur as a demand-side innovator and disassociating the entrepreneur from the risk-taker. However, as our brief survey of the historical roots of entrepreneurship reveals, while the early and persistent connection between risk and entrepreneurship was made by writers of the eighteenth and nineteenth centuries, the link between innovation and the entrepreneur was never far from mind, albeit from a supply-side perspective. Schumpeter switched emphasis to the demand side and made the entrepreneur the pivotal figure not only in the analysis of static market phenomena but in a sweeping theory of historical change.

Synthesis

It was left to Frank Knight (1885–1972) to revive the supply-side connection between entrepreneurship and risk-taking and integrate it with Schumpeter's demand-side innovator. To accomplish that task, Knight first provided a very useful emphasis on the distinction between insurable risks and non-insurable uncertainty, which is reminiscent of Baudeau's distinction between controllable and uncontrollable factors. Second, Knight advanced a theory of profit that related this non-insurable uncertainty to both rapid economic change and differences in entrepreneurial ability.

Knight charged that previous risk theories were ambiguous because they did not distinguish sufficiently between two very different kinds of risk. On the one hand, risk signifies a quantity capable of being measured, that is, the objective probability that an event will happen. Because this kind of risk can be shifted from the entrepreneur to another party by an insurance contract, it is not an uncertainty in any meaningful sense. On the other hand, risk is often taken to mean a non-measurable eventuality, because all possible outcomes cannot be specified and/or the probabilities of all possible outcomes are not known, such as the inability to predict the consumer demand. Knight dubbed the latter true uncertainty and geared his theories of profit and entrepreneurship to its magnitude. The best summary statement of this theory comes from Knight himself:

> Not all risks necessarily give rise to profit, or loss. Many kinds can be insured against, which eliminates them as factors of uncertainty.... The essential point for profit theory is that insofar as it is possible to

insure by any method against risk, the cost of carrying it is converted into a constant element of expense, and it ceases to be a cause of profit and loss. The uncertainties which persist as causes of profit are those which are uninsurable because there is no objective measure of the probability of gain or loss. This is true especially of the prediction of demand. It not only cannot be foreseen accurately, but there is no basis for saying that the probability of its being of one sort rather than another is of a certain value—as we can compute the chance that a man will live to a certain age. Situations in regard to which business judgment must be exercised do not repeat themselves with sufficient conformity to type to make possible a computation of probability. (1951, pp. 119–120)

By isolating the concept of risk and refining its meaning, Knight gave new clarity to Cantillon's theory of the entrepreneur as the bearer of uncertainty. He also attributed the evolutionary nature of enterprise organizations to the presence of uncertainty. He asserted that the mere presence of uncertainty transforms society into an "enterprise organization" that is characterized by specialization of functions. The function of the entrepreneur becomes paramount in this kind of organization as a specialized agent who reduces uncertainty (Knight 1921, p. 271).

This Knightian uncertainty is not easily compartmentalized, for it pervades all human decision-making. Yet, it helps establish a boundary between management and entrepreneurship. According to Knight (1921, p. 276), the function of manager does not in itself imply entrepreneurship, but a manager becomes an entrepreneur when his performance requires that he exercise judgment involving liability to error. Moreover, the assumption of responsibility for the correctness of his actions is a prerequisite to getting the other members of the firm to submit to an entrepreneur's direction.

An interesting corollary of Knight's theory is that profit could not exist without error. Entrepreneurial profit depends on whether an entrepreneur can make productive services yield more than the price fixed upon them by what other people think they can make them yield. Therefore, its magnitude is based on a margin of error in calculation by entrepreneurs as well as non-entrepreneurs who do not force the successful entrepreneurs to pay as much for productive services as they could be forced to pay. It is this margin of error in judgment that constitutes the only true uncertainty in the workings of the competitive organization. Furthermore, in Knight's view, it is this uncertainty that is borne by the true entrepreneur and explains profit.

Knight took the same position as Cantillon regarding the separation of the capitalist and the entrepreneur. Both agreed that the entrepreneur may or may not be a capitalist—usually he must of necessity own some property, just as all property owners can hardly be freed from risk and responsibility. The point both writers stressed is that whether or not an entrepreneur owns capital, the essence of entrepreneurship is not to be found therein. As Knight emphasized, "the only 'risk' which leads to [entrepreneurial] profit is a unique uncertainty resulting from an exercise of ultimate responsibility which in its very nature cannot be insured nor capitalized nor salaried" (1921, p. 310).

But Knight also connected the Cantillon entrepreneur who grapples with uncertainty to the Schumpeterian entrepreneur who innovates. Indeed, though Schumpeter seems not to have recognized it,[8] Knightian innovation by definition occurs in, or indeed creates, an uncertain environment.

Summary

Our survey of intellectual thought about the entrepreneur shows that throughout the ages theories of entrepreneurship have been both static and dynamic. However, upon reflection, it becomes obvious that only dynamic theories of entrepreneurship have any significant operational meaning. In a static world, there is neither change nor uncertainty in Knight's sense. The entrepreneur's role in a static state could not be anything more than what is implied in Table 2.1 by item 2 (supplier of financial capital), item 6 (a manager or superintendent), item 8 (the owner of an enterprise), or item 9 (an employer of factors of production). In a static world, the entrepreneur is a passive element because his actions merely constitute repetitions of past procedures and techniques already learned and implemented. Only in a dynamic world does the entrepreneur become a robust figure. A dynamic environment is implied in each of the remaining definitions.

Equally important is the nature of that dynamic environment and in particular whether the entrepreneur bears risk, uncertainty, or both. Early discussions made little or no distinction between risk and uncertainty, but that changed with the contribution of Frank Knight. Today there is growing consensus that non-entrepreneurial decision-making takes place under conditions of certainty or of risk, whereas entrepreneurial decision-making takes place under conditions of uncertainty (Alvarez and Busenitz 2001, Loasby 2002).

Schumpeter's defense notwithstanding (see endnote 8), other economists have criticized him for his relative neglect of the topic of uncertainty in the theory of entrepreneurship. Andreas Papandreou (1943) argued decades ago that uncertainty is fundamental to the understanding and appreciation of the environment in which entrepreneurs break away from the routine. To compensate for the deficiency in Schumpeter's theory, Papandreou posited an alternative definition that makes uncertainty more explicit: "The entrepreneur would be the one who carries out innovation under conditions of uncertainty and unpredictability (1943, p. 23)."

Under risk-based theories it may be reasonable to think of opportunities as objective phenomena waiting to be discovered by entrepreneurs (Kirzner 1973, Shane 2003). But under uncertainty-based theories, entrepreneurs do not so much discover profit opportunities as create them, often through their organizing efforts (Alvarez and Barney 2005). Alvarez and Barney recognized, among other ironies revealed by their research, that because the condition of uncertainty is often not stable over time, the bases of organizing entrepreneurial firms are not likely to be stable over time. In particular, uncertainty-based firms may turn into risk-based firms once the probability distribution of outcomes associated with uncertain exchanges are learned through experience. Entrepreneurial firms, in other words, may be temporary, but their persistence is nevertheless a prerequisite for the continual development of economic firms.

Toward a Theory of Public Sector Entrepreneurship

If you always do what you always did, you will always get what you always got.

—Albert Einstein

Introduction

In this chapter we outline a general theory of entrepreneurship and apply that theory to elucidate the fundamental characteristics of public sector entrepreneurship.[1] As we have previously argued, the notion of entrepreneurship is broad and subsumes both the notion of public sector entrepreneurship and the notion of private sector entrepreneurship from which the concept of public entrepreneurship stems in terms of intellectual development. We could simply take the summary list of entrepreneurial themes from Table 2.1 as our starting point, but such a borrowed approach would be rightly viewed as superficial. Indeed, such an approach would essentially assume that entrepreneurial behavior is exogenous and for the most part static.

The difficulty with a taxonomical approach to developing a general theory of entrepreneurship is that it provides little insight as to how the entrepreneur engages in his craft. This approach would implicitly suggest that little can be said regarding public policies that might foster increased entrepreneurial behavior and the benefits that arise from that behavior. Because we conclude this book with argument and evidence about the importance of policymakers thinking in terms of public sector entrepreneurship and how to stimulate it, it therefore behooves us to develop a theory of entrepreneurship that contains within an explanation of the entrepreneurial process itself. The application of that explanation to public sector behavior provides a meaningful foundation for our eventual conclusions.

To develop a theory of entrepreneurship, we build on our initial characterization of entrepreneurship from Chapter 1, namely that the entrepreneur is one who perceives an opportunity heretofore unexploited and acts on that opportunity. That process of opportunity recognition and exploitation, which can take place in both the private and public sectors, is the essence of what we mean by innovation, and the willingness to engage in an innovation process necessarily means that the entrepreneur must be willing to bear the inherent uncertainty that arises from the risk that characterizes the innovation process.

Knight (1921) characterizes uncertainty as a circumstance in which possible outcomes and their likelihoods are not known and cannot be determined deductively or through empirical inductive analysis (see Figure 3.1).[2] This situation, which is typical of technological development and other forms of innovation, is, Knight argued, in contrast to simple risk where the future may not be known, but all possible outcomes are known and their likelihoods can be estimated so that the future is known with at least probabilistic certainty.

In the face of such uncertainty, entrepreneurial processes such as technology development and other related forms of innovation will be based on the entrepreneur's subjective expectations regarding possible outcomes and their probabilities. For Knight (1921), the source of those subjective expectations is intuition, with intuition being the result of the entrepreneur's conscious and non-conscious reflections on knowledge gained from the entrepreneur's direct experiences as well as the knowledge gained from the experiences of others.[3] To the extent that such subjective probability estimates become stable or are shared by others, they may come to be viewed as objective. Nonetheless, such probabilities are by their very nature subjective, though in terms of explaining the formulation of entrepreneurial plans ex ante, whether these expectations are objective or subjective may not matter. However, the distinction between subjective and objective expectations is certainly relevant for explaining outcomes ex post. Indeed, Knight argued that it is the difference between subjectively expected outcomes and the eventual outcomes that provides the source of entrepreneurial returns. Were expectations objective, the entrepreneurial process would be predetermined, albeit with risk; the process would simply be one of production amenable to the usual market processes. Any risks that might be present would be managed through insurance—including the possibility of self-insurance—diversification, and other methods common to risk

		Identification of Future Outcomes	
		Known	Unknown
Probability of Outcomes	Known	Risk	Uncertainty
	Unknown	Uncertainty	Uncertainty

Figure 3.1 Risk versus Uncertainty

management. The result, then, is that the production would be devoid of the potential for entrepreneurial returns. Thus, the distinction between risk and uncertainty is crucial to understanding the entrepreneurial process and is a cornerstone of our theory of entrepreneurship.[4]

The formation of subjective expectations based on both past personal experiences as well as the experiences of others suggests that the entrepreneurial process is about using knowledge to create economically valuable outcomes, particularly new technologies and other innovations. Thus, we can characterize the innovation process as one in which knowledge is converted into what, following Arrow (1962), might be referred to using the term *economic knowledge*.[5] Our model of entrepreneurship is centered on the notion that an entrepreneur in both the public and private sector is one who acquires knowledge and converts it or, perhaps more accurately, uses it to produce economic knowledge. When the entrepreneur acquires more knowledge, there is a greater likelihood that his or her innovative activity both in terms of the perception of opportunities as well as in terms of the ability to act on such opportunities will be successful. This notion of the entrepreneur as one who searches for knowledge parallels the writings of Schumpeter in the following sense. Schumpeter (1928) argued that knowledge per se is not the key to innovation, but rather the key is the creative application of knowledge toward a task sui generis.

In our model below we envision that the entrepreneur engages in this process of knowledge conversion through his development of effective, experiential social relationships, which we shall refer to using the term *entrepreneur's social network*. Over time, the heterogeneity of those relationships engenders a creative spirit as to how that new knowledge can be applied, that is, how it can be transformed into economic knowledge.[6]

In the private sector, the outcome of this uncertain process of opportunity recognition and exploitation through the employment of the entrepreneur's social network manifests itself, as Schumpeter (1934) noted, in a variety of ways: the creation of a new good or new quality of good, the creation of a new method of production, the opening of a new market, the capture of a new source of supply, or even a new organization of industry. In the public sector, the outcome of this same innovation process manifests itself through new public policies that alter the private sector's rules of the game with the intent to improve overall economic performance. Particularly with respect to matters of economic growth and development, these policies will focus on stimulating entrepreneurial creativity through the enhancement of private sector entrepreneurial social networks that are the sine qua non for private sector entrepreneurial success.[7]

In keeping with the technology and innovation policy examples of public sector entrepreneurship that we discuss in later chapters, we argue that the process of developing a technology and seeing it through the innovation process (i.e., seeing it to commercialization) is wrought with both risk and uncertainty and therefore a worthy object of public sector entrepreneurship. There is technical risk and uncertainty in the technology phase, meaning that there is both a measurable and non-measurable chance that research to develop the technology will fail for technical reasons. And there is market risk and uncertainty as the entrepreneur attempts to commercialize the technology. Given the current state of public policies and the private sector entrepreneurial environment, public sector entrepreneurship can affect technology development and other innovations primarily by increasing the effectiveness of social networks, that is, by increasing the heterogeneity of experiential ties among economic units and the ability of those same economic units to exploit or learn from such diversity. This conclusion follows directly from our model of the innovation production process itself that heretofore has not been part of the discussion in the various private sector much less public sector entrepreneurship literatures. And, through policy initiatives that are characterized by public sector entrepreneurship, there will be more development of new technology and hence more innovation throughout the economy.

The Model

We characterize the entrepreneurial process of technology development and innovation as a process of discovery, and we describe it as a two-step process of problem formulation and search within and across sources of knowledge.[8] Our description below is heuristic and based in large part on the more formal and mathematical theory and model that can be found in Leyden et al. (2014).[9] But, before we present our model of public sector entrepreneurship, we reiterate our definition of that concept from Chapter 1. And, we will revisit our definition at the end of this chapter to emphasize threads from the model.

Public sector entrepreneurship as noted in Chapter 1 refers to innovative public policy initiatives that generate greater economic prosperity by transforming a status quo economic environment into one that is more conducive to economic units engaging in creative activities in the face of uncertainty. In today's economy, public sector entrepreneurship affects that transformation primarily by increasing the effectiveness of social networks, that is, by increasing the heterogeneity of experiential ties among economic units and the ability of those same economic units to exploit such diversity. Through policy initiatives that are characterized by public sector entrepreneurship, there will be more development of new technology and hence more innovation throughout the economy.

A Sequential Decision-Making Process

The entrepreneur's decision-making process is a costly one, developed sequentially against a background of social and professional experiences, as well as resource constraints. If we begin with the choice of the desired innovation already in place, we can conceive of the entrepreneur's efforts to achieve this innovation as being focused on the exploration of various combinations of knowledge, actions, and resources. For ease of exposition, we refer to possible knowledge, actions, and resources using the general and inclusive term *inputs*. Sequentially, then, the entrepreneur searches over time for a combination of inputs that will generate the desired innovation.[10] Guiding the entrepreneur in the choice of which input combinations to explore is the entrepreneur's subjective assessment of the likelihood of finding a successful input combination. If the initial exploration of input combinations believed to be most fruitful does not result in success, the entrepreneur will gradually widen the range of input combinations over which he searches.[11]

This sequence of increasing search areas is illustrated in Figure 3.2 for the case of two possible inputs, x_1 and x_2. The entrepreneur begins with a relatively small search region A_1, chosen because of the entrepreneur's subjective belief that the likelihood of finding a successful input combination lies within that region. If success is not achieved within that initial search region, the entrepreneur expands to a larger region A_2, and continues to search. This process of

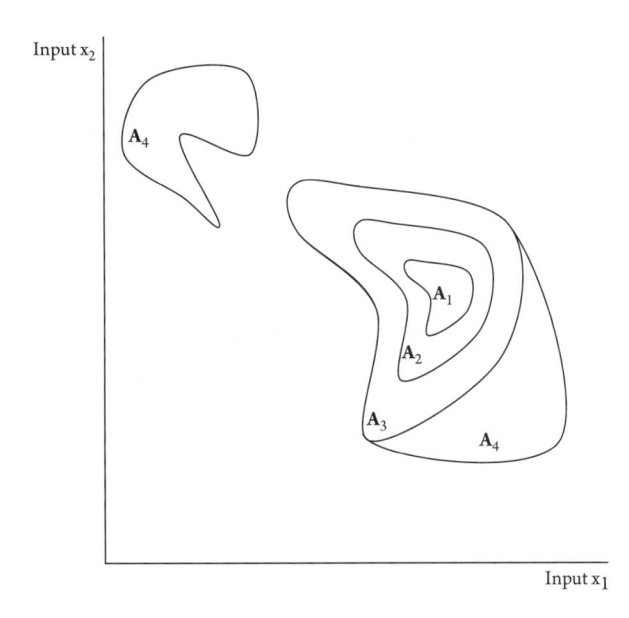

Figure 3.2 Regions of Entrepreneurial Search among Knowledge, Actions, and Resources

ever widening search regions continues until success is achieved or until the entrepreneur decides it is no longer desirable to continue to search.

Note that there is no reason to believe that the search regions are convex, or even connected. Thus, for example, Figure 3.2 includes the case of an entrepreneur who, after failing to find a successful input combination in regions A_1, A_2, and A_3, is of two minds about what combinations of inputs might be successful and concludes that the input combination most likely to be successful will either be a very high level of input x_1 with a very low level of input x_2, or a very low level of input x_1 with a very high level of input x_2. Hence, the entrepreneur's next search region, A_4, is a disconnected set.

If searching were a costless process, the entrepreneur would continue to search in ever-increasing regions until the desired innovation was found. However, searching is a costly process. We assume that the expected cost of searching increases as the size of the search region increases. The cost of searching will also depend on other factors, most notably the effectiveness of the entrepreneur's social network, which we assume is a positive function of the heterogeneity of the entrepreneur's social ties and past experiences. While the entrepreneur's social network may include individuals with various types of engineering and scientific knowledge, as well as knowledge of the entrepreneurial process, it will also include individuals of seemingly disparate areas of knowledge. Indeed, it is precisely the variety, and even incongruity, of ideas that gives rise to the creativity that underlies the innovation process. The crucial role of the entrepreneur's social network in the entrepreneur's innovation process is illustrated in Figure 3.3.

We assume that the cost of searching is generally lower the greater is the effectiveness of the entrepreneur's network. Thus, the cost of search can be represented by the function c(A, γ), where increases in A (which represents the size of the region **A)** result in greater cost, but increases in the effectiveness of the entrepreneur's social network (represented by γ) result in lower cost.

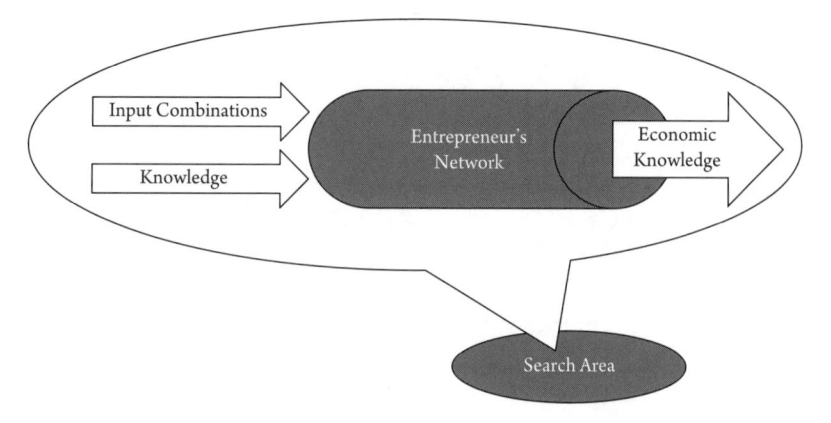

Figure 3.3 The Entrepreneur's Search Process

Because the search process is costly, the entrepreneur's choice of where to search will be determined by his subjective estimates of the likelihood of finding an input combination that succeeds in achieving the desired innovation. For a given search region of size A, the entrepreneur will choose the boundaries of that search region so as to maximize the subjective likelihood of successfully finding an input combination that results in successfully achieving the desired innovation. Thus, we can define the likelihood of finding an input combination in region **A** that has size A, that is successful by the subjective likelihood function $L(A \mid \gamma)$. Note that this subjective likelihood function, in addition to being a function of the size of the search region, will also be a function of the effectiveness of the entrepreneur's social network. The greater the effectiveness of this social network, the greater the entrepreneur's subjective assessment of the likelihood of success.

The Entrepreneur's Resource Constraint

Entrepreneurial activity requires financial capital. While self-funding is common, many entrepreneurs eventually secure funding from capital markets, particularly private equity markets (Link et al. 2013). We assume therefore that the entrepreneur seeks funding from the capital market, and that the entrepreneur's access to financial capital is constrained by the expectation (^{e}) that the suppliers of capital hold regarding the value of the entrepreneur's effort to achieve the desired innovation or project, V^e. Because the innovation process is by definition an uncertain one, the expected value of the project that the capital market holds will be a subjective one. Moreover, because there is no guarantee of success, this expected value can be defined as the subjectively determined value, V, of the innovation were it to be successfully achieved times the subjective probability of success $P(A \mid K)$, where K is the capital market's knowledge base.[12] Note that the assessment of the probability of success by the capital market will, like the entrepreneur's subjective assessment of success, be a function of the size of the entrepreneur's search region, A, but it will not be a function of γ, the effectiveness of the entrepreneur's social network.

The size of the search region, A, is included because this is information that can be relatively easily conveyed to the capital market; indeed, it is likely to be part of a proposal that the entrepreneur would put together in asking for financial support. The effectiveness of the entrepreneur's social network, γ, is not included because the amorphous nature of this variable would be difficult to convey to the capital market. In essence, γ is private information. As a result, the capital market will base its subjective assessment of the probability of success on its own knowledge base, K, comprised of methods for estimating the end value, V, of the innovation were it to be achieved and for estimating the chances of success using portfolio theory. Because this knowledge base is unlikely to be the same as knowledge embodied in the entrepreneur's social network and clearly does not include an understanding of the specific creative synergies that exist in the form of the entrepreneur's social network, the subjective probability of success, $P(A \mid K)$, held by the owners of private equity may not be the same as the subjective likelihood of success, $L(A \mid \gamma)$, held by the entrepreneur.[13] Thus, in choosing to engage in the uncertain innovation process, the entrepreneur will be constrained by the requirement that the cost of the project, $c(A, \gamma)$, not exceed the expected value, V^e, of the project held by the owners of private equity.

The Solution to the Entrepreneur's Problem

When entrepreneurs are asked about motivation and success, they generally respond that entrepreneurship requires passion and that solely seeking a monetary payoff will generally result in failure (Streitfeld 2012). Nabseth and Ray (1974) find in their study of individual industry process innovations that while profitability is correlated with innovation and its diffusion, the direction of causality is not clear. They observe, moreover, that while determining the profitability of an innovation ex post is often difficult, the difficulty of determining the same thing ex ante is even greater. The reasons for these difficulties are several—inability to anticipate ex ante the change in profits associated with the cascade of changes in the production process brought about by the employment of the innovation, future factor price changes, future changes in costs associated with selling additional output, and so on. While a desire for profits is clearly part of what motivates the entrepreneur, we see in these observations support for the argument that the motivation of the entrepreneur is better modeled as seeking to maximize the likelihood of success than simply maximize profits.

Given that the entrepreneur's objective is to maximize the likelihood of success, the entrepreneur's problem can be characterized as one of choosing a region of size A^* that will maximize the entrepreneur's subjective likelihood of successfully identifying an input combination that achieves the desired innovation, $L(A \mid \gamma)$, subject to the resource constraint that the expected cost to the entrepreneur, $c(A, \gamma)$, not exceed the expected value, V^e, of the project as assessed by the owners of private equity. Moreover, because increasing the size of a search region will always increase the entrepreneur's subjective assessment of the likelihood of success, the resource constraint will always hold as an equality, that is, $c(A \mid \gamma) = V^e$.

The entrepreneur's problem and its solution can be represented graphically by Figure 3.4. The condition that the expected cost, $c(A \mid \gamma)$, equals the expected value, V^e, of the project is equivalent to the condition that the expected average cost of the project per unit of area searched equals the expected average value of the project per unit of area searched, that is, $c(A \mid \gamma)/A = V^e/A$.

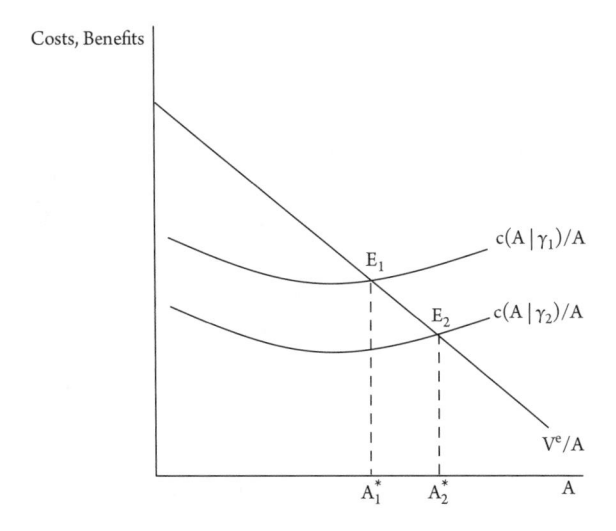

Figure 3.4 Optimal Solution to the Entrepreneur's Problem

We assume that the expected average cost of the project initially declines as the search region is expanded as a result of economies of scale in the innovation process and the ability to spread fixed costs over a greater and greater area of search. Eventually, however, the search process will be characterized by diminishing returns so that the expected average cost of the project will begin to rise. Thus, the average cost curves shown in Figure 3.4 are U-shaped. Likewise, while the capital market's subjective probability of success, $P(A \mid K)$, increases with the size of the area searched, we assume that it rises proportionately less than does the size of the search area. Thus, the expected average value of the project will decline as the area of search expands, as is illustrated by the downward-sloped expected average value of the project line in Figure 3.4.

Given that the effectiveness of the entrepreneur's social network is some γ_1, the solution to the entrepreneur's problem will be at point E_1 in Figure 3.4 where the expected average value line, V^e/A, intersects the average cost curve, $c(A \mid \gamma_1)/A$, thus implying an optimal search region of size A_1^*.

The solution to the entrepreneur's problem depends critically on the effectiveness of the entrepreneur's social network, γ. Because an increase in the quality of the entrepreneur's social network results in lower costs, all else held constant, we observe that an increase in the effectiveness of the entrepreneur's network from, say, γ_1 to γ_2, will result in a decrease in the expected average costs of the innovation to $c(A \mid \gamma_2)/A$. Thus, as illustrated in Figure 3.4, the solution to the entrepreneur's problem will be at point E_2 rather than E_1, and the optimal search region will increase in size to A_2^*. In other words—and this is the punch line of our model—the more effective the entrepreneur's social network, the greater the optimal search region and therefore the greater the chance of successfully finding an input combination that results in the desired innovation being successfully achieved.

Thus, as we first noted in Chapter 1, public sector entrepreneurship refers to innovative public policy initiatives that generate greater economic prosperity (that is, greater development of new technology and hence more innovation throughout the economy) by transforming a status-quo economic environment into one that is more conducive to economic units engaging in creative activities in the face of uncertainty. This transformation is affected primarily by increasing the effectiveness of social networks, that is, by increasing the heterogeneity of experiential ties among economic units and the ability of those same economic units to exploit such diversity.

Public Policy Implications of the Role of Networks

One implication of our theory is that it is not the accumulated knowledge of the entrepreneur that affects the entrepreneur's likelihood of success in identifying the input mix that succeeds in producing the innovation; rather, it is the effectiveness of the entrepreneur's network, γ.[14] This conclusion implies that directing public policies to achieving higher levels of entrepreneurial technical skill—a form of accumulated knowledge—in a particular area is not sufficient to increasing the chance of successfully achieving the desired innovation. Rather, public policies should be directed to increasing the heterogeneity of the social network that the entrepreneur relies upon.[15]

Therefore, an operational definition of public sector entrepreneurship, especially as it relates to technology and innovation policy, can be characterized in the following way. Public sector entrepreneurship focuses on the development of innovative public policies that affect the private sector innovation process, that is, the transformation of knowledge into economic knowledge. These public policies, whose outcomes are ex ante uncertain, work by increasing the effectiveness of entrepreneurial social networks, that is, the heterogeneity of experiential ties among economic units and the ability of those same economic units to exploit such diversity. Through technology and innovation policy initiatives that are characterized by public sector entrepreneurship, there will be more development of new technology and hence more innovation throughout the economy.[16]

As we noted in Chapter 1 and explored in detail in Chapter 2, the entrepreneur and his actions have been characterized by scholars in a variety of ways over time, and those characterizations are as varied as the scholars who have proffered them. However, while the entrepreneur, as Hébert and Link (1988, p. 41) phrased it, "has worn many faces and played many roles," the essence of what it means to be an entrepreneur is, as we have argued previously, to perceive an opportunity heretofore unexploited and act on that opportunity.[17]

Through this process of perception and action, the entrepreneur is thus a dynamic, not static, figure in economic activity.

It is important to note that, while we have been discussing the nature of the entrepreneurial experience as if it were a solitary endeavor, rarely is it the case, especially in the public sector, that the perception of opportunity and the ability to act on that perception are embodied in a single individual. This is to say that one individual entrepreneur may play off the entrepreneurial efforts of another and vice versa. Moreover, in this interplay of entrepreneurs, one may be more successful in his entrepreneurial efforts than another. Thus, Machlup noted that an entrepreneur is "alert and quick-minded, [one who perceives] what normal people of lesser alertness and perceptiveness would fail to notice" (1980, p. 179).

The reasons why one entrepreneur might succeed where another might not in pursuit of the same innovation—be it in the realm of technology and innovation policies or some other area—are typically complex. But particularly important are those reasons that can be traced to the successful entrepreneur having more and richer experiential ties than another entrepreneur. This greater effectiveness of the entrepreneur's social network results in an entrepreneur who is more quick-minded, alert, and perceptive than another. In short, it results in one who is more creative in this dynamic process both in opportunity recognition and in exploitation of the opportunities.

We illustrate a more creative individual within a dynamic process of opportunity recognition and exploitation in this chapter's appendix using the example of the development of Research Triangle Park, North Carolina.[18] We relegate this example to an appendix so as not to distract the intended flow of the book toward a discussion of U.S. technology and innovation policies. Yet, because the case of the development of Research Triangle Park humanizes our theory of entrepreneurship, we have included it for the interested reader.

Summary

This chapter outlined a general theory of entrepreneurship that is applicable to both private and public sector entrepreneurship. Beginning with the characterization of entrepreneurship as the process of opportunity recognition and exploitation, and based on the fundamental distinction between risk and uncertainty, our model argues that opportunity recognition and exploitation depend on the ability to engage in the creative application of existing knowledge to create new economic knowledge, and that the creation of new economic knowledge requires effective, heterogeneous social networks.

In the context of public sector entrepreneurship, this process will occur through the promulgation of innovative public policies that transform the status quo economic environment into one that is more conducive to economic units engaging in entrepreneurial creative activities in the face of uncertainty. Such public sector entrepreneurial policies often manifest themselves in terms of technology and innovation policy, though, as illustrated in the appendix by the case of Research Triangle Park in North Carolina, such policies are not limited to technology and innovation policy. Given the current state of public policies and the private sector entrepreneurial environment, public sector entrepreneurship thus affects the transformation of existing knowledge into new economic knowledge primarily by increasing the effectiveness of social networks, that is, by increasing the heterogeneity of experiential ties among economic units and the ability of those same economic units to exploit (i.e., to learn from) such diversity. Although this conclusion has heretofore not been part of the discussion in the various private and public sector entrepreneurial literatures, it is manifest in a number of technology and innovation policy initiatives that have occurred over the past several decades. It is to these policies that we now turn.

Appendix

Public Sector Entrepreneurship: The Case of Research Triangle Park

North Carolina's Research Triangle Park is an actual tract of land of approximately 6,800 acres located in the center of a scalene triangle formed by (alphabetically) Duke University, North Carolina State University,[19] and the University of North Carolina at Chapel Hill (see Figure A3.1). At present, there are about 170 global companies in the park employing nearly 39,000 individuals and contractors.

The Perception of a Park

Brandon P. Hodges was elected as state treasurer of North Carolina in November 1948 with the goal of bringing new types of industry, technology-based industries in particular, into the state. At that time, the North Carolina economy was centered on the traditional industries of furniture, textiles, and tobacco. In 1950, according to the U.S. Department of Commerce, there were only five states in the nation that had a per-capita income level lower than North

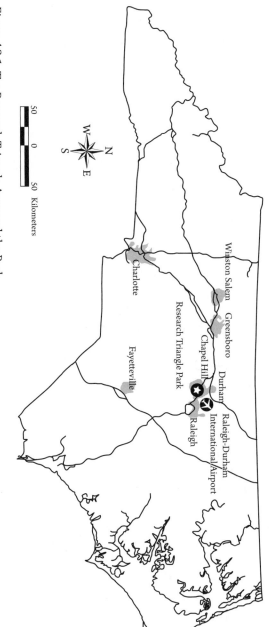

Figure A3.1 The Research Triangle Area and the Park

Carolina. By 1952, only two states did—Arkansas and Mississippi. There was justifiable concern that the economy needed to diversify in order to grow, and some thought that the state's university structure could possibly be used as a key element in an economic development plan.

Romeo Guest—a Greensboro, North Carolina, private sector contractor—is generally credited with the Research Triangle concept.[20] His idea was simple. For many years, North Carolina, and the South in general, lagged in scientific research and in the application of research to industry. Perhaps the triangle universities could act as a magnet to attract research companies into the area, and this in turn would lead to the development of new technology-based industries throughout the state.

Guest was able to sell his idea to Brandon Hodges, and in early December 1954 Brandon Hodges took the Research Triangle idea to Governor Luther Hodges (no relationship). But, the governor was at that time only lukewarm to the concept.

It has been argued (Link 1995) that the governor, because of his textiles background, did not fully understand the nature of research and development (R&D), much less its role in economic development. After the unsuccessful December meeting with the governor, William Newell, director of the North Carolina Textile Research Center and intimately familiar with the importance of R&D, prepared at the urging of Brandon Hodges and others a report entitled "A Proposal for the Development of an Industrial Research Center in North Carolina." The report was sent to the governor in late January 1955. Records from the ensuing meeting with the governor show that the meeting went well; archival communications suggest that thereafter the Research Triangle idea because simply known as "the Governor's Research Triangle" (Link 1995). Thus what initially was conceptualized as a private sector entrepreneurial opportunity was transformed into a public sector entrepreneurial opportunity to induce desirable behaviors on the private sector entrepreneurs through innovative public policies that alter the private sector market environment, that is, what we have labeled indirect public sector entrepreneurship.[21]

Management of the Perception

Guest took it upon himself to meet with the relevant leadership at the three triangle universities. These meetings were not simply an altruistic gesture. Rather, Guest saw a specific role for himself in the Research Triangle project. He hoped to become the contractor for all of the companies that would eventually locate in the park, so university commitment to the park idea was critical.

Throughout early 1955 there were numerous meetings about how to implement the governor's Research Triangle idea including the creation of several committees and working groups. For example, in May of that year, the Research Triangle Development Committee was established, and a formal statement of the relationship between the park and the three universities was articulated:[22]

> The basic concept of the Research Triangle is that North Carolina possesses a unique combination of educational and research resources and communication facilities eminently suitable to the fostering of industrial research. It is not anticipated that the three universities in the Triangle shall engage directly in the conduct of industrial research, except under carefully designated and administered policies. Rather, the principal functions of the Universities are to stimulate industrial research by the research atmosphere their very existence creates, and to supplement industrial-research talents and facilities by providing a wellspring of knowledge and talents for the stimulation and guidance of research by individual firms. (Link 1995, pp. 28–29)

In other words, universities from the outset saw their role as increasing the effectiveness of the social networks of those private sector enterprises that chose to locate in Research Triangle Park.

In March 1956, William Friday became acting president (and later president) of the University of North Carolina system. He, along with Governor Hodges, was instrumental in forming the Research Triangle Committee, Inc. This was a non-stock, nonprofit, benevolent, charitable, and educational corporation for the purpose of encouraging and promoting the establishing of industrial research laboratories in North Carolina primarily in the triangle area. This organization became the motivation for North Carolina representatives from the public sector and the university communities to publicize the research triangle concept and recruit companies into the area. But, a place was needed to demonstrate to research companies that the triangle concept was viable and was coming to fruition.

The Research Triangle Committee, Inc. attempted to identify investors in land that would eventually become the park. Simply put, it was believed that companies that were interested in the concept would want to visit North Carolina and see something tangible. One investor, Karl Robbins of New York, was found. Robbins had in his earlier years been involved in North Carolina's textile industry, so he knew people in the state as well as its citizenry. He initially invested $275,000, and those funds were used by Guest and others to option parcels of land under the name of Pinelands Company. By the end of 1957, just over 3,500 acres had been optioned with another 440 acres pending; the final purchase price would be $700,000. However, Robbins became reluctant to meet his promised $1 million investment. The reason for his waning interest in the project was the visible lack of North Carolina investors. Robbins would not send any additional moneys unless matched by investments by North Carolinians. But, such moneys were not to be forthcoming at that time.[23]

Action on the Perception

The for-profit Pinelands Company vehicle for obtaining land for the park did not seem to be working. While Guest's perception of the role of a research park as a driver for North Carolina's future economic development was widely accepted as sound, neither Guest nor the governor's office had the ability to act on that perception in a way that would make the idea a reality.

Robert Hanes, president of Wachovia Bank and Trust Company, who was a supporter of the triangle idea, and Governor Hodges realized that it was time for a change in course. They approached Archie Davis, chairman of Wachovia Bank and Trust Company, to sell stock in Pinelands Company.

Davis, who knew nothing about Research Triangle or Pineland Company before his meeting with Hanes and Hodges in August 1958, realized immediately on hearing about what had transpired that Guest's perception of the role of a research park for the state was sound but the management of the park idea to date was flawed. As Davis noted:

> To me, I just felt without knowing anything about it, [the park idea] just didn't make sense. If this [park] indeed was designed for public service, then it would be much easier to raise money from corporations and institutions and the like, who were interested in serving the State of North Carolina, by making a contribution. (Link 1995, p. 68)

At an October 1958 meeting of the Research Triangle Committee, Inc., Davis pointed out that the idea of a research park has a public character and should be a nonprofit undertaking. It was agreed that Davis would raise $1 million for the committee plus $250,000 for a main building. Within a thirty-day period Davis traveled the state, at his own expense, speaking one-on-one with people about supporting a research park for the good of North Carolina. By the end of December, he had exceeded his fundraising goal.

What Davis did, Guest could never have done. While Guest was entrepreneurial in his perception of the idea of a research park, it took Davis's ability to act on that perception to raise sufficient funds to launch the park. His ability to do this came from his experiential ties with the business community in North Carolina, that is, his entrepreneurial success in exploiting the opportunity first conceived of by Guest was due to the superiority of his social network. Figure A3.2 shows the geographic breadth from which he was able to raise the needed moneys.

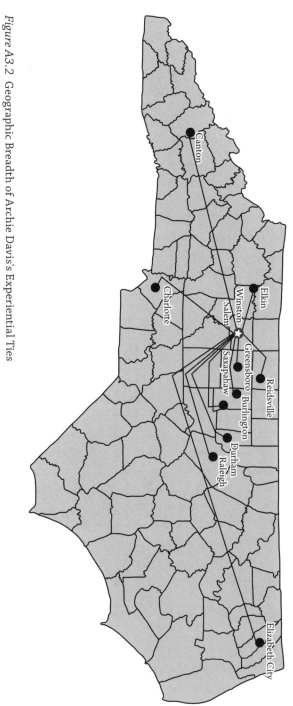

Figure A3.2 Geographic Breadth of Archie Davis's Experiential Ties

The Strategic Management of the Park

One of the most significant events in the history of North Carolina took place on January 9, 1959, in Raleigh. Governor Hodges announced that Davis had raised $1.425 million. These funds were to be used for three purposes:

- To establish the Research Triangle Institute to do contract research for business, industry, and government.
- To construct a new building to house the Institute in the park.
- To acquire the land that was assembled by Robbins and to pass control of Pinelands Company to the nonprofit Research Triangle Foundation.

Soon thereafter, Guest resigned from his role in Pinelands Company and watched, as an outsider, what was to happen.

In early October 1959, Chemstrand Corporation purchased 100 acres and broke ground on a research facility later that month. However, it was not until April 1965 that the park idea was validated. IBM announced that it would locate a 600,000-square-foot research facility on 400 acres in the park. That event became the prologue for the future.

Research Triangle Park is arguably the most successful research park in the nation (Link 2002), and perhaps this is due to a unique management strategy. It was written into the certificate of incorporation of the Research Triangle Committee, Inc. in 1956:

> It is the intent and purpose of the corporation to promote the use of the research facilities of the [Duke University, North Carolina State, and University of North Carolina at Chapel Hill] ... through cooperation [among] the three institutions and cooperation [among] the institutions and industrial research agencies. ... The corporation is a nonprofit, benevolent, charitable, and educational corporation and has no capital stock. Upon the dissolution of the corporation, all assets of the corporation shall be divided equally among [the institutions] for the purpose for which [the] institutions were founded. (Link 2002, p. 63)

In 1974, Davis, in his role as president of the Research Triangle Foundation, realized that the universities needed a presence or home in the Park noting (Link 2002, p. 64): "It would be a shame ... for the principal beneficiaries of the Park—the universities—not to have some land in the Park for their own use." In 1975, the Triangle Universities Center for Advanced Studies, Inc. (TUCASI), a nonprofit corporation, was established on 120 acres in the center of the park.

A unique undertaking, TUCASI, represents the nation's first three-university corporation designed to plan and develop joint research and educational activities in a major research park ... The major purpose of [TUCASI is] to assist in and facilitate the planning and execution of non-profit research and educational programs that utilize and enhance the productivity of the intellectual and physical resources of [three world-class universities]. (Link 2002, pp. 72–73)

In a sense, TUCASI is the universities' home within Research Triangle Park. TUCASI is an ever-present symbol that the universities are at the heart of the park's mission and therefore at the heart of its success. TUCASI is like a park within a park.

Setting the Stage

So long as the mother, Ignorance, lives, it is not safe for Science, the offspring, to divulge the hidden causes of things.
—Johannes Kepler

Introduction

Having completed our characterization of entrepreneurship and explained why private sector entrepreneurship manifests itself indirectly through policies that focus on making the general economic environment more conducive to public sector entrepreneurial efforts—particularly those associated with U.S. technology development and other related innovations—we now turn to an empirical examination of technology and innovation policy over the past several decades. This chapter sets the stage for that examination by characterizing the overall patterns of behavior that provide a context for the examples of public sector entrepreneurship that follow in later chapters.

The Productivity Slowdown

Perhaps the most significant events over the past half century in the United States from a technology and innovation perspective were the two productivity slowdowns that occurred in the mid-1970s and the late 1970s/early 1980s. Beyond the negative impact that these productivity slowdowns had on the prospects for future economic growth, these events set in motion a debate on how to curtail and reverse these trends. The result was the adoption of innovative public policies that we now know had a significant impact on improving productivity. What made these policies innovative was their focus on fundamentally changing the general economic environment in a way that stimulated technology development and other innovative activity. Thus, we can mark this period of productivity slowdown as the starting point for contemporary technology and innovation policy and our focus on public sector entrepreneurship.

In broad terms, the notion of productivity is a relatively intuitive notion and can be thought of as the amount of output associated with a given amount of input(s). However, further consideration suggests that there are a number of complications that have made the study of productivity, and how to measure it, an interesting one. For example, should productivity be measured in marginal or average terms? How should the general notion of productivity be adapted to account for more than one input? And, what complications need to be dealt with when thinking in terms of the productivity of an entire economy rather than an individual firm's production process?

Perhaps the most common way to measure productivity at an economy-wide level is in terms of the degree to which there has been technological advancement. In that regard, total factor productivity (TFP) is considered by many to be an appropriate index of technological advancement because of its ability to account in an economy-wide setting for the simultaneous employment of more than one input.[1] TFP is generally measured in terms of value-added output per a measure of the combined use of multiple input units. In the simplest case, TFP can be defined as output (Q) per the functionally (f) combined number of units of capital (K) and labor (L):

$$TFP = Q/f(K, L). \tag{4.1}$$

A more detailed derivation of a TFP index is presented in the appendix in terms of two inputs, K and L. The approach that underlies equation (4.1) is a general one, so that it is possible to expand the number of inputs to account more finely for the overall production process. Thus, a more complete functional (F) version of equation (4.1) is:

$$TFP = Q/F(K, L, M, E, S), \tag{4.2}$$

where M refers to material inputs, E to energy inputs, and S to purchased business services.[2] Figure 4.1 shows an index of TFP, normalized to 2005 (2005 = 100), for the private U.S. business sector from 1948 through 2011. As noted above, the two time periods in the figure that are associated with productivity slowdowns are particularly important for motivating the technology and innovation policy examples in this book. The first time period is from 1973 through 1974, and the second time period is from 1978 through 1982.

The slowdown in measured productivity, specifically in terms of the downturn in the TFP index in 1973 and 1974, was presumed by many economists, and likely many policymakers as well, to be a result of a nonrecurring, periodic event. The nonrecurring event was associated with the energy crisis of 1973: "Energy prices stand as the single most important contributor to the 1973 [productivity] break" (Siegel 1979, p. 60). Many thought at the time that such events were normal, one-time cyclical shocks to the economy, and

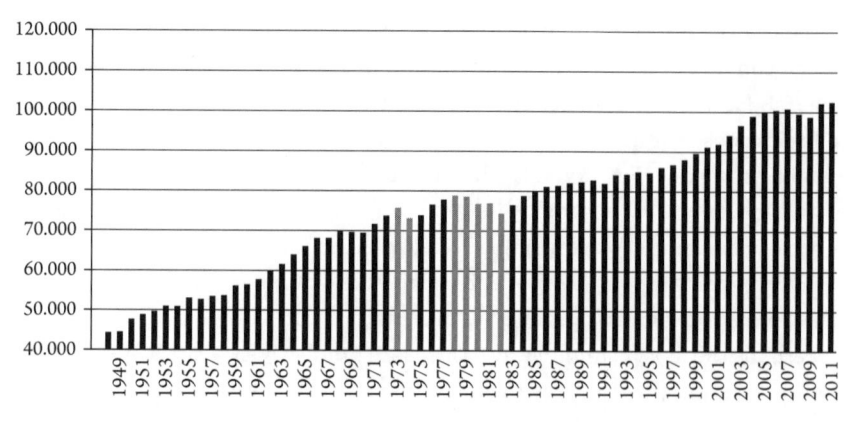

Figure 4.1 U.S. Total Factor Productivity Index, 1948–2011 (2005 = 100)

movement in the TFP index was accordingly a normal cyclical response around a more stable, long-term growth in productivity.

More important, however, from both an economic and a policy perspective, was the productivity slowdown that began in 1978 and ended in 1982. In fact, in 1978 the Bureau of Labor Statistics TFP index was 78.906, the highest it had been in the post-World War II period. By the end of 1982, the TFP index was 74.401, only slightly higher that it had been a decade earlier.

Many explanations have been offered for this precipitous and unprecedented decline in productivity or technological advancement from 1978 through 1982, as summarized in Link (1987). Link and Siegel, reflecting the concern that the slowdown was not a response to cyclical, one-time, and temporary shocks but rather a more fundamental and enduring change in long-term growth prospects, wrote:

> In the early 1980s there was great concern among economists and policymakers in the United States regarding the pervasive slowdown in productivity growth and the concomitant decline in the global competitiveness of American firms in key high-technology industries. One of the alleged culprits of this productivity slowdown was a decline in the rate of technological innovation, which is a reflection of declining entrepreneurship. (2003, p. 58)

As we will discuss in Chapter 9, the U.S. House of Representatives' report about the proposed High Technology Research and Development Joint Ventures Act of 1983 (H. R. 3393) noted:

> A number of indicators strongly suggest that the position of world technology leadership once firmly held by the United States is declining. The United States, only a decade ago, with only five percent of the

world's population was generating about 75 percent of the world's technology. Now, the U.S. share has declined to about 50 percent and in another ten years, without fundamental changes in our Nation's technological policy ... the past trend would suggest that it may be down to only 30 percent.

Public Sector Responses to the Productivity Slowdown

Congress was quick to respond at the beginning of what would become the second productivity slowdown, perhaps in an effort to avert another episode in the economy like the one that occurred in 1973–1974. Congress' first technology-based initiative began with the consideration of the Dole-Bayh bill

Table 4.1 **Summary of the Post-Productivity Slowdown Technology and Innovation Related Policies**

Legislation	Targeted Parties	Direct Impact on R&D	Indirect Impact on R&D
University and Small Business Patent Procedure Act of 1980 (known as the Bayh-Dole Act of 1980)	Universities Private sector firms		Yes
Stevenson-Wydler Technology Innovation Act of 1980 (known as the Stevenson-Wydler Act of 1980)	National laboratories and other research organizations Private sector firms		Yes
Economic Recovery Tax Act (ERTA) of 1981 (relevant portion known as the R&E Tax Credit of 1981)	Firms conducting R&D	Yes	
Small Business Innovation Development Act of 1982	Small firms (< 500 employees)	Yes	
National Cooperative Research Act of 1984	Firms of all sizes and their research partners		Yes
Omnibus Trade and Competitiveness Act of 1988	Firms all of sizes conducting focused R&D	Yes	

in late 1978 (see Chapter 5) in light of what appeared to be another slowdown like that in 1973 and 1974.[3] This initiative was quickly followed by the promulgation of a number of other innovative pieces of legislation in the 1980s, in large part as an immediate effort to reverse the productivity slowdown and rebuild the technology base of the United States to prevent another such decline.

Table 4.1 lists the six post-productivity slowdown, technology, and innovation related legislations that were passed in the 1980s and that we discuss in the later chapters. Also shown in the table are the affected parties and whether the legislation affected R&D activity directly or indirectly.[4] Policymakers at that time understood that investments in R&D are fundamental to rebuilding the U.S. technology base.

One possible taxonomy for these six post-productivity slowdown policies is provided in Table 4.2. Certainly, there is an element of subjectiveness to our placement of these policies in the labeled cells, especially the cells under the heading "Advancement of Knowledge." However, as will be evident in the chapters that follow, we find that this taxonomy provides a useful structure for analyzing each of the policies listed in Table 4.1.

Table 4.2 **Taxonomy for the Impact of the Six Post-Productivity Slowdown Technology and Innovation Related Policies**

Impact on Technology and Innovation

	Immediate	Long term
Advancement of Knowledge High		ERTA of 1981 (R&E Tax Credit of 1981) Small Business Innovation Development Act of 1982 National Cooperative Research Act of 1984 Omnibus Trade and Competitiveness Act of 1988
Low	University and Small Business Patent Procedure Act of 1980 (Bayh-Dole Act of 1980) Stevenson-Wydler Technology Innovation Act of 1980 (Stevenson-Wydler Act of 1980)	

In the chapters that follow, we will therefore refer back to Table 4.2 in our discussion of each policy and why, based on our theoretical model of entrepreneurship in Chapter 3, each is an example of public sector entrepreneurship.

Government's Role in the Support of Technology and Innovation

Were the six technology and innovation policies introduced above justifiable, in concept, from an economic perspective? That is, is there a theoretical foundation to substantiate the public sector entering into market activities?[5]

Market failure is typically offered as the theoretical basis for government's role in market activity, and the most common way in economics is to attribute market failure to the presence of market power, imperfect information, externalities, or public goods. Interestingly, however, the explicit application of market failure to justify government's role in technology and innovation—in R&D investment activity in particular—is a relatively recent phenomenon within the public policy community.

President William Clinton articulated this theoretical position in his 1994 *Economic Report of the President*:

> The goal of technology policy is not to substitute the government's judgment for that of private industry in deciding which potential 'winners' to back. Rather, the point is to correct market failure. (Council of Economic Advisers 1994, p. 191)

Subsequent Executive Office policy statements have echoed this theme; *Science in the National Interest* (Executive Office of the President 1994) and *Science and Technology: Shaping the Twenty-First Century* (Executive Office of the President 1998) are among such examples. President Clinton's 2000 *Economic Report of the President* elaborated upon the concept of market failure as part of U.S. technology policy:

> Rather than support technologies that have clear and immediate commercial potential (which would likely be developed by the private sector without government support), government should seek out new technologies that will create benefits with large spillovers to society at large. (Council of Economic Advisers 2000, p. 99)

Relatedly, Martin and Scott observed:

> Limited appropriability, financial market failure, external benefits to the production of knowledge, and other factors suggest that strict

reliance on a market system will result in underinvestment in innovation, relative to the socially desirable level. This creates a prima facie case in favor of public intervention to promote innovative activity. (2000, p. 438)

At a more general level, market failure refers to the market—including both the R&D-investing producers of a technology and the users of the technology—underinvesting, from society's standpoint, in a particular technology or technology application. Such underinvestment occurs because conditions exist that prevent organizations from fully realizing or appropriating the benefits created by their investments. Those conditions, as Munger (2000) argues, can be categorized in a hierarchy based on the nature of the cause. At the lowest level, type 3 sources of market failure (those most closely related to problems associated with the characteristics of markets themselves) are those market failures that we have noted above—the presence of market power, imperfect information, externalities, or public goods. At a higher level, type 2 sources of market failure (those that are removed from the characteristics of markets themselves) are failures attributable to governmental policies and may be thought of as failures of commission that interfere with the ability of markets to act efficiently. Thus, government policies that result in the creation of monopolies that are not justified by type 3 market failures would be examples of type 2 market failures. And finally, at the most fundamental level, type 1 sources of market failure are those that stem from government neglecting to establish the general environment for the efficient functioning of markets. They might be thought of as failures of omission. They arise in the absence of well-defined and comprehensive property rights, clear and effective contract laws, systems of enforcement, and so on.

There is some overlap in types of market failure that indirect public sector entrepreneurship seeks to redress. Thus, for example, the problem of incomplete markets associated with the presence of risk or uncertainty may be due to imperfect information—a type 3 market failure—or a flawed system of property rights and contract laws—a type 1 market failure. However, it is clear that indirect public sector entrepreneurship has a stronger focus on type 1 sources of market failure than do traditional forms of economic regulation and policy, which focus on redressing type 3 market failures.

One example of a type 1 market failure follows closely on Arrow's (1962, p. 609) seminal work identifying three sources of market failure related to knowledge-based innovative activity: "indivisibilities, inappropriability, and uncertainty."

To elaborate on these sources of market failure, consider a marketable technology to be produced through an R&D process where conditions prevent the R&D-investing firm from fully appropriating the benefits from its technological advancement. Other firms in the market, or in related markets, because of their ability to learn of the new marketable technology and to one extent or another exploit it, will realize some of the benefits (i.e., revenues in excess of the opportunity costs of the resources used by these other firms) from the innovation. The original R&D-investing firm will then calculate, because of such conditions, that the marginal benefits it can receive from a unit investment in such R&D will be less than could be earned in the absence of the conditions that reduce the appropriated benefits of R&D below their potential, namely the ability of other firms to exploit the R&D of the original firm. In other words, the original R&D-investing firm will calculate that the marginal benefits received from a unit investment in such R&D will be less than the full social benefits of their R&D. Thus, the R&D-investing firm is likely to underinvest in R&D relative to what it would have chosen as its investment in the absence of the conditions, that is, relative to what it would have chosen to invest had it been able to exploit fully the benefits of its R&D investment. Indeed, if the R&D-investing firm determines that its private rate of return is less than its private hurdle rate (the rate of return necessary to justify such investment), it would not undertake socially valuable R&D at all.

The standard textbook approach to such problems is to view them as problems associated with prices not being right, that is, as type 3 market failure problems. The policy typically proposed to solve the problem is a subsidy, a tax, or some form of regulation. While such an approach may help in many markets, the decision to engage in R&D is a decision to engage in innovation and, as we have argued, is fundamentally characterized by uncertainty. Thus, the correct tax, subsidy, or form of regulation is not only not known, it is not knowable ex ante. Hence, to correct for underinvestment in R&D, one needs to view the problem as a type 1 market failure problem and therefore engage in changing the economic environment of the firm fundamentally by engaging in indirect public sector entrepreneurship as we have defined it in Chapter 3. This use of public sector entrepreneurship is justified precisely because it addresses a fundamental failure to adequately define the economic environment of firms—in this case, those that engage in R&D—so that they may act efficiently.

Summary

From a technology and innovation perspective, the most significant economic events of the past half century in the United States were the two productivity slowdowns in the mid-1970s and the late 1970s/early 1980s. To redress the slowdowns, Congress promulgated a number of innovative public policies. Included in this set of policies were the Bayh-Dole Act of 1980, the Stevenson-Wydler Act of 1980, the R&E Tax Credit of 1981, the Small Business Innovation Development Act of 1982, the National Cooperative Research Act of 1984, and the Omnibus Trade and Competitiveness Act of 1988.

What was remarkable about these policies was that they broke new ground. Rather than focusing on traditional policies of providing subsidies, taxes, or regulations based on the assumption that the world is at least probabilistically determinate, they focused on redefining the economic environment in which R&D decisions are made to make it more receptive and encouraging for technology and innovation development. Such policies, at least implicitly, recognize the fundamental role of uncertainty in the entrepreneurial process and are examples of indirect public sector entrepreneurship as we defined it in Chapter 3. We now turn in the next several chapters to an examination of each of these policies.

Appendix

Derivation of a Total Factor Productivity Index

The academic model underlying the calculation of a TFP index is based on a generalizable production function applicable to the ith firm, i^{th} industry, i^{th} sector, or i^{th} country, written as:[6]

$$Q_i = A_i F(K_i, L_i), \qquad (A4.1)$$

where Q represents output, and K and L represent the stock of physical capital and labor, respectively. In equation (A4.1), A_i is a neutral disembodied shift factor that can be interpreted as a general measure of the productivity common to all inputs, that is, as a measure of TFP.

Many, if not most, of the early empirical studies of the technology-productivity growth relationship employed a simplified Cobb-Douglas production function to give a tractable structure to the general production function represented in equation (A4.1):

$$Q = A_0 e^{\lambda t} K^\alpha L^\beta, \qquad (A4.2)$$

where A_0 is a constant, λ is a disembodied rate of growth parameter, and α and β are output elasticities. Constant returns to scale were typically assumed, which implies that $\alpha + \beta = 1$. Notice, moreover, that in terms of equation (A4.1), A_i, the variable representing TFP, is equal to $A_0 e^{\lambda t}$. Hence, λ represents the growth rate in TFP.

Assuming K and L are both functions of time, t, and letting $X' = (dX/dt)$, the growth rate of output can be decomposed into three components—that which is attributable to the growth in capital, that which is attributable to the growth in labor, and that which is attributable to a general increase in productivity (TFP):

$$Q'/Q = \lambda + \alpha K'/K + \beta L'/L. \qquad \text{(A4.3)}$$

While it is possible to measure the growth rate of output, and of capital and labor, from an empirical perspective, it is difficult to measure λ, our measure of the TFP growth rate. But solving equation (A4.3) for λ reveals that one can calculate λ as the difference between overall growth rates and the (weighted) growth rates in capital and labor: [7]

$$\lambda = Q'/Q - \alpha K'/K - \beta L'/L. \qquad \text{(A4.4)}$$

Thus, λ is an index of the residually measured growth rate in TFP:

$$\text{TFP}'/\text{TFP} = Q'/Q - \alpha K'/K - \beta L'/L. \qquad \text{(A4.5)}$$

PART II

POLICY EXAMPLES OF PUBLIC SECTOR ENTREPRENEURSHIP

5

The Bayh-Dole Act of 1980

The ornament of a house is the friends who frequent it.
—Ralph Waldo Emerson

Legislative Background

In the 95th Congress, Senator Robert Dole (R, KS) and Senator Birch Bayh (D, IN) introduced the Dole-Bayh bill. In his introductory remarks on September 13, 1978, Senator Bayh said:[1]

A wealth of scientific talent at American colleges and universities—talent responsible for the development of numerous innovative scientific breakthroughs each year—is going to waste as a result of bureaucratic red tape and illogical government regulations. ... The problem, very simply, is the present policy followed by most government agencies of retaining patent rights to inventions. ... Government sponsored research is often basic rather than applied research. Therefore, many of the resulting inventions are at a very embryonic stage of development and require substantial expenditures before they actually become a product or applied system of benefit to the public. ... It is not government's responsibility—or indeed, the right of government—to assume the commercialization function. Unless private industry has the protection of some exclusive use under patent or license agreements, they cannot afford the risk of commercialization expenditures. As a result, many new developments resulting from government research are left idle. (Stevens 2004, p. 95)

On December 12, 1980, President Jimmy Carter signed Public Law 96-517, amendments to the patent and trademark laws formally known as the University and Small Business Patent Procedure Act of 1980. This legislation is commonly known as the Bayh-Dole Act of 1980, and this innovative legislation may possibly be "the most inspired piece of legislation to be enacted in America over the past half-century" (*The Economist* 2002, p. 3). According to the Act (emphasis added in italics),

> it is the policy and objective of the Congress to use the patent system to promote the utilization of inventions arising from federally supported research or development; to encourage maximum participation of *small business firms* in federally supported research and development efforts; to promote collaboration between commercial concerns and *nonprofit organizations*, including *universities*; to ensure that inventions made by nonprofit organizations and small business firms are used in a manner to promote free competition and enterprise; to promote the commercialization and public availability of inventions made in the United States by United States industry and labor; to ensure that the Government obtains sufficient rights in federally supported inventions to meet the needs of the Government and protect the public against nonuse or unreasonable use of inventions; and to minimize the costs of administering policies in this area.

According to the Congressional Research Service, only about 5 percent of government-owned patents have ever been used in the private sector, though a portion of the government's intellectual property portfolio had potential applications: "The Bayh-Dole Act was constructed, in part, to address the low utilization rate of these federal patents" (Schacht 2009a, p. 2). As a result of the Act, small businesses and nonprofit organizations—especially universities—could now take ownership of inventions and explore their commercial exploitation with other parties.

University Technology Transfer

Technology transfer offices (TTOs) facilitate the transfer of faculty inventions and technologies to the private sector either through licensing arrangements or through the creation of spinoff or startup companies.[2, 3]

The technology transfer process, incentivized through the passage of the Bayh-Dole Act, has evolved over time and is now a rather complex one. A schematic of what might be called the traditional model of university technology transfer (UTT), or more simply the traditional model, is presented in Figure 5.1 (Bradley et al. 2013a). The numbered processes in the figure are discussed sequentially below. This model is a synthesis of dominant paradigms and the extant literature in several disciplines related to technology transfer within the academic and professional landscape. We refer to this synthesis of existing thought in its totality as a description of the entire technology transfer process.

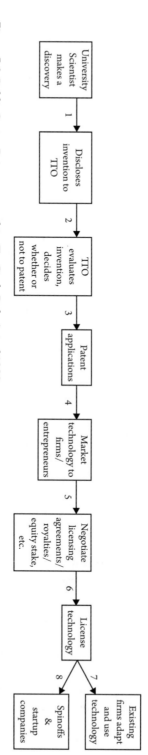

Figure 5.1 Public Sector Entrepreneurship: The Bayh-Dole Act of 1980

This representation of the technology transfer process has pedagogical value for at least three reasons: (1) it is a useful construct for segmenting the academic and professional literature on UTT;[4] (2) it establishes a straw man for our discussion of the limitations of traditional views about the technology transfer process; and (3) it serves as a point of departure for a more in-depth and complete model of technology transfer that accounts for the variety of ways by which rights are assigned and exploited, the special role that governments at all levels play under the Bayh-Dole Act, and more subtle but important feedback effects. An expanded model of technology transfer is discussed in the appendix.

The traditional model of the technology transfer process in Figure 5.1 is illustrated as a linear model, and it begins with the process of discovery by a university scientist. The term *scientist* is used as a descriptor for any university researcher. Of course, academic research could come from any discipline or any department or campus structure.

The scientist discloses his technology or invention to the university's TTO at process 1. As stipulated by the Bayh-Dole Act, the federally funded faculty member who recognizes or discovers a new technology or invention that has commercialization potential is required to disclose the invention to their university's TTO. The Bayh-Dole Act mandates that "the contractor disclose each subject invention to the Federal agency within a reasonable time after it is made and that the Federal Government may receive title to any subject invention not reported to it within such time."[5] However, the rule that university scientists must file an invention disclosure is rarely enforced even when detected, and disclosure depends largely on the incentive structures in place within the university.

Once the invention is disclosed, the TTO evaluates the invention and decides whether or not to pursue acquiring a patent—process 2. The TTO must consider the commercial potential of the invention, as well as its prospective interest from the public or private sector. If the TTO decides to invest in the invention, the next step is the patent application process as noted by process 3. If the patent is awarded, the TTO markets the technology to organizations and entrepreneurs. The goal of this marketing effort is to match the technology with an organization that or entrepreneur who can best utilize the technology and provide an opportunity for revenues to flow back to the university. This is process 4.

When a suitable partner is found, the university works with the organization or entrepreneur to negotiate a licensing agreement—process 5. The licensing agreement typically includes a royalty to the university, an equity stake in the startup, or other such compensation. When an agreement is reached, the technology is officially licensed in process 6. In the final stage of the model, the organization—process 7—or faculty entrepreneur—process 8—adapts and uses the technology, and hopefully will commercialize it as an innovation.

The original invention typically undergoes extensive adaptation during the process to commercialization. The university, and sometimes the inventing scientist, might continue to be involved with the organization or entrepreneur to help develop the technology or to maintain the licensing agreement.

Several existing paradigms underlie this so-called traditional model. Miller and Acs (2013) have characterized traditional technology transfer as an organization-centric model that combines Etzkowitz's (2003) triple helix model and Kerr's (2001) concept of the multiversity.

Under the triple helix model of university-industry-government relations, reciprocal relationships are formed among the three institutions in which each attempts to enhance the performance of the others. The multiversity is a modular institution centered on undergraduate and graduate schools with multiple activities and organizations, including science parks and research institutes, integrated or released depending on the needs of the students, faculty, and regional communities. Miller and Acs's organization-centric model extends the path from Bush's (1945) implicit linear model (see Chapter 11) to the Bayh-Dole Act, and achieves technology transfer through connections between university researchers and both federal funding and potential commercial opportunities.

The Bayh-Dole Act as an Example of Public Sector Entrepreneurship

The relevant question to ask to determine if the Bayh-Dole Act meets our criterion for public sector entrepreneurship is whether it is an innovative public policy that improves the social network for the affected parties operating in an uncertain economic environment, that is, whether it increases the number and quality of heterogeneous experiential ties for the affected parties, thus resulting in those parties having an enhanced ability to identify heretofore unexploited opportunities and to exploit those same opportunities.

We first describe the Bayh-Dole Act in Table 5.1 in terms of four characteristics, the first two of which come from the taxonomy of technology and innovation policies proffered in Chapter 4 and summarized in Table 4.2: advancement of knowledge and impact on technology and innovation.[6] The third characteristic, targeted parties, emphasizes the segment of the innovation system spectrum targeted by this initiative (see Table 4.1). And the fourth characteristic reflects our definition of public sector entrepreneurship by emphasizing the heterogeneity of the experiential ties to the social networks that are improved by the Act.[7]

Table 5.1 **Public sector Entrepreneurship: The Bayh-Dole Act of 1980**

Characteristics	*Descriptor*	*Comment*
Advancement of knowledge	Low	Existing knowledge, as embodied in the technology or invention, is being transferred; new knowledge is not being created.
Impact on technology and innovation	Immediate	Because the technology already exists, its impact outside of the university could be immediate.
Targeted parties	Universities	Universities benefit from the transfer of own technology in terms of licensing revenues, private sector ties, and regional development. University faculty benefit in terms of licensing revenues.
	Private sector firms	Private sector firms that license the university's technology benefit in terms of having saved on the cost of the underlying R&D—although adoption and implementation are not costless—and they possibly benefit in terms of exclusive licensing arrangements.
Heterogeneity of experiential ties	Significant	Experiential ties that enhance the university come in the form of future possible industry research partners. Experiential ties that enhance the licensing private sector firm come in the form of future possible university research partners or graduate hires.

The Bayh-Dole Act achieved such a significant improvement through a redefinition of property rights that facilitated the transfer of existing knowledge from universities to the private sector—be it to existing firms, startups, or spinoffs—for commercial exploitation. Several issues are of relevance in this process.

First, while one might think that the transfer of existing knowledge rather than the creation of new knowledge does not fit the notion of innovation, recall Schumpeter's observation:

> To carry any improvement into effect is a task entirely different from the inventing of it, and a task, moreover, requiring entirely different

kinds of aptitudes. Although entrepreneurs of course may be inventors just as they may be capitalists, they are inventors not by nature of their function but by coincidence and vice versa. Besides, the innovations which it is the function of entrepreneurs to carry out need not necessarily be any inventions at all. (1934, pp. 88–89)

There is, in fact, invention embodied in the transfer of knowledge facilitated by the Bayh-Dole Act, but that invention typically occurs before the actual transfer process is initiated. But, as Schumpeter noted, such invention is not the hallmark of entrepreneurial innovation. Rather, it is the exploitation of opportunities heretofore unexploited. Such opportunities may be based on newly created knowledge or knowledge that is, figuratively speaking, lying on the ground ready to be picked up. Indeed, one particular advantage of existing knowledge is that it is more likely to be immediately exploitable.

Second, the social networks of both those in the university and those in the private sector are significantly enhanced. For those in the university, the ability to engage in the transfer of knowledge to the private sector opens them, albeit with considerable uncertainty, to input from those in the private sector, a perspective typically missing from those in the university community. This private sector perspective is often quite different from that of the university scientist, and with that divergence come the creative synergies and dynamics that can result in additional transfer of existing knowledge in the future as well as the creation of new knowledge that can also be exploited for commercial gain. Likewise, those in the private sector gain for similar reasons. The ability to access existing university knowledge creates, again with uncertainty, a distinct perspective that is often absent within the private sector. And with that come the creative synergies and dynamics that can result in new, unexploited opportunities being recognized and ways to exploit such opportunities for commercial gain being discovered. In addition, with the enhancement in the social networks of the university and of the private sector comes the possibility of additional knowledge synergies in the form of future research partners and the hiring of university graduates who bring with them university knowledge and perspectives.

The Economic Impact of the Bayh-Dole Act

The economic impact of the Bayh-Dole Act has been substantial. Figure 5.2 shows the number of TTOs opened, by year of founding. Clearly, the number of TTOs in each of the two decades following the passage of the Bayh-Dole Act was greater than in any other decade. Of the 166 TTOs documented by the Association of University Technology Managers (AUTM) through 2011, 5 of which were founded prior to 1970, 34 percent were started between 1980 and 1989, and 41 percent were started between 1990 and 1999.

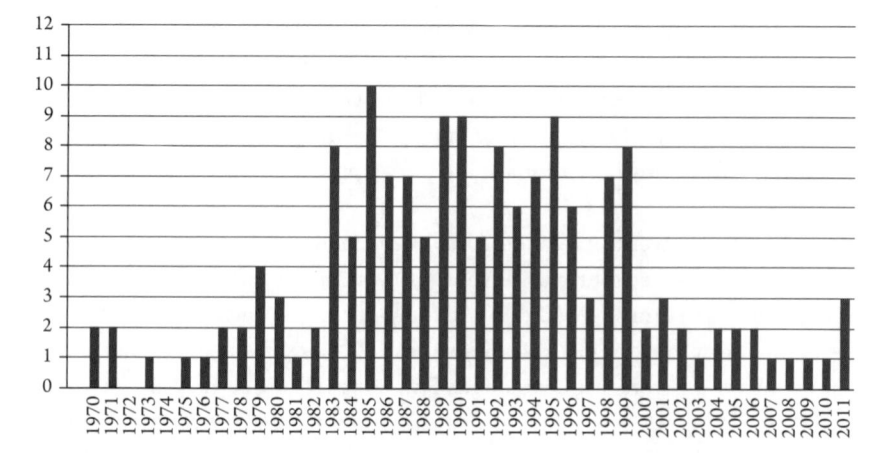

Figure 5.2 Number of University Technology Transfer Offices Founded, 1970–2011

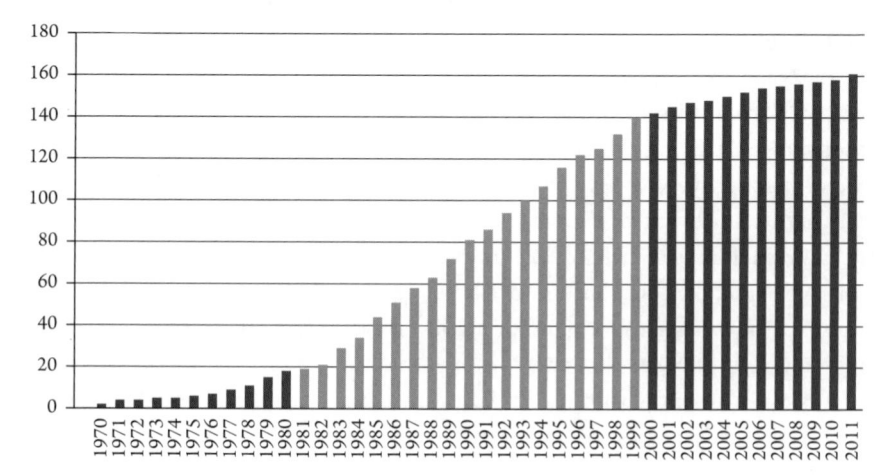

Figure 5.3 Cumulative Number of University Technology Transfer Offices Founded, 1970–2011

Figure 5.3 shows the cumulative number of TTOs founded over the 1970–2011 period, based on the data underlying Figure 5.2. There are at least three sub-periods of activity with these 40 plus years. The first sub-period, which begins in 1970 and goes through 1980, the year that the Bayh-Dole Act was passed, was a period of gradual, rather non-dramatic growth in the total number of TTOs. However, in the second sub-period, which begins in 1981 and goes through 1999, the growth in the total number of TTOs increased dramatically. We suggest that this increase was attributable to the passage of the Bayh-Dole Act. Finally, in the third period, which begins in 2000 and goes through 2011, we see a leveling off in the growth of the total number of TTOs. There are, of course, physical limits to cumulative growth in TTOs; after all, the number of universities and colleges that appropriately would have interest in and ability to create and operate a TTO is fixed. Thus, by the year 2000, the university population was approaching what might be thought of as a saturation point with many, if not most, members of that community for whom a TTO is both desirable and feasible having created one. If a dimension of the economic impact of the Bayh-Dole Act is the establishment of TTOs, the metric illustrated in Figure 5.3 suggests that the Act has had its intended economic impact.[8] And with this large improvement in university-private sector social networks has come a broad increase in the level of private sector entrepreneurial behavior and hence the development of new technology and innovations throughout the economy.

University Proof of Concept Centers

Since the passage of the Bayh-Dole Act in 1980, there has been widespread and growing public sector support for the commercialization of university-based research. Evidence of this, as shown in Figures 5.2 and 5.3, is most visible in the trend at universities to establish and operate TTOs and offices of innovation and commercialization.

Though one might think that the influence of the Bayh-Dole Act has run its course, interest in exploring possible ways to further expand on the Act's impact led to the Obama Administration in September 2009 to reiterate the federal government's support for commercialization of university-based research through the release of *A Strategy for American Innovation: Driving towards Sustainable Growth and Quality Jobs* (Executive Office of the President 2009).[9] Shortly thereafter, in March 2010, a Request for Information (RFI) was published in the *Federal Register*:

> This RFI is designed to collect input from the public on ideas for promoting the commercialization of Federally funded research. ... the RFI seeks public comments on how best to encourage commercialization of university research ... [and] on whether PoCCs [Proof of Concept Centers] can be a means of stimulating the commercialization of early-stage technologies. (75 [57], p. 14,476)

The impetus for this RFI was, of course, the conjecture that PoCCs, as a means of enhancing UTT beyond the levels seen through TTOs, would also have significant positive economic development consequences for the nation.

PoCCs gained broader recognition as a potentially important element of the nation's technology infrastructure when President Obama announced in March 2011, as part of the Startup America initiative, the i6 Green Challenge.[10] Under this proposal, a total of $12 million will be awarded to establish or expand PoCCs that have the potential to enhance the commercialization of technology and entrepreneurship in support of a green economy, to increase U.S. competitiveness, and to leverage job growth. Six organizations received initial public funding.[11]

Despite this flurry of policy interest and activity, discussions as to the basic definition and specific role of PoCCs are conspicuously absent from both policy conversations and the academic and professional literatures. And there is a void of any systematic investigation of the structure and analysis of the economic impact of these centers. And while, broadly speaking, we can describe a PoCC as a collection of infrastructure services intended to improve the dissemination and commercialization of new knowledge from universities in order to spur economic development and job growth, this description amounts to little more than a black box whose purpose is understood but whose method of functioning remains hidden. In short, this description simply says that a PoCC is an investment by a university or universities for improved technology transfer.

Toward Understanding Proof of Concept Centers

To better understand what PoCCs are, at least at a conceptual level, we define here the current population of university-related PoCCs in the United States and place PoCCs within our framework of public sector entrepreneurship.[12]

From a firm-level perspective, Maia and Claro (2013, p. 2), building on Auerswald and Branscomb (2003), argue that the most critical phase in technology commercialization

> occurs between invention and product development, when commercial concepts are created and verified, appropriate markets are identified, and protectable Intellectual Property (IP) may have to be developed. This Proof of Concept ... phase has a funding gap, caused by information and motivation asymmetries and institutional gaps between the Science and Technology and Business enterprises.

Relatedly, in their examination of the definition offered by the University of California at San Diego's von Liebig Center and MIT's Deshpande Center, Gulbranson and Audretsch define a PoCC as an institution "devoted towards facilitating the spillover and commercialization of university research" (2008, p. 250). In other words, PoCCs seem to be taking aim at improving the transfer and development of technologies derived from public R&D funding, especially from universities and public laboratories.[13]

In short, if the Bayh-Dole Act implicitly envisaged the process of technology transfer as linear, with the key being the legal act of transferring copyright or patent rights, the formation of PoCCs seems to demonstrate the recognition of an inherently more complex technology transfer structure. PoCCs focus on facilitating that transfer process through the development of additional mechanisms linked to that complex structure.

While PoCCs are focused on relatively early stages of university technology development, they have the potential to impact most of the UTT process. Typically, PoCC services include seed funding, business and advisory services, incubator space, and market research. The university's TTO coordinates with the PoCC by assisting with IP and licensing responsibilities, providing representatives for advisory services, and connecting inventors with outside funding sources.

Thus, PoCCs enable inventors to evaluate the commercial potential of their research; within PoCCs, early stage products can be developed and prototypes can be tested. Proving a concept makes it easier for inventors to obtain funding from outside investors, such as angel investors or venture capitalists, for further product development.[14]

We offer in Table 5.2 an initial taxonomy of the challenges that PoCCs are intended to address in an effort to move toward a more systematic understanding of their economic role. This taxonomy comes from a review of the extant literature and from our model of entrepreneurship in Chapter 3.

Proof of Concept Centers: An Inferential Analysis

Reflecting on a broader view of technology transfer, we conceptualize PoCCs as a critical piece of the infrastructure that facilities the recognition and especially exploitation of heretofore unexploited commercial opportunities in an uncertain economic environment. PoCCs are important not only for remediating technology transfer challenges but also for accelerating the advancement of proofs of concept into the market application stage, like the Bayh-Dole Act. Thus, PoCCs are a prime example of public sector entrepreneurship.

To better understand this technology infrastructure, 32 PoCCs were identified from public sources based on the definitions discussed above.[15] Table 5.3 describes what we have identified from public domain sources as the current

Table 5.2 **Challenges in Technology Transfer Potentially Addressed by Proof of Concept Centers**

1. University entrepreneurs tend to be older and often lack relevant business skills.

2. Research productive faculty are not always inclined to redirect their research toward transferable technologies.

3. University faculty often lack the social networks necessary for successful technology transfer.

4. University policies (e.g., promotion and tenure, financial, and IP) do not always provide sufficient incentives for faculty to engage in technology transfer.

5. External funding for startups is often difficult to obtain and thus hinders the success of technology transfer.

Table 5.3 **Description of the U.S. University-related Proof of Concept Center**

Center	Location	Year Founded	Initial Funding
von Liebig Entrepreneurism Center	San Diego, CA	2001	$10-million donation from the William J. von Liebig Foundation
Deshpande Center	Cambridge, MA	2002	$17.5-million donation from Jaishree and Gururaj Deshpande
VentureLab	Athens, GA	2002	From 2002 to 2010, Georgia Research Alliance directed $19 million of state funding into VentureLab
Ohio Third Frontier	Columbus, OH	2002	$1.6-billion, 10-year commitment by the State of Ohio Extended through 2015 in May 2010
St. Louis BioGenerator	St. Louis, MO	2003	McDonnell Family Foundation, the Danforth Foundation, Bunge North America, the Monsanto Fund, and CORTEX

University Affiliation	Types of Services	# Projects Funded	Partners/Affiliates
Jacobs School of Engineering, University of California, San Diego	Seed funding, advisory services, educational programs, technology acceleration programs	10–12 annually	Center for Commercialization of Advanced Technologies, CONNECT, UCSD $50K Entrepreneurship Competition
MIT School of Engineering	Grant program, catalyst program, innovation teams, special events	90 + to date	Lockheed Martin, Sanofi Aventis
University of Georgia, Georgia Tech, Emory University, Georgia State University, Medical College of Georgia, Clark Atlanta University	Seed funding awarded in three phases: Phase 1—$50,000 grants. Develop business plans, market assessments, proof of concept studies Phase 2—$100,000 grants with matching funds required. IP licensing, develop prototypes Phase 3—$250,000 loans. Field trials, product distribution, facility and staffing, marketing	107 +	Georgia Research Alliance
Kent State University, University of Akron, Cleveland State University, University of Dayton, University of Toledo, Case Western Reserve University, Ohio State University, Wright State University	Comprehensive state-wide system of programs and organizations that support the development and commercialization of new technologies, expand Ohio's technology-based R&D capabilities, provide risk capital, and promote entrepreneurial skills Focus on developing 5 key technology clusters: advanced energy, advanced materials, biomedical instruments, controls and electronics, power and propulsion	700 + companies created, capitalized, or attracted to Ohio by Third Frontier funds	
Washington University, Saint Louis University, University of Missouri	Provide pre-seed or seed funding at the early stages of new company formation, continued support to milestones of follow-on funding or sustainable revenue, professional services (lawyers, accountants), management support	27	Danforth Plant Science Center, Missouri Botanical Gardens, Coalition for Life Sciences, Missouri Technology Corporations, InnovateVMS, CORTEX Life Science District, St. Louis Arch Angels, Skandalaris Student Venture Fund

(continued)

Table 5.3 **(Continued)**

Center	Location	Year Founded	Initial Funding
University of Colorado Proof of Concept Program	Boulder, CO	2004	Income generated from commercialization of University of Colorado IP
Commercial Ventures and Intellectual Property Technology (CVIP) Development Fund	Massachusetts	2004	Created and maintained through licensing revenues, initial $50,000 contribution from the president's office of CVIP
Alabama Innovation and Mentoring of Entrepreneurs Center	Tuscaloosa, AL	2007	Reconstitution of the Alabama Institute for Manufacturing Excellence
Boston University-Fraunhofer Alliance for Medical Devices, Instrumentation and Diagnostics	Boston, MA	2007	$5-million, 5-year initiative jointly funded by Fraunhofer Gesellschaft and Boston University

University Affiliation	Types of Services	# Projects Funded	Partners/Affiliates
University of Colorado	Four types of grants: Proof of Concept small grants (POCsg), Proof of Concept investments (POCi), Proof of Concept State of Colorado Bioscience matching grants (POCmbg), Renewable and Sustainable Energy Institute (RAESI) Proof of Concept energy grants (POCeg) (includes a Market Assessment Program [MAP] element)	139	University License Equity Holdings, Inc. (ULEHI) (nonprofit organization that manages private equity for CU)
University of Massachusetts	Awards given annually to faculty members across all five University of Massachusetts campuses to accelerate commercialization of early stage technologies developed there	66	
University of Alabama	Entrepreneurial training, Center for Green Manufacturing, Manufacturing Information Technology Center, Machine Process and Product Design Center, Operations Research and Statistical Analysis Center, teams of staff / students to conduct market research and business model plan/development, idea database, idea selection committee		Bama Technology Incubator
Boston University	Fraunhofer Center for Manufacturing Innovation engineers work with Boston University researchers to develop medical innovations from Boston University labs into functional instruments and devices that can attract venture capital investment for a new venture creation or be licensed to existing companies in their space		Fraunhofer Gesellschaft

(continued)

Table 5.3 **(Continued)**

Center	Location	Year Founded	Initial Funding
Stevens Institute for Innovation	Los Angeles, CA	2007	$22-million donation from Mark and Mary Stevens
Biomedical Accelerator Fund	Cambridge, MA	2007	$6 million in private donations
Vermont Experimental Program to Stimulate Competitive Research Innovation Fund Awards	Burlington, VT	2007	Vermont EPSCoR funded by National Science Foundation
Institute for Advancing Medical Innovation	Kansas City, KS	2008	$8.1-million gift from the Kauffman Foundation $8 million matching from University of Kansas's endowment fund
Medical Devices Center	Minneapolis, MN	2008	$10-million, 5-year investment from the University of Minnesota

University Affiliation	Types of Services	# Projects Funded	Partners/Affiliates
University of Southern California	Coaching, mentoring, networking and showcase opportunities for startups, connecting innovators with funding, IP management, University of Southern California Student Innovator Showcase, Ideas Empowered program, planned "Innovation Fund" for faculty and researchers in health sciences to develop proofs of concept		University of Southern California Office of the Provost
Harvard University	Development gap funding awarded to Harvard investigators to propel emerging technologies originating from Harvard's biomedical and life science research community into clinical development	27	
University of Vermont	Provide funding and support for high-risk research that could revolutionize a science, technology, engineering, or math (STEM) field	Awards up to $12,000	
University of Kansas	Annual request for proposals seeking POC projects, $50–100 thousand funding per project, one-on-one support from project directors		Kauffman Foundation, Leukemia & Lymphoma Society, National Institues of Health, Kansas Bioscience Authority, Children's Mercy Hospitals and Clinics, Frontiers: The Heartland Institute for Clinical and Translational Research, Bioscience & Technology Business Center
University of Minnesota	Provide technical assistance and facilities for prototype development and testing to refine technology and ensure finished product is commercially viable. 1-year Fellows Program	8 fellows funded per year	Minnesota Department of Employment and Economic Development, Maslowski Family Trust,

(continued)

Table 5.3 **(Continued)**

Center	Location	Year Founded	Initial Funding
Blue Highway	Syracuse, NY	2008	Wholly owned subsidiary of Welch Allyn, Inc.
QED Proof of Concept Program	University City, Philadelphia, PA	2009	$300,000 grant from the Commonwealth of Pennsylvania's Ben Franklin Technology Development Authority $300,000 grant from the William Penn Foundation $1.8-million commitment from University City Science Center and participating institutions
New Hampshire Innovation Commercialization Center	Portsmouth, NH	2010	$165,000 per year (2010–2012) seed investment from University of New Hampshire Undisclosed private backers
Agile Innovation System	Pittsburgh, PA	2010	$1-million grant from Economic Development Administration

University Affiliation	Types of Services	# Projects Funded	Partners/Affiliates
Syracuse University	Invention triage, technical evaluations, product development, rapid prototyping, IP landscape and valuation studies, Original Equipment Manufacturing	100 + active collaborations with academia, government, and industry	Welch Allyn, Inc.
Delaware State University, Drexel University, Harrisburg University of Science & Technology, Lehigh University, New Jersey Institute of Technology, Penn State College of Medicine Hershey, Philadelphia College of Osteopathic Medicine, Philadelphia University, Rutgers University, Temple University, Thomas Jefferson University, University of Delaware, University of Medicine & Dentistry of New Jersey, University of Pennsylvania, University of the Sciences in Philadelphia, Widener University	Solicits life science R&D project proposals from the region's research centers and selects the most promising technologies for funding designed to bridge the valley of death	12	Fox Chase Cancer Center, Lankenau Institute for Medical Research, Monell Chemical Senses Center, New Jersey Institute of Technology, The Wistar Institute
University of New Hampshire	Select early stage ventures with high commercialization potential and grow them into companies by providing business resources, seed capital, and management expertise	6	Elevate Communications, Pease Development Authority, PixelMEDIA, Whaleback Systems
Carnegie Mellon University	Workshops, mentoring, funding through translational research grants, accelerator space	25	Innovation Works

(continued)

Table 5.3 **(Continued)**

Center	Location	Year Founded	Initial Funding
Oregon Innovation Cluster	Oregon	2010	$1-million grant from EDA $1-million grant from Oregon Innovation Council $400,000 supplemental awards from NIH/NSF
Innovative Solutions for Invention Xceleration	Akron, Ohio	2010	$1-million grant from EDA
Maryland Proof of Concept Alliance	Maryland	2010	$5.1 million in federal funding
Iowa Innovation Network i6 Green Project	Ames, Iowa	2011	$1-million grant from EDA
Proof of Concept Center for Green Chemistry Scale-Up	Holland, MI	2011	$580,000 grant from EDA $500,000 from Michigan Economic Development Corporation Former pharmaceutical R&D and pilot plant facility donated by Pfizer
iGreen New England Partnership	New England	2011	$1.25-million grant from EDA

University Affiliation	Types of Services	# Projects Funded	Partners/Affiliates
Oregon State University, Oregon Health & Science University, University of Oregon, Portland State University	Technical and business assistance services, proof of concept grants, intern/ sabbatical program for students and researchers, business accelerator and capital development fund		Oregon Nanoscience and Microtechnologies Institute, Oregon Translational Research and Development Institute, Oregon Built Environment and Sustainable Technologies, Pacific Northwest National Laboratory
University of Akron Research Foundation	Proof of concept prototyping in ABIA's Medical Device Development Center and Center for Clinical and Community Health Improvement, design/ manufacturing services, commercialization and marketing plans		Austen BioInnovation Institute in Akron
University of Maryland system	Identifies and funds promising technologies developed through University System of Maryland institutions	21	U.S. Army Research Laboratory
Iowa State University	Adding a next-stage proof of commercial relevance center to help start businesses bring product to market		Iowa Innovation Council, Iowa Innovation Corp.
Bioeconomy Institute of Michigan State University	Business support services, green technology incubation, assist client firms in obtaining U.S. Department of Agriculture BioPreferred designations		Lakeshore Advantage, Prima Civitas Foundation, NewNorth Center
University of Maine	Networking roundtables, applied research in university labs, incubator space for start-ups, online tools (forums, stakeholder network, etc.)	20–30 expected over the next 2 years	40 + including New England Clean Energy Foundation, ME Technology Institute, ME Regional Redevelopment Authority, MA Clean Energy Center, CT Clean Energy Finance and Investment Authority, NH Office of Energy and Planning, RI Renewable Energy Fund, VT Agency of Commerce and Community Development

(continued)

Table 5.3 **(Continued)**

Center	Location	Year Founded	Initial Funding
Igniting Innovation (I2) Cleantech Acceleration Network	Orlando, FL	2011	$1.3-million grant from EDA Matching funds from Space Florida and the Florida High Tech Corridor Council
Louisiana Tech Proof of Concept Center (LA_i6)	Ruston, LA	2011	$1.1-million grant from EDA
Washington State Clean Energy Partnership Project	Washington State	2011	$1.3 million grant from EDA
University of California Proof of Concept Program	California	2011	$2.7 million invested by University of California in 2011, $2.6 million invested by University of California in 2012
Global Center for Medical Innovation	Atlanta, GA	2012	$1.3-million grant from EDA $1.3-million match from Georgia Research Alliance

University Affiliation	Types of Services	# Projects Funded	Partners/Affiliates
University of Central Florida	Virtual network linking Florida-based universities, business incubators, investors, and industry resources, 3-month I2 Accelerator Program (kickoff business bootcamp, 1-on-1 mentoring, presentations to I2 Ventures network)	150 + companies have participated	Florida Energy Systems Consortium, Technological Research and Development Authority
Louisiana Tech	Support for field testing and prototyping, engage private sector partners, collaborate with researchers and organizations at Enterprise Campus research park	3 pilot projects: geopolymer concrete, solar cell power conversion, piezoelectric generators	Louisiana Tech Enterprise Center, companies along I-20 Innovation Corridor
South Seattle Community College	Annual analysis and reports on policy alignment, help eliminate regulatory barriers limiting clean energy development, assist Pacific Northwest energy companies in deploying products to global markets, build the Building Efficiency Testing and Integration (BETI) Center and Demonstration Network		Washington Clean Energy Regional Innovation Cluster, Puget Sound Regional Council's Prosperity Partnership, Cleantech Open Mentoring Program, Innovate Washington
University of California system	Funds innovations based on IP owned by University of California that are within 12 months of commercialization	35	Lawrence Berkeley National Lab
Georgia Tech	Product-specific project teams, prototyping/design/engineering/product development, preclinical testing, clinical trials	2	Piedmont Healthcare, Georgia Research Alliance, Saint Joseph's Translational Research Institute, MetricIreland, Atlanta Pediatric Device Consortium, Interoperability & Integration Innovation Lab

(*continued*)

Table 5.3 **(Continued)**

Center	Location	Year Founded	Initial Funding
Proof of Concept Fund	Lawrence, KS	2012	Funding from University of Kansas
Proof of Concept Gap Funding Initiative	Chicago, IL	2012	$500,000 from the Office of the Vice President for Research, the Office of the Vice Chancellor for Research, the Colleges of Engineering, Medicine and Pharmacy, and the Office of Technology Management
Proof of Concept Program	Tucson, AZ	2012	Revenue from University of Arizona licensing and options
Oklahoma Proof of Concept Center	Oklahoma	Forthcoming	Capital from i2E and Cowboy Technologies

University Affiliation	Types of Services	# Projects Funded	Partners/Affiliates
University of Kansas	Provide funding (up to $50 thousand per proposal) to mature research projects for 1 year. The fund will support projects in all areas of technology—including electronics, software, communications and engineering—that aren't eligible for POC funding through University of Kansas's Institute for Advancing Medical Innovations (IAMI)	Will award a total of $200,000 in funding in 2012, award notifications to be made February 2013	KU Center for Technology Commercialization
University of Illinois at Chicago	Commercial product development/testing, address technical or commercial risks, attract potential licensees or additional third-party funding	4 projects were funded in the 1st round of the POC Initiative, an estimated 4–5 projects are anticipated to be funded in the 2nd round	University of Illinois at Chicago Office of Technology Management
University of Arizona	Generate data to support the potential commercial value of the invention, prototype development and testing, validate academic software code for commercial application, design, construct, and evaluate a prototype device, delivery system, software, etc.	Funding selections to be announced December 17, 2012, for research to begin January 7, 2013	Tech Launch Arizona
Oklahoma State University, Oklahoma University	Virtual center that will accelerate products to the marketplace through coordinating efforts to validate markets, developing prototypes, obtaining guidance and feedback from industry mentors, and providing access to capital necessary		I2E Inc., Cowboy Technologies LLC

Table 5.3 **(Continued)**

Center	Location	Year Founded	Initial Funding
Downstate Regional Energy Technology Accelerator	New York, NY	Forthcoming	$5 million awarded by New York State Energy Research and Development Authority
NYC Clean Economy Center for Proof of Concept	Brooklyn, NY	Forthcoming	$5 million awarded by New York State Energy Research and Development Authority
High Tech Rochester, Inc.'s NYSERDA Proof of Concept Center	Rochester, NY	Forthcoming	$5 million awarded by New York State Energy Research and Development Authority
Proof of Concept for Technology Commercialization Award Program	Piscataway Township, NJ	Forthcoming	
ICE Commercialization GAP Fund Program 2012	Iowa City, IA	Forthcoming	Seed funding provided by the Iowa Centers for Enterprise in conjunction with the Office of the Vice President for Research

Source: Bradley et al. 2013b.

University Affiliation	Types of Services	# Projects Funded	Partners/Affiliates
Columbia University	Fund the development of sustainable technologies and clean energy solutions		Brookhaven National Laboratory, Stony Brook University, Cornell University's NYC Tech
Polytechnic Institute of New York University partnered with City University of New York	Support applied science research that focuses on challenges specific to an urban environment		PowerBridge, New York University Center for Urban Science and Progress
University of Rochester, Rochester Institute of Technology, Alfred University, Cornell University, Clarkson University, University at Buffalo, SUNY Research Foundation	Accelerate the creation and growth of clean energy startups across Western and Central New York		
Rutgers	Enable Rutgers investigators to develop a commercializable product based upon Rutgers IP that has not yet been licensed	Awards up to $50,000	
University of Iowa	Support a range of stages in technology development, from initial concept (prior to IP disclosure), through proof of concept, to licensing and commercialization	Awards from $10,000 to $75,000	

(as of the end of 2012) U.S. population of university-related PoCCs. Also shown at the end of Table 5.3 are six additional PoCCs that are termed as forthcoming.

From the description of the PoCCs in Table 5.3 it is clear that commercialization of university-generated technology is an important goal of each center, and that this goal is being approached differently in different PoCCs. For example, some PoCCs are based at a single university and others have an integral relationship with several universities. Differences in achieving commercialization success through a PoCC infrastructure underscores the relevance of our contention above that the economic role of the PoCC—accelerating innovation from the laboratory to the market—can occur throughout the UTT process.

As with any public sector entrepreneurial effort, consideration should be given to the potential economic impact of PoCCs. Table 5.4 provides suggestive evidence of this impact. For each single university-related PoCC in Table 5.4, we calculated the number of university startups before and after the PoCC's founding.[16] Table 5.4 shows that for the nine PoCCs for which sufficient data were available, the number of new university startups generally increased in the years after the PoCC's founding. Of course, no other factors related to changes in the number of university startups are held constant in this descriptive comparison.

Summary

The Bayh-Dole Act of 1980, which authorized universities (among others) to take ownership of inventions that were at least in part funded by the federal government and to explore their commercial exploitation with other parties, represents an important example of public sectorpublic sector entrepreneurship. It led to a dramatic increase in university TTOs, which have played a significant role in enhancing the social networks of both universities and private sector firms, thereby stimulating increased entrepreneurial behavior in the form of new technology development and other commercially valuable innovations. The legislation has also given rise to PoCCs that, through an improved recognition of the complexities of the technology transfer process, have in recent years built on the role that TTOs play in enhancing technology development and other commercially valuable innovations.

Appendix

An Expanded Model of University Technology Transfer

This appendix builds on the traditional linear model of technology transfer in Figure 5.1 by addressing its limitations and incorporating the concept of

Table 5.4 **University Startups Before and After the Establishment of the Proof of Concept Center**

PoCC	University	Year Founded	Number of Startups before Founding*	Number of Startups after Founding*
Deshpande Center	MIT	2002	119	125
Commercial Ventures and Intellectual Property Technology Development Fund	University of Massachusetts	2004	3	5
University of Colorado Proof of Concept Program	University of Colorado	2004	17	60
Boston University-Fraunhofer Alliance for Medical Devices, Instrumentation and Diagnostics	Boston University	2007	15	24
Biomedical Accelerator Fund	Harvard University	2007	25	43
Stevens Institute for Innovation	University of Southern California	2007	35	24
Vermont Experimental Program to Stimulate Competitive Research Innovation Fund Awards	University of Vermont	2007	11	14
Institute for Advancing Medical Innovation	University of Kansas	2008	4	8
Medical Devices Center	University of Minnesota	2008	11	21

* The number of university startups before and after the founding of the PoCC was determined by counting the number startups from the date of the PoCC's founding to 2011, the latest available year of data from the AUTM, and then comparing that count to the number of startups for the same number of years prior to the date of the PoCC.

the entrepreneurial university and models of open innovation as applied to UTT.[17]

To formulate an alternative model of technology transfer, it is useful to identify the various factors that contribute to the technology transfer process. Factors that enhance technology transfer include greater rewards for faculty involvement in technology transfer activities, proximity to regions with a concentration of high technology firms, and the experience of the TTO.

Mechanisms of technology transfer include joint laboratories between academia and business, spinoffs, IP licensing, research contracts, mobility of researchers, joint publications, conferences, expositions and special media, informal contact within professional networks, and a flow of graduates to the industry. Sponsored research, hiring of students, and serendipity are other mechanisms of technology transfer. All of these mechanisms create pathways of technology transfer that do not necessarily have to flow in one linear direction.

Figure A5.1 illustrates our expanded model of UTT. The solid black arrows indicate processes of technology transfer, while the gray dashed arrows indicate factors that influence these processes.

This alternative model begins with a scientific discovery, as does the traditional model in Figure 5.2, but the expanded model distinguishes between different inventors—university scientists, graduate students, and research teams—that exist in practice. Also indicated in the beginning of this heuristic are the possible funding sources that facilitate discovery, including federal contracts, federal grants, private grants, corporate contracts, donations, and venture capital funds.

Once a discovery is made, the technology transfer process follows one of two paths:

- The inventor can choose to disclose his invention to the university's TTO— process 1.
- The inventor can choose not to disclose his invention, bypassing the TTO— process 2.

The inventor's decision to disclose is influenced by the university's reward systems and culture, as noted by the gray dashed arrows. If the university has a reward system in place that provides incentives for faculty to engage in commercialization activities, the inventor might be more likely to disclose and participate in the formal mechanisms of technology transfer. If there are too many perceived barriers and disadvantages to involving the TTO and going through official channels, the inventor might circumvent disclosure and adopt informal mechanisms of technology transfer.

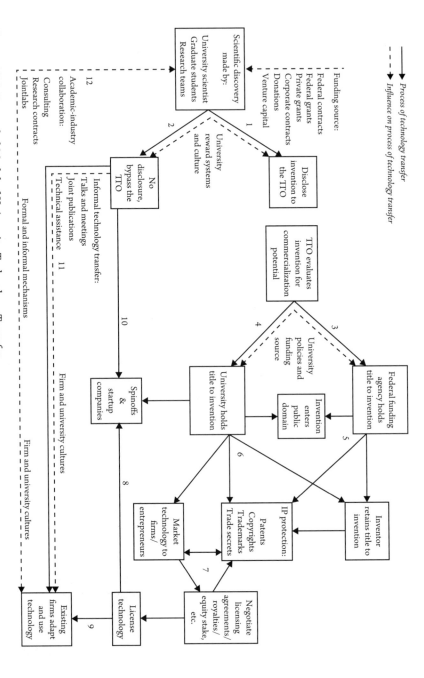

Figure A5.1 Expanded Model of University Technology Transfer

Once the inventor decides to disclose to the TTO, the office will evaluate the invention's commercialization potential, including the time it will take to bring the invention to market and its market potential (i.e., profitability). If the TTO decides to pursue the invention, the issue of which entity holds title to the invention becomes relevant. It is important to note that process 3 in Figure 5.4 shows the case where the federal funding agency rather than the university holds title to the invention (process 4). This possibility is included in order to depict a complete technology transfer process, as federal funding is still the most common source of funding.

As acknowledged at the beginning of the model, there are certainly other sources of funding. For the private sources of funding (i.e., private grants, corporate contracts, and donations), the university automatically holds title to the invention. Thus, the technology transfer process would simply move from the TTO to the decision on how to commercialize the invention (process 6).

When the discovery results from a federally funded research project, under the Standard Patent Rights Clause (SPRC),[18] one of two paths might be followed:

- The university can decline to retain title; the federal funding agency can then request title to the invention—process 3.
- The university can retain title to the invention—process 4.

If the university declines to retain title to the invention, the responsibility goes to the federal agency that funded the discovery and the federal funding agency has three options (process 5):

- Request the title to the invention and let it enter the public domain, effectively ending the technology transfer process.
- Allow the inventor to retain title to the invention, as long as the university approves. The inventor is then free to file his own application for IP protection.
- Request the title to the invention and file an application for IP protection, typically a patent.

Or, the university can choose to hold title to the invention and decide how to proceed with commercialization (process 6):

- In some cases, it may be decided early on that a spinoff or startup is the best way to develop the invention.
- In other cases, the university may market the technology to firms or entrepreneurs to develop the technology.
- The university may also begin the process of acquiring IP protection in the form of patents, copyrights, trademarks, trade secrets, and so on.

- The university may, with the funding agency's approval, allow the inventor to retain title to the invention.
- If the invention is not federally funded, it may be allowed to enter the public domain. This outcome typically occurs when the invention is unlikely to have significant commercial value, or there is no market interest or need for the invention.

Whether or not the university chooses to retain title to the invention depends largely on the technology transfer policies of the university. Some universities may take a more hands-off approach to technology transfer and limit their involvement to conducting the research. In such a case, the choice of what to do is left to the federal funding agency. Other universities may prefer to stand in for the federal agency and hold on to the title to the invention so they can undertake the responsibility of commercialization themselves. The extent to which a university traditionally engages in technology transfer activities may indicate which path to commercialization the discovery will likely follow. Process 3, in which the federal funding agency holds title to the invention, is only an option if the inventor's research is in fact federally funded.

The processes of marketing the invention, acquiring IP protection, and negotiating licensing agreements and pecuniary returns do not necessarily follow a linear path. These processes can overlap and occur simultaneously (process 7):

- The invention can be marketed before IP protection is acquired if the university wants to gauge market interest before investing significant time and resources to protecting the invention. Or, if the invention seems especially promising, the university might choose to apply for patents, copyrights, and so on before or even while marketing it to potential investors. The university could successfully market the invention, lock in an interested firm or entrepreneur, and begin licensing negotiations before the IP protection process is completed.
- If the federal funding agency holds title to the invention, its next step is to file patent applications.
- Similarly, if the inventor is permitted to retain title, he will likely seek IP protection before taking steps to commercialize and develop his invention.

Once the technology has been protected and successfully marketed, and a licensing agreement is concluded, the technology is officially licensed to a firm, organization, or entrepreneur.

- If the technology has been licensed to an entrepreneur, such as the inventing faculty member or an outside party, a spinoff or startup company is established around the invention—process 8.

- If the technology has been licensed to an existing firm, the firm then adapts and uses the technology. Recall that the technology is typically embryonic and requires significant further development before reaching the market— process 9.

If the inventor chose to bypass the TTO (process 2), the technology transfer process is carried out through informal mechanisms. Informal technology transfer mechanisms include consulting, joint publications, presentations and conferences, and other communication processes between and among faculty members and industry contacts.

Informal technology transfer is more abstract than formal technology transfer in that it involves the exchange of ideas and knowledge rather than the property of a specific invention. However, similar to the path of formal technology transfer, the ideas and knowledge that are passed along through informal mechanisms can also result in

- A spinoff or a startup company being established that utilizes the knowledge passed on from the university scientist—process 10.
- The inventor's discovery, idea, or knowledge being adapted and used by an existing firm—process 11.
- Other forms of knowledge dissemination, including the disclosure of the invention into the public domain for others to use without cost.

When the university scientist chooses not to be involved in the formal technology path, he can take advantage of preexisting relationships with industry contacts and present his idea or discovery directly to them. Or, a person in industry may reach out to their university contact regarding a specific research interest or idea, thus initiating a two-way flow of communication. The firm has a connection to the resources and innovations within the university, and the university scientist has the opportunity to share his knowledge with industry contacts that can utilize it without the bureaucratic red tape of going through the TTO's official channels. Again, the decision to engage in informal technology transfer might depend on incentives to engage in formal technology transfer.

The firm's culture also impacts its decision to engage in informal technology transfer. Firms that are located near research universities, and firms that have long-term, well-established working relationships with universities, will be more likely to engage university faculty members in informal mechanisms of technology transfer.

Finally, the university scientist and the firm developing the invention often maintain a continued working relationship by means of academic-industry collaboration. The firm and university cultures must be favorable toward maintaining a partnership and engaging in technology transfer activities in order for collaborations to be successful.

Academic-industry collaborations can involve consulting, research contracts, the establishment of joint laboratories, and other partnerships between the university and the firm (process 12). These collaborations can involve both formal and informal mechanisms of technology transfer. Maintaining these relationships over time ensures that the university scientist continues to work with the firm to develop the embryonic invention and to bring it to market, thus providing a foundation for future technology transfer activities.

The expanded model of technology transfer includes many of the same processes as the traditional model, but expands upon them and incorporates more elements of technology transfer in practice. Technology transfer is a complicated and dynamic process, and no single model can capture all its nuances perfectly. However, we believe that this is one alternative view that improves on the traditional model described in Figure 5.2.

The paradigm of open innovation, conceptualized by Chesbrough (2003), ties into academic entrepreneurship and can be applied to alternative methods and views of technology transfer. The open innovation paradigm was originally directed toward innovation in large multinational corporations, such as Proctor and Gamble and IBM, but there is increasing interest in applying open innovation to other types of firms and institutions, including universities.

In contrast to open innovation is the paradigm of closed innovation. Closed innovation strategies were the norm for most of the 20th century, wherein a company generates, develops, and commercializes its own ideas. Closed innovation is hindered by its linearity and restrictiveness, which recalls the limitations of the traditional model of technology transfer discussed above. Toward the end of the 20th century, as the number and mobility of knowledge workers rose and the availability of private venture capital increased, the effectiveness of closed innovation began to deteriorate. Many industries are now transitioning from closed to open innovation, and this paradigm is increasingly relevant for the 21st-century university as well.

The foundation of the open innovation concept is that innovators integrate their ideas, expertise, and skills with those of others outside the organization to deliver results to the marketplace using the most effective means possible. For universities, this means obtaining innovations from outside sources to augment their own R&D and entrepreneurial activities. For example, the university spinoff can license technology from other companies, their home university, and other research institutions and adopt a proactive, commercialization-centric approach to technology transfer. Or, if a firm has a specific technical problem, it can extend its research channels and open up the problem to universities; ideas can originate outside the firm's laboratories and then be brought inside for commercialization. TTOs can facilitate this process by acting as knowledge and technology brokers, marketing patents and licenses to the interested firms.

Employing open innovation strategies can introduce multidirectional flows of knowledge and technology, allowing for more effective academic-industry collaborations. When knowledge and technology are able to flow freely to society and be transformed into useful applications, the innovations generated by universities will have the most efficient and significant impact on economic growth. Firms and universities that can embrace open, collaborative innovation strategies beyond the boundaries of their institutions will enjoy a competitive edge in today's global, decentralized technology transfer environment.

Another identifiable, and somewhat more experimental, practice of technology transfer is what might be referred to as the collaborative view of knowledge and technology transfer. Building on the concept of open innovation, a new method of technology transfer is gaining popularity. It is characterized by low-cost, streamlined, transparent collaboration between participants. The collaborative model is better suited to the transfer of knowledge than of physical inventions, although both can be accomplished within the view. The collaborative view is constructed from the examination of several collaborative organizations that have developed legal and technical infrastructures which allow participants to engage in knowledge- and idea-sharing.

The original and most well-known of such organizations is Creative Commons. Creative Commons is a nonprofit organization that releases Creative Commons licenses, which allow creators to communicate which rights they reserve and which rights they waive for the benefit of recipients or other creators. Creative Commons licenses can be used in addition to traditional IP protections, with the added benefits of a standardized way for participants to keep their copyrights while allowing certain uses of their creative, educational, or scientific works.[19]

Another organization employing similar practices is GreenXchange. GreenXchange is a project launched by Creative Commons in collaboration with industry giants Nike and Best Buy. It helps holders of patents share IP assets to accelerate sustainability innovations. GreenXchange provides a standardized patent license structure, whereby asset holders can control what levels and to whom their intellectual assets are available.[20] Participants are able to make both patented innovations and unpatented know-how available for use in research and commercialization while retaining the ability to choose their licensing approach. Both Creative Commons and GreenXchange focus on utilizing the Internet as a means of universal access to research and education, which drives innovation, economic growth, and productivity.

Similarly, the Sustainability Consortium is an organization launched by Walmart and jointly administered by Arizona State University and the University of Arkansas for the purpose of representing government, academic, and business interests by developing a framework for sustainability product standards to enhance technology transfer.[21] The Sustainability Measurement and Reporting System framework is a common, global platform for companies to measure and report on product sustainability. The Sustainability Consortium is an example of a collaborative knowledge transfer model in action; it is a conglomeration of institutions cooperating to develop methodologies, tools, and strategies that facilitate product development and innovation.

6

The Stevenson-Wydler Act of 1980

> Bodily exercise, when compulsory, does no harm to the body;
> but knowledge which is acquired under compulsion obtains no
> hold on the mind.
>
> —Plato

Legislative Background

Whereas the Bayh-Dole Act of 1980 provided a mechanism and incentive system for universities and nonprofit organizations to transfer their technology to private sector firms, the Stevenson-Wydler Technology Innovation Act of 1980, Public Law 96-480 (hereafter the Stevenson-Wydler Act), provided a similarly innovative and more specific infrastructure for technologies to flow from federal laboratories to industry. Although the Stevenson-Wydler Act was passed two months before the Bayh-Dole Act,[1] its implications have garnered significantly less attention from scholars in the academic and policy literature on technology transfer. According to the Act,

> Congress finds and declares that: Technology and industrial innovation are central to the economic, environmental, and social well-being of citizens of the United States. Technology and industrial innovation offer an improved standard of living, increased public and private sector productivity, creation of new industries and employment opportunities, improved public services and enhanced competitiveness of United States products in world markets. Many new discoveries and advances in science occur in ... Federal laboratories, while the application of this new knowledge to commercial and useful public purposes depends largely upon actions by business and labor.... The Federal laboratories and other performers of federally funded research and development frequently provide scientific and technological developments of potential use to State and local governments and private industry. These developments should be made accessible

to those governments and industry. There is a need to provide means of access and to give adequate personnel and funding support to these means.... It is the purpose of this Act to improve the economic, environmental, and social well-being of the United States by ... promoting technology development through the establishment of centers for industrial technology [within Federal laboratories and] stimulating improved utilization of federally funded technology developments by State and local governments and the private sector.... It is the continuing responsibility of the Federal Government to ensure the full use of the results of the Nation's Federal investment in research and development. To this end the Federal Government shall strive where appropriate to transfer Federally owned or originated technology to State and local governments and to the private sector.

Thus, the Act called for federal laboratories to actively promote technology transfer to the private sector for commercial exploitation. And while this mandate was not explicitly focused on manufacturing, the nature of the technology research in federal laboratories has meant a clear connection to the U.S. manufacturing sector.

Prior to the Stevenson-Wydler Act, technology transfer was not an explicit mission of federal laboratories.[2] But because of the Act, each national laboratory was mandated to establish an Office of Research and Technology Applications.

Each Federal laboratory shall establish an Office of Research and Technology Applications. Laboratories having existing organizational structures which perform the functions of this section may elect to combine the Office of Research and Technology Applications within the existing organization.

The function of each Office of Research and Technology Applications is to

prepare an application assessment of each research and development project in which that laboratory is engaged which has potential for successful application in State or local government or in private industry;... provide and disseminate information on federally owned or originated products, processes, and services having potential application to State and local governments and to private industry;... cooperate with and assist the Center for the Utilization of Federal Technology and other organizations which link the research and development resources of that laboratory and the Federal Government as a whole to potential users in State and local government and private industry;

and ... provide technical assistance in response to requests from State and local government officials.

The mandate to actively promote technology transfer to the private sector for commercial exploitation was not without controversy,[3] and in 1986, the Stevenson-Wydler Act was amended by the Federal Technology Transfer Act of 1986, Public Law 99-502, to provide financial incentives to laboratory scientists of "at least 15 percent of the royalties or other income the agency receives on account of any invention to the inventor ... if the inventor ... was an employee of the agency at the time the invention was made."[4, 5]

In addition, the Federal Technology Transfer Act enables the laboratories to enter into cooperative R&D agreements (CRADAs) with outside organizations or parties:

> Each Federal agency may permit the director of any of its Government-operated Federal laboratories—(1) to enter into cooperative research and development state and local agreements on behalf of such agency ... with other Federal agencies; units of State or local government; industrial organizations (including corporations, schools and partnerships, and limited partnerships, and industrial development organizations); public and private foundations; non-profit organizations (including universities); or other persons (including licensees of inventions owned by the Federal agency); and (2) to negotiate licensing agreements.

Commenting on CRADAs, Mowery wrote:

> The U.S. "industrial competitiveness crisis" of the 1980s spawned a number of experiments in civilian technology policy. Among these was the Cooperative Research and Development Agreement (CRADA), an instrument that was created in the Technology Transfer Act of 1986. A CRADA is a contractual arrangement between a federal laboratory and participating firm that enables the laboratories to conduct joint R&D projects with private firms. Federal agencies are prohibited from providing direct funding to the industrial participants in CRADAs, but federal funds can be used to support the overhead and other expenses of the government research facilities participating in CRADAs. Under the terms of a CRADA, the private-firm partner can be assigned the rights to any intellectual property resulting from the joint work, while the federal government retains a nonexclusive license to the intellectual property. (2001, p. 93)

In subsequent legislation, the activities that fall under a CRADA and related licensing arrangements were expanded. This legislation included the National Competitiveness Technology Transfer Act of 1989, Public Law 101-189; the National Technology Transfer and Advancement Act of 1995, Public Law 104-113; and the Technology Transfer Commercialization Act of 2000, Public Law 106-404.

Federal Laboratory Technology Transfer Activities

Few scholars have studied technology transfer from federal laboratories because of—or so we conjecture—the difficulty in obtaining detailed information about the technology and the transfer partners. Many times the transfer process is prolonged as research relationships are developed among participants. And, often what is transferred is technical knowledge rather than discrete technologies, as the following two examples illustrate.

Plasma Spray Technology

Plasma is a gas in an excited state, and it is used to heat coating materials to a molten state. Plasma spray is a type of thermal spray, a generic term for coating processes used to apply metallic and non-metallic coating, and has been used since the early 1900s. The purpose of spraying a coating on a component at a high temperature is to make it wear longer by changing its surface characteristics.

In 1967, Sandia National Laboratories began research on plasma spray technology[6] with a focus on defense applications. Then, in 1988–1989, Fisher-Barton, a Wisconsin-based manufacturer of lawnmower blades, wood chippers, and agriculture equipment, transferred knowledge about plasma spray technology from Sandia. While the transfer, which was the result of a Fisher-Barton scientist conducting research at Sandia, was of advantage to Fisher-Barton, it did not involve a specific technology but rather a method.

Polycrystalline Diamond Compact Bits

From 1973 to 1977, General Electric (GE) worked with Sandia National Laboratories to improve the performance of a prototype of a polycrystalline diamond compact (PDC) bit.[7] The bit was commercialized by GE in 1977 and diffused rapidly throughout the drilling industry from 1980 onward.

A PDC bit is a type of drill bit used for oil and gas well drilling. Drillers confront sticky clay, soft shale, and brittle limestone. The technological advancement of PDC bits is that their cutting surface is covered with a layer of synthetic diamonds, which increases the durability of the bits and thus the speed with which wells can be drilled.

The specific knowledge about PDC bits that was transferred from Sandia to GE was about the physics and hydraulics of PDC bit operation, force, wear, and failure patterns. The only discrete technology that was transferred was in the form of computer codes to aid in bit design.

The Stevenson-Wydler and Federal Technology Transfer Acts as Examples of Public Sector Entrepreneurship

The relevant question to ask to determine if the Stevenson-Wydler Act and its follow-up, the Federal Technology Transfer Act, meet our criterion for being examples of public sector entrepreneurship is to ask whether these two acts are innovative public policies that improve the social network for the affected parties operating in an uncertain economic environment. That is, the relevant question is whether they increase the number and quality of heterogeneous experiential ties for the affected parties, resulting in those parties having an enhanced ability to identify and take advantage of heretofore unexploited opportunities.

Both Acts are clearly innovative pieces of legislation, whose time effects were initially uncertain. And, as Table 6.1 summarizes, both do in fact create improvements in social networks.

More specifically, the Stevenson-Wydler and the Federal Technology Transfer Acts, by facilitating the formation of CRADAs that enhance the social networks for both federal laboratories and private sector firms, enhance the transfer of existing knowledge from federal research laboratories to private sector industries.[8] For federal laboratories, such enhancement comes in the form of possible future private sector industry research partners who participate in those CRADAs.

As with the enhancements that universities receive as a result of the Bayh-Dole Act, this private sector industry perspective is often quite different from that of the federal research laboratory, and with that divergence come the creative synergies and dynamics that can result in future transfer of existing knowledge as well as the creation of new knowledge that can also be exploited for commercial gain. Such advantages are made all the more attractive to federal

Table 6.1 **Public Sector Entrepreneurship: The Stevenson-Wydler Act of 1980 and the Federal Technology Transfer Act of 1986**

Characteristics	Descriptor	Comment
Advancement of knowledge	Low	Existing knowledge, as embodied in the technology or invention, is being transferred; new knowledge is not being created.
Impact on technology and innovation	Immediate	Because the technology already exists, its impact outside of the federal laboratory could be immediate.
Targeted parties	Federal laboratories	Federal laboratories benefit from the transfer of own technology in terms of licensing revenues, private sector ties, and regional development. Federal laboratory scientists benefit in terms of licensing revenues.
	Private sector firms	Private sector firms that license the federal laboratory's technology benefit in terms of having saved on the cost of the underlying R&D, although adoption costs and implementation is not cost-less, and they possibly benefit in terms of exclusive licensing arrangements.
Heterogeneity of experiential ties	Significant	Experiential ties that enhance the federal laboratory come in the form of future possible industry research partners through CRADAs.
		Experiential ties that enhance the licensing private sector firm come in the form of future possible federal laboratory research partners through CRADAs.

research laboratories and their scientists through the receipt of licensing revenues from the transfer of laboratory technology to private sector industries. Those private sector industries gain for similar reasons. The ability to access existing federal research knowledge creates—again, with uncertainty—an often distinct perspective that does not exist within private sector industries. Finally, such benefits are reinforced by other associated advantages such as partial savings on the cost of the underlying R&D and exclusive licensing arrangements.

The Economic Impact of the Stevenson-Wydler Act and Federal Technology Transfer Act

The Bayh-Dole Act established an incentive for universities to engage in technology transfer as evidenced by the formation of technology transfer offices, whereas the Stevenson-Wydler Act mandated that federal laboratories establish an Office of Research and Technology Applications. Under Bayh-Dole, the incentives for university faculty to participate in university technology transfer were established by each university in terms of the sharing percentage of licensing revenues between the inventor and the university. The Federal Technology Transfer Act, however, mandated a minimum allocation of royalties or licensing fees to the inventive scientist.

To the best of our knowledge, there has only been one empirical study of the economic impacts of the Stevenson-Wydler Act and the Federal Technology Transfer Act. The Link et al. (2011) case-based study focused on the patent application patterns at Sandia National Laboratories in Albuquerque, New Mexico, and at the National Institute of Standards and Technology (NIST) in Gaithersburg, Maryland.[9]

Sandia has an annual budget of $2.4 billion and 8,500 employees compared to NIST's annual budget of $900 million and 2,800 employees.[10] Sandia is a government-owned, contractor-operated (GOCO) laboratory; NIST is a government-owned, government-operated (GOGO) laboratory.

Sandia National Laboratories

The roots of Sandia trace to the Z-Division at Los Alamos National Laboratory in New Mexico, which was formed in July 1945 for ordinance engineering and assembly as part of the nation's postwar planning.[11] In the fall of 1945, units of the Z-Division were moved to Sandia Base near Albuquerque due to overcrowding at Los Alamos.[12] Building 828 was constructed in 1946 to house mechanical test activities related to the design of new weapons. Under the leadership of Paul Larsen, then director of Z-Division, Sandia Base became Sandia Laboratory in April 1948. After the Soviet Union exploded an atomic weapon, President Eisenhower "promoted the use of nuclear weapons like any other strategic weapon in the military arsenal" (Sullivan 2010, p. 2). As a result, the Sandia Laboratory's role in bomb and warhead applications greatly increased. Sandia Laboratory became Sandia Laboratories in 1956 after establishing a second research facility in Livermore, California. In 1979, it was designated a Department of Energy (DOE) federal laboratory.[13]

Sandia's funding comes primarily from the DOE with supplementary funding from the Department of Homeland Security and the Department of Defense. Research is conducted in five major areas: nuclear weapons, energy and infrastructure assurance, nonproliferation, defense systems and assessments, and homeland security and defense.[14] As a GOCO laboratory, Sandia Corporation, a Lockheed Martin company, manages Sandia for the DOE's National Nuclear Security Administration.[15]

National Institute of Standards and Technology

The creation of NIST stems from a long history of U.S. leaders calling for uniformity in science. The clarion call for uniformity is traceable to several formal proposals for a federal department of science in the early 1880s, along with the explosion of documentary standards in all aspects of federal and state activity. Due to these trends, the establishment of a standards laboratory was inevitable.[16] The political force for the establishment of this laboratory was Lyman Gage, secretary of the Treasury under President William McKinley. Gage's original plan, announced in 1900, was for a separate agency to be called the National Standardizing Bureau. This bureau would maintain custody of standards; compare, construct, and test standards; and resolve problems in connection with standards. Finally, the Act of March 3, 1901, also known as the Organic Act, established the National Bureau of Standards (NBS) within the Department of the Treasury.

In the period after World War I, the bureau's research focused on assisting in the growth of industry. Research was conducted on ways to increase the operating efficiency of automobile and aircraft engines, electrical batteries, and gas appliances. Work was also begun on improving methods for measuring electrical losses in response to public utility needs. This latter research was not independent of international efforts to establish electrical standards similar to those established over 50 years before for weights and measures. After World War II, significant attention and resources were allocated to the bureau. NBS moved from Washington, DC, to Gaithersburg, Maryland, in 1958, and it was renamed NIST under the guidelines of the Omnibus Trade and Competitiveness Act of 1988.[17] Through the Act, the scope of NIST's research mission was expanded.

NIST's mission is to promote U.S. economic growth by working with industry to develop and apply technology, measurements, and standards. NIST carries out this mission primarily through its eight measurement and standards research laboratories. NIST laboratories provide technical leadership for vital components of the nation's technology infrastructure needed by U.S. industry to continually improve its products and services.

Patent Application Activity at Sandia and the National Institute of Standards and Technology

The patent applications and patent applications per R&D dollar (billions, 2009 dollars) trends from 1970 through 2009 at Sandia and NIST are in Figures 6.1 and 6.2, respectively.[18] In both laboratories, patent applications and patent applications per R&D dollar increased during the post-1980 period, following a pattern observed at U.S. research universities following the enactment of the Bayh-Dole Act. However, at Sandia and NIST, the rise in patenting did not occur immediately after the Stevenson-Wydler Act; rather, it began in the mid-1980s.

With respect to Sandia's patent applications and patent applications per R&D dollar, as shown in Figure 6.1, activity remained constant and very low until 1985. Following 1985, there was a slight increase until 1990/1992. From 1990/1992 to 2000 there was a more substantial increase, and there has been a steady decline in patent applications and patent applications per R&D dollar since 2000.

Regarding the patenting activity trend at NIST in Figure 6.2, there was a slight but erratic increase from 1970 to 1988, followed by a significant increase until 1992. After 1992, both series declined steadily. Thus, at both Sandia and NIST, the immediate post-Stevenson-Wydler Act period did not show significant patent application activity. The post-1986 Amendment period of increases appears to have been dampened by other events during the 1990s and later.

Link et al. (2011) estimated regression equations using the data that underlie Figure 6.1 and Figure 6.2, controlling for the timing of the 1980 Stevenson-Wydler Act of 1986 and 1986 Federal Technology Transfer Act, as

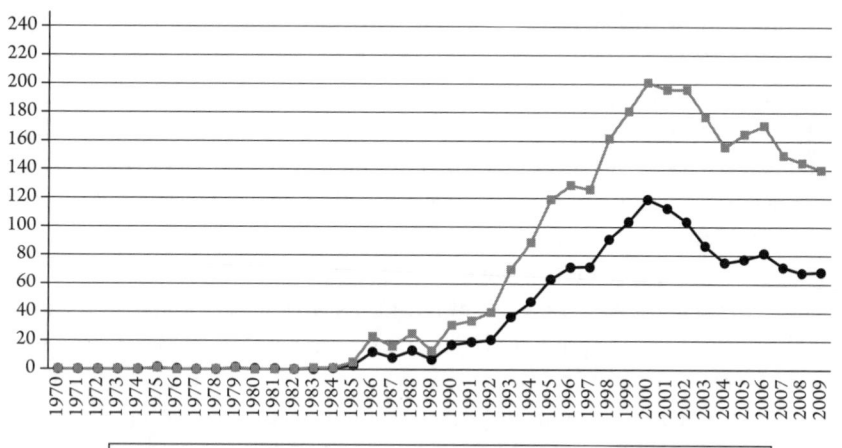

Figure 6.1 Patent Applications at Sandia National Laboratories, 1970–2009

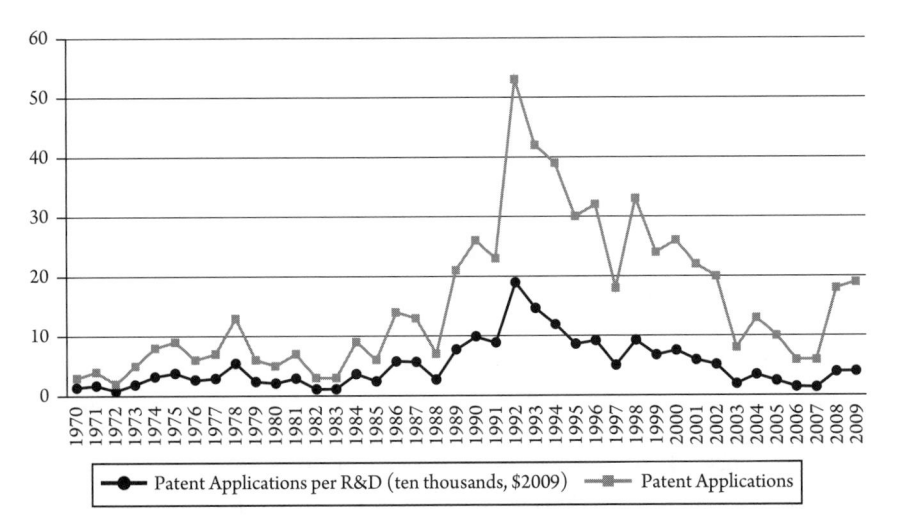

Figure 6.2 Patent Applications at the National Institute of Standards and Technology, 1970–2009

well as for any laboratory-specific factors. Two relevant institutional events that could conceptually have an impact on a laboratory's potential applications are the time when the technology transfer effects actually began in response to the Stevenson-Wydler Act and its 1986 amendment and the timing of a mission change in a laboratory.

The Office of Intellectual Property Management, Alliances, and Licensing at Sandia (i.e., the technology transfer office) did not ramp up until the mid-1990s. This does not mean that technology transfer activities were less important prior to, say, 1995, but it does indicate that more resources were devoted to the internal laboratory infrastructure to promote technology transfer after that year.

The Omnibus Trade and Competitiveness Act of 1988 (discussed in Chapter 10) not only changed NIST's name from NBS but also broadened its research mission. In that year there was also a ramp-up in the sense that the Office of Research and Technology Assessment was formalized. In addition to these increases in the allocation of internal resources devoted to technology transfer, the mission of each laboratory also changed over time.

Production activities at Sandia began in the early 1990s on a limited scale, but these activities were first seen in Sandia's accounting budgets in 2004. In that year, Sandia's accounting department began to separate production operating costs from research laboratory operating costs. Production operating costs averaged nearly 6 percent of total R&D costs over the 2004–2009 period.[19] Diverting scientists from research to design, prototyping, and production could reduce the time available to undertake patentable research, and thus patent applications could decrease over time.

At NIST, there had long been an open policy toward scientists patenting, and the directors had a broad interpretation of the laboratory's research mission. However, beginning in the early 1990s until about 2007, the various NIST directors embraced a more narrow interpretation of NIST's mission. In response, patenting was not as encouraged as it had been before or currently is.

The regression results reported by Link et al. (2011) show statistically that the patenting activity in these two laboratories is primarily related to the financial incentives established through the Federal Technology Transfer Act and the availability of internal resources. The statistical impact of the Stevenson-Wydler Act is insignificant in comparison to the Federal Technology Transfer Act.[20] Thus, unlike the Bayh-Dole Act, which was a dramatically successful example of public sector entrepreneurship, the Stevenson-Wydler Act and the Federal Technology Transfer Act—while clearly examples of public sector entrepreneurship—have been less successful. As the discussion above indicates, the smaller success of the Stevenson-Wydler and Federal Technology Transfer Acts can be attributed, at least in part, to the smaller incentives for entrepreneurial behavior that were either embodied directly in the acts or that were generated as the acts were implemented. As is the case for private sector entrepreneurship, the presence of an uncertain economic environment means that there is no guarantee that public sector entrepreneurship will succeed.

The Never-Ending Task of Public Sector Entrepreneurship and the Revival of the U.S. Manufacturing Sector in the 21st Century

As Figure 4.1 in Chapter 4 reveals, total factor productivity in the United States revived after the downturns of the 1970s and early 1980s. However, by the turn of the 21st century, concerns began to rise that the United States was on the cusp of another possible productivity slowdown. Such a slowdown should not necessarily be interpreted as a failure of past public sector entrepreneurship efforts, such as the Bayh-Dole Act and the Stevenson-Wydler Act. Like private sector entrepreneurship, and particularly in an increasingly competitive global economy, success may require constant innovations. But if new public sector entrepreneurial initiatives were called for, how should they be focused?

One reason some had concerns about yet another slowdown in total factor productivity was a fall in the support for R&D in the United States relative to the economy's size and relative to the support for R&D in other nations. Figure 6.3 shows gross expenditures on R&D (GERD) as a share of gross domestic product (GDP) for the United States, the European Union (EU), and selected Asian countries. The solid line in the figure represents the United States; it

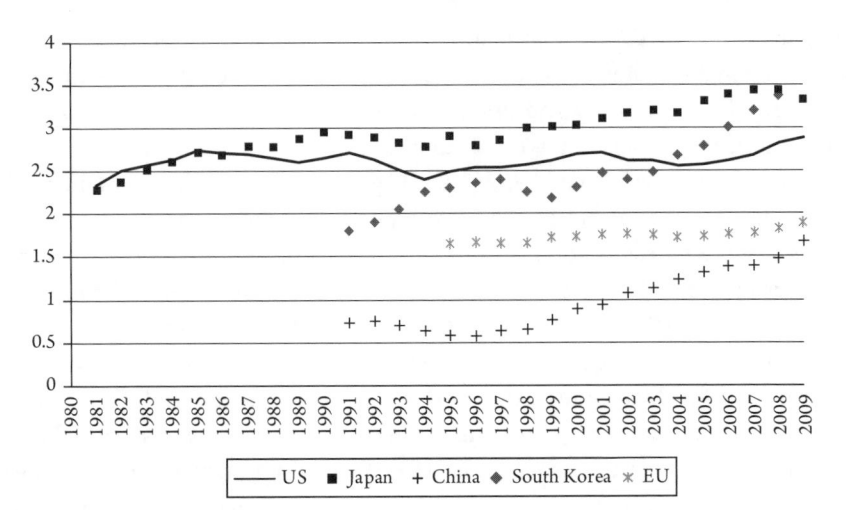

Figure 6.3 Gross Expenditures on R&D as a Share of Gross Domestic Product (%), Selected Countries, 1981–2009

shows an increase in GERD/GDP for the first half of the decade of the 1980s. Perhaps this half-decade trend reflects an immediate economic impact from several of the post-productivity slowdown technology and innovation policies discussed in this book. The pattern of GERD/GDP has been sporadic since the mid-1980s, although the trend since 2004 has been upward.

Regarding our theme of public sector entrepreneurship, more relevant than the overall trend in relative U.S. investments in R&D is the comparative pattern for China and South Korea. For more than a decade, the GERD/GDP ratio for China and South Korea has been increasing, and the rate of increase has been visibly greater than for any post-1980s period in the United States.

An Emphasis on the Manufacturing Sector

At the 2005 meeting of the councils of the National Academy of Sciences and the National Academy of Engineering, concern was widely expressed about the weakness of U.S. science and technology.[21] After a series of meetings and discussions, many of which included members of Congress, the National Academies' Committee on Science, Engineering, and Public Policy (COSEPUP) established the Committee on Prospering in the Global Economy of the 21st Century: An Agenda for American Science and Technology. The committee was charged to prioritize actions for policymakers that would "enhance the science and technology enterprise so that the United States can successfully compete, prosper, and be secure in the global community in the 21st century" (National Academies 2007, p. xi). The recommendations, which were presented in *Rising Above the Gathering Storm: Energizing and Employing America for a*

Brighter Economic Future (National Academies 2007), called for still another effort at what we refer to as public sector entrepreneurship, this time directed at improving technology and innovation policies. And this effort had a relationship to the activities in federal laboratories.

The response was quick. Congress began to address the recommendations in *Gathering Storm*, as the National Academies' report is commonly called, and Congress's actions resulted in the passage of the America Creating Opportunities to Meaningfully Promote Excellence in Technology, Education, and Science (COMPETES) Act of 2007, Public Law 110-69. Among the many elements in the America COMPETES Act, the Office of Science and Technology Policy (OSTP), which advises the president, was charged to study "structures that could effectively encourage long-term value creation and innovation" and to study "incentives to encourage participation among institutions of higher education ... to encourage innovation." Many provisions within the Act focused on STEM-related educational and job-training programs.

The America COMPETES Reauthorization Act of 2010, Public Law 111-358, also emphasized STEM education and authorized funding of such a program until 2013, at which time it would need to be reauthorized. The Reauthorization Act of 2010 also emphasized advanced manufacturing R&D. In particular, OSTP was to "develop, and update every 5 years, a strategic plan to guide Federal programs and activities in support of advanced manufacturing research and development."

In July 2011, the President's Council of Advisors on Science and Technology (PCAST), the external advisory body of OSTP and thus of the president, released its report, *Ensuring American Leadership in Advanced Manufacturing*. The report stated:

> The Nation's historic leadership in manufacturing ... is at risk. ... The United States is lagging behind in innovation in its manufacturing sector [which accounts for over 60 percent of R&D funded and over 70 percent of R&D performed]. ... Our trade deficit in advanced technology manufactured products ... shifted from a surplus to deficit starting in 2001. In addition, the United States has been steadily losing the research and development activity linked to manufacturing ... to other nations, as well as our ability to compete in the manufacturing of products that were invented and innovated here. (PCAST 2011, p. i)

The report correctly—at least from an economic perspective as discussed in Chapter 4—emphasized that the United States should invest to overcome market failures by, among other things, supporting applied research programs in "new technologies with the potential for transforming impact" (p. iii), supporting "investment in shared technology infrastructure that would help U.S. companies improve their manufacturing" (p. iv), and supporting "a robust basic research enterprise" (p. iv).

Building on *Ensuring American Leadership in Advanced Manufacturing*, the Executive Office of the President released *A National Strategic Plan for Advanced Manufacturing* in February 2012. The proposed national strategy had five objectives:

> Objective 1: Accelerate investment in advanced manufacturing technology, especially by small and medium-sized manufacturing enterprises, by fostering more effective use of Federal capabilities and facilities (i.e., federal laboratories), including early procurement by Federal agencies of cutting-edge products.

> Objective 2: Expand the number of workers who have the skills needed by a growing advanced manufacturing sector and make the education and training system more responsive to the demand for skills.

> Objective 3: Create and support national and regional public/private, government-industry-academic partnerships to accelerate investment in and deployment of advanced manufacturing technologies.

> Objective 4: Optimize the Federal government's advanced manufacturing investment by taking a portfolio perspective across agencies and adjusting accordingly.

> Objective 5: Increase total U.S. public and private investments in advanced manufacturing research and development (R&D). (Executive Office of the President 2012, p. 1)

On the heels of this White House report came a follow-up PCAST report, *Capturing Domestic Advantage in Advanced Manufacturing* (PCAST 2012) that had a similar focus.

Follow-Up Reports to the America COMPETES Act as an Example of Public Sector Entrepreneurship

While the reports that followed from the America COMPETES Act of 2007 and its 2010 reauthorization do not imply that Congress will authorize or fund any of the recommendations, they are nonetheless examples of public sector entrepreneurship. In particular, the July 2012 PCAST report recommended that manufacturing innovation institutes (MIIs) be established. These institutes would not have the status of a federal laboratory, but they would perform similar transfer tasks. Specifically, these institutes would bridge the gap between basic/applied research performed in federal laboratories and applied research/development conducted in innovative companies, especially smaller ones. Specifically, "MIIs would function as embedded nodes within a distributed network of research institutes concurrently anchoring both a national and a regional innovation system" (PCAST 2012, p. 22). Companies could use the resources in an MII—the institute's human and technical capital—to test their innovations and to interact with other companies pursuing similar technologies.[22] Like the Bayh-Dole, Stevenson-Wydler, and Federal Technology Transfer Acts, this is an example of efforts to enhance the social networks of private sector, entrepreneurial firms interested in developing new technology and other related innovations.

Summary

Like the Bayh-Dole Act, the Stevenson-Wydler Act, which mandated that federal laboratories establish an Office of Research and Technology Applications, represents an important example of public sector entrepreneurship. Unlike the Bayh-Dole Act, however, the Stevenson-Wydler Act did not give rise to a dramatic and sustained increase in innovative activity. In part, this difference was due to the lack of incentives for federal research laboratories and their scientists to engage in technology transfer activities. To provide those incentives, the Federal Technology Transfer Act was passed six years later. In the decades after the passage of the Bayh-Dole, Stevenson-Wydler, and Federal Technology Transfer Acts, productivity in the United States resumed its upward path. But by the beginning of the 21st century, concerns once again arose that the United States was heading toward a new productivity decline, particularly with respect to manufacturing. This concern precipitated the passage of the America COMPETES Act in 2007, and a reauthorization in 2010. These acts represent the most recent round of public sector entrepreneurial efforts by a federal government focused on the nation's economic health.

The R&E Tax Credit of 1981

So far as my coin would stretch; and where it would not, I have
used my credit.
　　　　　　—William Shakespeare (*King Henry the Fourth*)

Legislative Background

Section 174 of the Internal Revenue Code, adopted in 1954, codified and
expanded tax laws pertaining to the R&D expenditures by firms. This provision of the tax code permitted businesses to fully deduct research and experimentation (R&E) expenditures but not development or research application
expenditures in the year incurred.[1, 2]

Dissatisfaction with Section 174 of the Internal Revenue Code led to the
passage of the Economic Recovery Tax Act (ERTA), Public Law 97-34, in 1981,
which was signed by President Ronald Reagan on August 13 of that year. The
Joint Committee on Taxation offered the following reasons for the Act:

> The Congress concluded that a program of significant multi-year tax
> reductions was needed to ensure economic growth in the years ahead.
> This tax reduction program should help upgrade the nation's industrial
> base, stimulate productivity and innovation throughout the economy,
> lower personal tax burdens, and restrain the growth of the Federal
> Government. Lower tax burdens on individuals and businesses, main-
> tained over a period of years, should help restore certainty to economic
> decision-making and provide a sound basis for a sustained economic
> recovery. Accordingly, the Congress chose a program of broadly based
> tax cuts that it believed would improve incentives to work, produce,
> save, and invest, consistent with the goal of eliminating the Federal
> budget deficit by 1984.
>
> The Congress was concerned that the performance of the economy
> had fallen far below its potential and that this condition would con-
> tinue if there was no change in policy. The real growth of the economy,

which had slowed in 1978 and again in 1979, came to a halt in 1980. (1981, p. 17)

Clearly, according to the Joint Committee, the productivity slowdown that was discussed in Chapter 4 was one motivating factor for changes in U.S. tax policies. More specifically, as related to technology and innovation in general, and to Section 174 of the Internal Revenue Code in particular, the focus was on R&E/R&D expenditures. The Joint Committee noted:

> Research and experimentation are basic activities that must precede (1) the development and application to production of new techniques and equipment, and (2) the development and manufacture of new products. In recent years, the Congress concluded, spending for these purposes had not been adequate.
>
> In the case of research and development activities conducted by business, company-financed and Federal expenditures over the 12-year period 1968–1979 remained at a fairly stable level in real terms, fluctuating between $19 and $22.8 billion in constant dollars. Relative to real gross national product, such expenditures for company research declined from 2.01 percent in 1968 to 1.58 percent in 1975, essentially remaining at that level since then.
>
> Aggregate research and development spending in this country has experienced a similar period of decline. In 1967, total expenditures reached a high of 2.91 percent of GNP before declining over ten years to 2.26 percent in 1977, and then increasing to an estimated 2.30 percent in 1980.. . . .
>
> In order to reverse this decline in research spending by industry, the Congress concluded that a substantial tax credit for incremental research and experimental expenditures was needed to overcome the reluctance of many ongoing companies to bear the significant costs of staffing and supplies, and certain equipment expenses such as computer charges, which must be incurred to initiate or expand research programs in a trade or business. While such costs have characteristics of investment activity, the relationships between expenditures for research and subsequent earnings often are less directly identifiable, and many businesses have been reluctant to allocate scarce investment funds for uncertain rewards. (1981, p. 119)

In terms of our model of public sector entrepreneurship from Chapter 3, research and experimentation are inputs in the process of opportunity recognition and exploitation—both of which, as Congress recognized, are inherently uncertain.

Figure 7.1 illustrates this concern using a longer time period of data for the ratio of aggregate R&D expenditures to GDP in constant 2005 dollars. Measured this way, the 1967–1977 period of decline referenced by the Joint Committee (although the decline continued through 1978) is obvious. R&D expenditures as a percentage of GDP declined throughout the referenced period, all the way down to 2.12 percent in 1978. The ratio of R&D expenditures to GDP has not been that low since that year. In fact, its minimum in recent years was 2.39 percent in 1994.

The 1967–1978 decline turned out, in retrospect, to be a leading indicator of what was to come, namely the decline in total factor productivity from 1978 through 1982 as discussed in Chapter 4 and shown in Figure 4.1. The decline in relative R&D expenditures, which was on the minds of many economists, was the motivating force behind the technology and innovation policy initiatives of the 1980s; those policy initiatives are at the heart of this book.

ERTA included a 25 percent marginal tax credit, that is, a 25 percent tax credit for qualified R&E expenditures in excess of the average amount spent during the previous three taxable years or 50 percent of the current year's expenditures (called the R&E base). The initial R&E tax credit had several limitations, including the fact that it did not cover expenses related to the administration of R&D or to research conducted outside of the United States.

As with the Bayh-Dole Act and the Stevenson-Wydler Act, experience with ERTA led to follow-up reforms, most notably the Tax Reform Act of 1986, Public Law 99-514, which modified the limitations on expenses related to the administration of R&D and research conducted outside the United States. But it also reduced the marginal tax credit rate for qualified R&E expenditures from 25 to 20 percent,[3] and lowered the credit on payments for basic research for "certain basic research by colleges, universities, and certain research organizations."

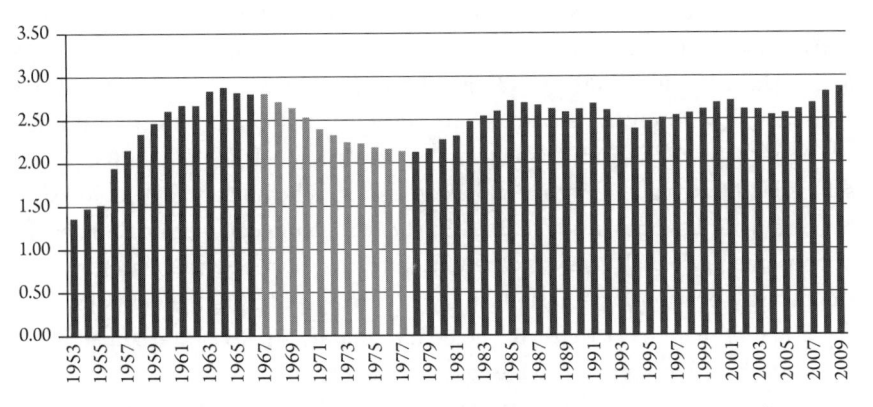

Figure 7.1 Aggregate R&D Expenditures as Percent of Gross Domestic Product, 1953–2009 Data.

Source: National Science Board 2012, Tables A4-1, A4-3.

Interestingly, given the ostensible motivation for reducing business uncertainty, the R&E tax credit has never been made permanent. As chronicled in Table 7.1, the credit has expired and been renewed retrospectively a number of times. As discussed below, the effect of such institutionally induced uncertainty is surely not positive. The degree to which it has mitigated the measurable and nonmeasurable benefits of the tax credit in practice, however, is not clear.

The Economics of the R&E Tax Credit

Bozeman and Link (1984) noted that tax incentives in general or, in this case, tax credits are a mechanism that government uses to stimulate or leverage private sector R&D.[4] Like any policy tool, tax incentives have advantages and disadvantages. Advantages include the following (Bozeman and Link 1984): tax incentives entail less interference in the marketplace than many other mechanisms, thus affording private sector recipients the ability to retain autonomy regarding the use of the incentives; tax incentives require less paperwork than other programs; tax incentives obviate the need to directly target individual firms in need of assistance; tax incentives have the psychological advantage of achieving a favorable industry reaction; tax incentives may be permanent and thus do not require annual budget review (but recall the impermanence of the R&E tax credit); and tax incentives have a high degree of political feasibility. Some disadvantages of tax incentives are: tax incentives may bring about unintended windfalls by rewarding firms for what they would have done in the absence of the incentive; tax incentives often result in undesirable inequities; tax incentives raid the federal treasury; tax incentives frequently undermine public accountability; and the effectiveness of tax incentives often varies over the business cycle.

Figure 7.2 illustrates the economics of an R&E tax credit. Measured on the vertical axis is the marginal rate of return, and measured on the horizontal axis is the amount of R&E spending. Both the marginal social return and the marginal private return schedules are downward sloping, reflecting diminishing returns to R&E investments in a given time period. The social return schedule is drawn greater than the private return schedule for all levels of R&E because firms cannot appropriate all the benefits from conducting R&E; some of those benefits spill over to other firms in the current time period and in the post-innovation time period, thus generating additional benefits to society. The marginal private cost to the firm to undertake R&D is assumed to be constant; hence, marginal private cost is shown as a horizontal line.

As shown, the firm will equate the marginal private cost of conducting R&E with the marginal private return associated with this activity, and the firm will invest at level RE_0. Society wishes to push the firm to invest at level RE_1 in order

Table 7.1 **Legislative History of the R&E Tax Credit**

Legislation	Public Law	Time Period	Comment
Economic Recovery Tax Act of 1981	P. L. 97-34	July 1, 1981, through December 31, 1985	
Tax Reform Act of 1986	P. L. 99-514	January 1, 1986, through December 31, 1988	Lowered the credit's rate from 25% to 20%
Technical and Miscellaneous Revenue Act of 1988	P. L. 100-647	January 1, 1989, through December 31, 1989	
Omnibus Budget Reconciliation Act of 1989	P. L. 101-239	January 1, 1990, through December 31, 1990	
Omnibus Budget Reconciliation Act of 1990	P. L. 101-508	January 1, 1991, through December 31, 1991	
Tax Extension Act of 1991	P. L. 102-227	January 1, 1992, through June 30, 1992	
Omnibus Budget Reconciliation Act of 1993	P. L. 103-66	July 1, 1992, through June 30, 1995	Enacted on August 10, 1993 and extended the credit retrospectively to July 1, 1992
Small Business Job Protection Act of 1996	P. L. 104-188	July 1, 1996, through May 31, 1997	Enacted on August 20, 1996, and extended the credit retrospectively to July 1, 1996; there was a 1-year gap in the credit's coverage from July 1, 1995, through June 30, 1996
Taxpayer Relief Act of 1997	P. L. 105-34	June 1, 1997, through June 30, 1998	Enacted on August 5, 1997, and extended the credit retrospectively to June 1, 1997

(*continued*)

Table 7.1 **(Continued)**

Omnibus Consolidated and Emergency Supplemental Appropriations Act of 1998	P. L. 105-277	July 1, 1998, through June 30, 1999	
Ticket to Work and Work Incentives Improvement Act of 1999	P. L. 106-170	July 1, 1999 through June 30, 2004	
Working Families Tax Relief Act of 2004	P. L. 108-311	July 1, 2004, through December 31, 2005	
Energy Policy Act of 2005	P. L. 109-58	—	Enacted on August 8, 2005 and included in eligible R&E a 20% credit on energy research performed under contract by a qualified research consortia, university, federal laboratory, or small business
Tax Relief and Health Care Act of 2006	P. L. 109-432	January 1, 2006, through December 31, 2007	
Emergency Economic Stabilization Act of 2008	P. L. 110-343	January 1, 2008, through December 31, 2009	Enacted on October 3, 2008, and extended retrospectively to January 1, 2008
Tax Relief Unemployment Compensation Reauthorization, and Job Creation Act of 2010	P. L. 111-312	January 1, 2010, through December 31, 2011	
American Taxpayer Relief Act of 2012	P. L. 112-240	January 1, 2012, through December 31, 2013	Enacted on January 2, 2013, and expended retrospectively to January 1, 2012

Source: Based on Guenther 2013, pp. 16–19.

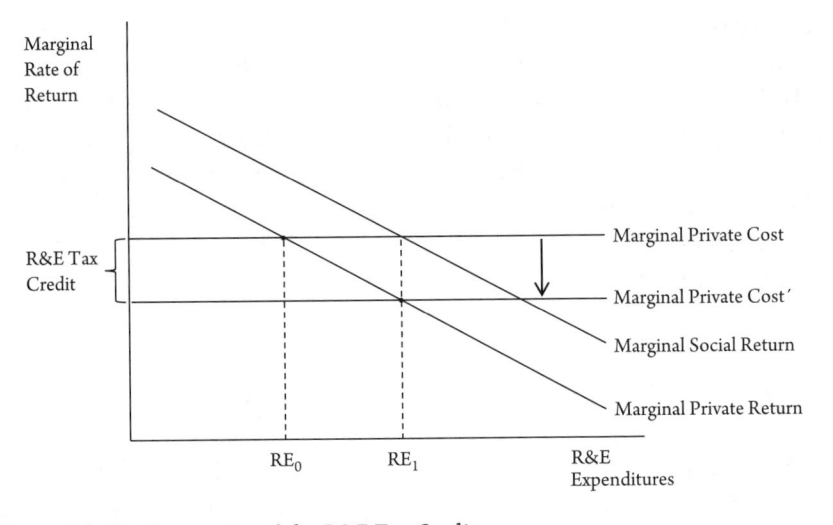

Figure 7.2 The Economics of the R&E Tax Credit

to maximize social benefits.[5] Hence, the optimal tax credit is one that provides an incentive to the firm to increase its R&E expenditures to level RE_1.

One way to induce the firm to increase its R&E expenditures to level RE_1 is to reduce the firm's marginal private cost of undertaking additional R&E. In fact, receipt of a tax credit can be thought of as such a reduction. Hence, with an appropriately sized R&E tax credit as shown in Figure 7.2, the firm's marginal private cost will fall sufficiently so that when the firm re-equates its tax-affected marginal private cost (i.e., marginal private cost') with its marginal private return, it will end up investing at the efficient level of RE_1.

Note, however, that while the tax credit—and tax incentives in general—will increase the firm's level of R&E from RE_0 to RE_1, the credit will not alleviate the technical or market risk that characterizes the firm's portfolio of projects. Its effect on the level of uncertainty associated with the innovation process, however, is a more complex issue both because of the inherent nonmeasurability of uncertainty and the indirect mechanism by which the tax credit affects the innovation process. This indirect mechanism, by increasing the firm's willingness to expand its social network due to the reduced net marginal cost of such activities, would, in terms of our model of public sector entrepreneurship, result in an expansion of the search region (see Figure 3.2) and thereby presumably result in a greater chance for innovation success, even if the size of that increase cannot be formally measured.

Other issues that give rise to concern center on the fact that R&E and R&D are not homogeneous activities. As Mansfield (1980) and Link (1981) have shown, the research (R) portion of R&E and R&D has a greater impact on productivity growth and hence economic growth than does experimentation (E) or development (D).[6] Any uniform tax incentive that treats either R&E or R&D as if it were a homogeneous activity will likely encourage the firm to maintain its ongoing portfolio of R&E or R&D, which it arrived at through its profit-maximizing strategy, not society's maximizing strategy. That may not necessarily be a bad thing, because economic studies have suggested that the marginal private return from R&D in total is still greater than the marginal cost of conducting R&D. Clearly, a tax credit on research (R) as opposed to experimentation (E) or development (D) is socially more desirable. Nevertheless, it could be cumbersome to administer. We revisit this issue in more detail in Chapter 9.

International Comparisons

As our discussion in Chapter 6 about the America COMPETES Act and attempts to increase U.S. productivity in general, and manufacturing productivity in particular, reveals, the effectiveness of public sector entrepreneurship that focuses on technology development and other related innovations in a globally competitive economy depends on a country's own efforts relative to those of other countries.

Table 7.2 shows a sample of countries that have a tax credit for R&E or R&D, along with the ratio of tax revenue foregone because of the credit as a percentage of GDP. Only three nations—Canada, the United States, and South Korea—forego at least 0.18 percent of GDP as a result of their R&E or R&D tax credits; Canada gives up the most, 0.22 percent. The other countries in the sample sacrifice 0.12 percent or less—the average for this group is 0.06 percent—with Poland having the lowest figure.

It is not clear, however, whether foregoing a larger percent of GDP results in greater impact on firm cost or behavior. Table 7.3 shows a sample of countries with R&D tax credits, and it shows the value of the flat and marginal rate.[7] Only two countries in the table—Ireland and the United States—have a marginal rate, but, as discussed below, there are arguments against the marginal rate aspect of an R&D tax credit. That issue aside, there is little correlation between the rates employed and the size of the GDP sacrifice associated with R&E and R&D tax credits.

The R&E Tax Credit as an Example of Public Sector Entrepreneurship

The relevant question to ask to determine if the R&E tax credit meets our criterion for being an example of public sector entrepreneurship is whether it is an innovative public policy that improves the social network for the affected

Table 7.2 International Comparison of Foregone Tax Revenues from the R&E/R&D Tax Credit as a Percentage of Gross Domestic Product (rounded, various years)

Country	Foregone Tax Revenue as a Percentage of GDP (year)
United States	0.18 (2008)
Japan	0.12 (2007)
Canada	0.22 (2008)
South Korea	0.19 (2008)
France	0.08 (2008)
United Kingdom	0.06 (2008)
Netherlands	0.07 (2008)
Spain	0.02 (2008)
Hungary	0.09 (2008)
Portugal	0.09 (2009)
Ireland	0.09 (2007)
Norway	0.07 (2008)
Poland	0.00 (2008)

Note: Order in which countries are listed is preserved from OECD 2010.

Data Source: OECD 2010, pp. 22–26.

Table 7.3 R&D Tax Credits by Country, 2011–2012

Country	Flat R&D Credit	Marginal R&D Credit
Austria	10%	—
Canada	20–35%	—
Ireland	—	25%
Italy	10%	—
Japan	8—12%	—
Korea	3—25%	—
Portugal	32.5%	—
Spain	25%	—
United States	—	20%
Taiwan	15%	—

Note: When a credit rate range is shown, the smaller value is relevant to large firms and the larger value is relevant to small firms.

Data Source: Stewart et al. 2012, pp. 13–16.

parties operating in an uncertain economic environment. That is, the question to ask is whether the credit increases the number and quality of heterogeneous experiential ties for the affected parties, thus resulting in those parties having an enhanced ability to identify and take advantage of heretofore unexploited opportunities.

The R&E tax credit certainly is innovative. While the mechanism of tax credits is one that had been employed for various purposes over the years, it had never before been applied in the manner embodied in ERTA. Moreover, the effects of the R&E tax credit were at the time uncertain. In addition, as summarized in Table 7.4, the R&E tax credit has resulted in improved social networks, even if the credit is not directly focused on enhancing such networks, as the Bayh-Dole, Stevenson-Wydler, and the Federal Technology Transfer Acts were.

There are two specific mechanisms by which R&E tax credits enhance existing knowledge. The first works through the basic research tax credit component of R&E tax credit programs. To the extent that the basic research of the firm is conducted along with university faculty, the increased access to existing university knowledge ability, which follows from the lower net cost of engaging in basic research, creates—though with uncertainty—increased access to an often distinct perspective that does not typically exist within a private sector

Table 7.4 **Public Sector Entrepreneurship: The R&E Tax Credit Portion of the Economic Recovery Tax Act of 1981**

Characteristics	*Descriptor*	*Comment*
Advancement of knowledge	High	The tax credit expands the research base of affected firms, thus having the potential to advance the knowledge base of the firm and of society as new technologies diffuse through the economy.
Impact on technology and innovation	Long term	The R&E or R&D process, especially the basic research portion of R&E, is long. Thus, any impact on technology and subsequently on innovation will be long term.
Targeted parties	All firms	All taxpaying firms engaged in R&E can benefit from the tax credit. Those firms that are not profitable and do not pay taxes will not benefit from a tax credit.
Heterogeneity of experiential ties	Marginal to moderate	Only the basic research tax credit for R&E conducted with universities has the potential to enhance experiential ties if the R&E conducted is with university faculty.

firm. With that increased access to a different perspective come creative syner-gies and dynamics that can result in discovery of new opportunities and ways to exploit them for commercial gain. Likewise, for those in the university, the increased ability to engage in the transfer of knowledge with the private sec-tor opens them up—again with uncertainty—to increased input from those in the private sector, a perspective otherwise typically missing in the univer-sity community. This private sector perspective is often quite different from that of the university, and with that divergence come the creative synergies and dynamics that can result in additional transfer of existing knowledge in the future, as well as the creation of new knowledge that can be exploited for commercial gain.

The second mechanism works through the expansion in the research base of affected firms. While the direct effect of the R&E tax credit is to increase the level of R&E expenditures, as shown in Figure 7.2, this increase in R&E expen-ditures will typically include increased effort at exploiting, and even expand-ing, the firm's social network. This more intensive exploitation of the firm's social network results in a more effective one.

Together, these mechanisms mean that the R&E tax credit can be expected to result in a greater level of opportunity recognition and exploitation. For the firm, this means a greater chance at commercial success. But more than that, it means advances in the knowledge base of the firm and, as new technologies diffuse through the economy, advances for society as well.

The Economic Impact of the R&E Tax Credit

In 1996, the Office of Technology Assessment released a report on the effec-tiveness of the R&E tax credit in the United States. The report concluded:

- There is not sufficient information available to conduct a complete benefit-to-cost analysis of the effectiveness of the R&E tax credit on the economy.
- The econometric studies that have been done to date conclude that the credit has been effective in the sense that for every dollar lost in federal revenue there is an increase of a dollar in private sector R&D spending. These studies concluded that the credit would be more effective if it were made permanent. Hall and van Reenen (2000) concluded from their review of the literature that the tax elasticity of R&D is about unity, meaning that a one percent increase in the credit will increase industry R&D by about one percent.
- The R&E tax credit represents a small fraction of federal R&D expenditures, about 2.6 percent of total federal R&D funding and about 6.4 percent of federal R&D for industry. (Office of Technology Assessment 1996b)

Since the time of the report, more evaluations of the impact of the credit have been done. The general consensus is that the credit is effective. According to Guenther:

> One can argue the credit may have boosted [R&D] spending [from 1999 to 2009] somewhere between 2.1% and 4.2%, compared with investment that might have taken place in the absence of the credit. (2013, p. 22)

Regarding the tax credit's effectiveness, most economists agree that the credit should be made permanent so firms can make their long-run investment decisions in a more certain tax environment. Some economists further argue that the tax credit should be based on a flat rate, as is more common in other nations, rather than on a marginal rate. For example, Tassey takes the position:

> As a policy instrument, a tax incentive for R&D should be most effective if its form is a flat rate applied to all R&D. (2007a, p. 605)

Atkinson agrees, but explains:[8]

> If the United States is to remain globally competitive in R&D-based activities, increasing the generosity of the R&E credit will be important. How to do that is not as clear. Perhaps the most important issue in the design of an R&D tax credit is whether it should be a volume credit, an incremental credit, or some mix of the two. An incremental credit defines some base level of R&D with incremental R&D defined as R&D above this base level. Most economists favor an incremental credit because it rewards only increases in research investments. As a result, for the same amount of tax expenditures the incentive value of the incremental credit can be higher than a flat credit.
>
> However, an incremental credit has three main disadvantages. First, as discussed below, determining the appropriate base level can be difficult. That is even more difficult now that it is so easy for firms to locate R&D in a wide number of nations. In this case, all of a firm's R&D may be incremental in the sense that a firm may choose to perform the research in the United States or outside of it. Second, the compliance costs for industry and government from incremental credits can be higher. Finally, because of the complexity and lack of transparency, incremental credits can send an uncertain signal to business managers who decide on R&D levels, reducing its effectiveness. (2007, p. 624)

A flat R&E tax credit will also have marginal effects because it is applicable to both marginal and infra-marginal R&E expenses. The debate over whether a flat R&E credit is more effective than a marginal R&E credit centers on two issues: (1) the size of the income and substitution effects associated with the flat R&E credit versus the size of the substitution effect associated with the marginal R&E tax credit, and (2) the revenue cost of employing a flat R&E credit rather than a marginal R&E credit. Ultimately, this is an empirical issue. However, as Tassey (2007a) and Atkinson (2007) point out, there are reasons to believe that because of complications associated with the implementation of the marginal form of the R&E tax credit, the flat version of the R&E tax credit may be more effective overall. As the data in Tables 7.2 and 7.3 hint, the flat version of the R&E tax credit may be more efficient at well.

Summary

The R&E tax credit, which reduces a firm's marginal and perhaps average cost of engaging in qualifying R&E and R&D expenses, represents still another example of public sector entrepreneurship, albeit one less directly focused on social networks than are the Bayh-Dole, Stevenson-Wydler, and Federal Technology Transfer Acts. Initially passed in 1981 as a temporary measure, but modified and renewed several times since, the tax credit has been effective, according to empirical studies, in stimulating additional private sector R&E activity and thus innovation. There are, to be sure, debates about the effectiveness of the R&E tax credit, but those debates center not on the value of the R&E tax credit per se but on whether it should be permanent to provide a more reliable stimulus, and on whether a flat version of the R&E tax credit—which is more common outside the United States—is superior to the marginal version used in the United States. Much of the argument for the flat version hinges on problems associated with implementing a marginal R&E tax credit from a practical perspective.

The Small Business Innovation Development Act of 1982

The vitality of thought is in adventure. Ideas won't keep.
Something must be done about them. When the idea is new,
its custodians have fervor, live for it, and, if need be, die for it.
—Alfred North Whitehead

Legislative Background

Since 1953, when the Small Business Administration was established through the Small Business Act of 1953, Public Law 85-536, Congress has singled out small business for special treatment as a vehicle for stimulating economic growth. By the early 1980s, no doubt in part due to the reaction to the productivity slowdowns that gave rise to the Bayh-Dole and Stevenson-Wydler Acts, concerns arose in Congress that small business was a neglected but important sector for economic growth policies. In particular, the Congress found:[1]

(1) Technological innovation creates jobs, increases productivity, competition, and economic growth, and is a valuable counterforce to inflation and the United States balance-of-payments deficit;

(2) While small business is the principal source of significant innovations in the Nation, the vast majority of federally funded research and development is conducted by large businesses, universities, and Government laboratories; and

(3) Small businesses are among the most cost-effective performers of research and development and are particularly capable of developing research and development results into new products. (Public Law 97-219)

The result was the passage of the Small Business Innovation Development Act of 1982, Public Law 97-219, which has come to be referred to simply as the 1982 Act. The purposes of the 1982 Act are

(1) to stimulate technological innovation;

(2) to use small business to meet Federal research and development needs;

(3) to foster and encourage participation by minority and disadvantaged persons in technological innovation; and

(4) to increase private sector commercialization innovations derived from Federal research and development.

To raise funds to support these purposes, the Act stated that

> each Federal agency which has an extramural budget for research or research and development in excess of $100,000,000 for fiscal year 1982, or any fiscal year thereafter, shall expend not less than 0.2 per centum of its extramural budget in fiscal year 1983 or in such subsequent fiscal year as the agency has such budget, not less than 0.6 per centum of such budget in the second fiscal year thereafter; not less than 1 per centum of such budget in the third fiscal year thereafter, and not less than 1.25 per centum of such budget in all subsequent fiscal years with small business concerns specifically in connection with a small business innovation research program which meets the requirements of the Small Business Innovation Development Act of 1982 and regulations issued thereunder.

But, to assure that such funding not come at the expense of crippling funding for basic research and other R&D, the Act also stated that

> a Federal agency shall not make available for the purpose of meeting the requirements of this subsection an amount of its extramural budget for basic research or research and development which exceeds the percentages specified herein.

With the funding mandated by the 1982 Act, Small Business Innovation Research (SBIR) program awards were created with three designed phases of outlays. Phase I awards were small, generally less than $50,000 for the six-month award period. The purpose of Phase I awards was and still is to assist businesses as they assess the feasibility of an idea's scientific and commercial potential in response to the funding agency's objectives. According to the Act, Phase I is: "a first phase for determining, insofar as possible, the scientific and technical merit and feasibility of ideas submitted pursuant to SBIR Program solicitations." Or, as it has been described earlier in our characterization of the entrepreneurial process, the purpose of Phase I grants is to facilitate opportunity recognition.

Phase II awards, which are focused on support for the initial steps of opportunity exploitation, were capped at $500,000; they generally last for two years. These awards were and still are for the business to further develop its proposed research, ideally leading to a commercializable product, process, or service. According to the Act, Phase II is

> a second phase to further develop the proposed ideas to meet the particular program needs, the awarding of which shall take into consideration the scientific and technical merit and feasibility evidenced by the first phase and, where two or more proposals are evaluated as being of approximately equal scientific and technical merit and feasibility, special consideration shall be given to those proposals that have demonstrated third phase, non-Federal capital commitments.

Further work on the projects launched through the SBIR program occurs in what is called Phase III, which does not involve SBIR funds. At this stage, firms needing additional financing—to ensure that the product, process, or service can move into the marketplace—are expected to obtain it from sources other than the SBIR program. According to the Act, Phase III is

> a third phase in which non-Federal capital pursues commercial applications of the research or research and development and which may also involve follow-on non-SBIR funded production contracts with a Federal agency for products or processes intended for use by the United States Government.

As stated in the 1982 Act, to be eligible for an SBIR award, the small business must be independently owned and operated; not the dominant firm in the field in which it is proposing to carry out SBIR projects; organized and operated for profit; the employer of 500 or fewer employees, including employees of subsidiaries and affiliates; the primary source of employment for the project's principal investigator at the time of award and during the period when the research is conducted; and at least 51 percent owned by U.S. citizens or lawfully admitted permanent resident aliens.

Because the 1982 Act was not permanent, the Act has witnessed a number of reauthorizations over the years, along with occasional amendments to modify the structure of the SBIR program. In 1986, the 1982 Act was extended through 1992 as a part of the Department of Defense Appropriation Act of 1986, Public Law 99-443. Then in 1992, the SBIR program was reauthorized again until 2000 through the Small Business Research and Development Enactment Act, Public Law 102-564. The 1992 reauthorization also modified the program's structure. Recall that under the 1982 Act, the set-aside rate imposed on government agencies to fund the SBIR program gradually increased to 1.25 percent over time. The 1992 reauthorization raised that maximum set-aside rate to 2.50 percent and re-emphasized the commercialization intent of SBIR-funded technologies (see point (4) from the 1982 Act above). The reauthorization also increased Phase I awards to $100,000 and Phase II awards to $750,000, and broadened objective (3) to also focus on women: "to provide for enhanced outreach efforts to increase the participation of ... small businesses that are 51 percent owned and controlled by women."

Further reauthorizations and changes occurred after the turn of the century. The Small Business Reauthorization Act of 2000, Public Law 106-554, extended the SBIR program until September 30, 2008; kept the 2.50 percent set-aside rate; and did not increase the amounts of Phase I and Phase II awards.

In 2008, however, difficulties reauthorizing the 2000 Act arose. Congress did not reauthorize the SBIR program by the legislated date of September 30, 2008; rather, Congress temporarily extended the program until March 20, 2009, with Public Law 110-235. The Senate version of the failed reauthorization bill (S. 3029) included, among other things, an increase in Phase I funding to $150,000 and an increase in Phase II funding to $1,000,000, with provisions for these funding guidelines to be exceeded by 50 percent. Also, the current 2.50 percent set-aside rate would have increased at a rate of 0.10 percent per year over 10 years up to 3.50 percent (except for the National Institutes of Health, which would have stayed at 2.50 percent).

Then, on March 19, 2009, the House and Senate reauthorized the SBIR program until July 31, 2009 (Public Law 110-10); it was again reauthorized through September 30, 2009, through a Senate continuing resolution (S. 1513). On September 23, 2009, a House bill (H. R. 3614) extended SBIR until October 31, 2009; a Senate bill (S. 1929) again extended the program until April 30, 2010. A Senate bill (S. 3253) extended the program to July 31; the House (H. R. 5849) extended the program to September 30, 2010; and S. 3839 and H. R. 366 extended the program to January 31 and then May 31, 2011, respectively.

Still to be decided at that time was whether the existing Phase I, Phase II, and Phase III processes should remain; whether the dollar size of Phase I and Phase II awards should be changed; and whether venture capitalists should be involved in the SBIR process. While this debate lingered in Congress, the Small Business Administration on March 30, 2010, amended the SBIR Policy Directive to allow the threshold amount to increase to $150,000 for Phase I awards and to $1,000,000 for Phase II awards, as was proposed in the Senate version of the reauthorization bill.

On May 31, 2011, the program was yet again temporarily extended through September 30, 2011, by S. 1082, The Small Business Additional Extension Act of 2011. H. R. 2608 extended the program until November 18, 2011; H. R.

Table 8.1 **Legislation Related to the SBIR Program**

Legislation	Public Law	Relevant Time Period
Small Business Innovation Development Act of 1982	P. L. 97-219	1982–1986
Department of Defense Appropriation Act of 1986	P. L. 99-443	1986–1992
Small Business Research and Development Enactment Act of 1992	P. L. 102-564	1992–2000
Small Business Reauthorization Act of 2000	P. L. 106-554	2000–2008
Temporary Extensions	—	2008–2012
National Defense Authorization Act of 2012	P.L. 112-81	2012–2017

2112 extended it again until December 16, 2011. On December 15, 2011, the program was reauthorized by Congress, and on December 31, 2011, President Obama signed the National Defense Authorization Act of 2012, Public Law 112-81. That Act codified the reauthorization of the SBIR program to September 30, 2017. Thus, after many multi-month extensions of the program because Congress failed to reauthorize it in 2008, the SBIR program was eventually reauthorized for six years. The major legislations leading to the December 31, 2011, authorization are summarized in Table 8.1.

The December 31, 2011, legislation reauthorizing the SBIR program introduced some controversial changes, including the provision that small firms that are majority owned by venture capital operating companies, hedge funds, or private equity firms are eligible to participate in the program.

Eleven agencies currently participate in the SBIR program: the Environmental Protection Agency (EPA); National Aeronautics and Space Administration (NASA); National Science Foundation (NSF); and the Departments of Agriculture (USDA), Commerce (DoC), Defense (DoD), Education (ED), Energy (DOE), Health and Human Services (HHS, particularly NIH), Transportation (DoT), and most recently the Department of Homeland Security (DHS).

The Economics of the SBIR Program

As we discussed in Chapter 4, firms underinvest in R&D because of market failures.[2] Of particular concern in this regard are failures due to the presence of risk and uncertainty. A natural approach to correcting such failures is to focus public sector entrepreneurial policies on reducing a firm's exposure to the risk and uncertainty associated with engaging in R&D and that gives rise to the problem.

Risk and uncertainty may arise in the R&D production process (i.e., technical risk/uncertainty) or in the process of participating in input or output markets (i.e., market risk/uncertainty). Technical risk and uncertainty are attributable to the physical R&D process and the fact that the outcomes of the R&D process are not certain. If that physical process is not certain but probabilistically predictable, then it is technical risk; if that physical process is not certain so that it is not possible to enumerate all possible outcomes and/or quantify the probabilities of all possible outcomes, then it is technical uncertainty. Likewise, market risk and uncertainty are attributable to the vicissitudes of participating in the marketplace. Such lack of certainty is typically the result of a lack of certainty about a combination of factors: demand for the firm's output, supply for the firm's inputs, ability to appropriate returns, market structure, and so on. If that market process is not certain but probabilistically predictable, then it is market risk; if that physical process is not certain so that it is not possible to enumerate all possible outcomes and/or quantify the probabilities of all possible outcomes, then it is market uncertainty.

Both risk and uncertainty will result in difficulties for the firm. In the case of risk, while insurance markets may, if they exist, allow the risk to be shifted to others, that shifting comes at a price that reduces the return the firm can expect to receive. And this reduction may result in the firm's expected return falling below its minimum rate of return, that is, its hurdle rate, required to go forward with the project. Even more problematic is the case of an incomplete market associated with a high level of risk. In that case, the risk is sufficiently high that there is no available insurance market. Of course, the firm can decide to bear the risk itself. However, in that case, particularly if the firm is risk averse, the effect can be much the same, with that risk lowering the expected return below the firm's hurdle rate and the firm thus choosing not to engage in the innovation project.

In the case of uncertainty, the result is even more stark. Because of the lack of knowledge about possible outcomes and their probabilities, no insurance market will exist. In other words, there will be an incomplete markets problem. As a result, the firm will be forced to bear the effect of the uncertainty, and depending on the firm's subjective estimation of the likelihood of success, this uncertainty may also result in the firm deciding not to engage in the innovation process.[3]

The SBIR program represents a way of correcting for these market failures by helping the firm over its hurdle rate so that it invests in a particular R&D project that it would not have invested in without the award. To understand

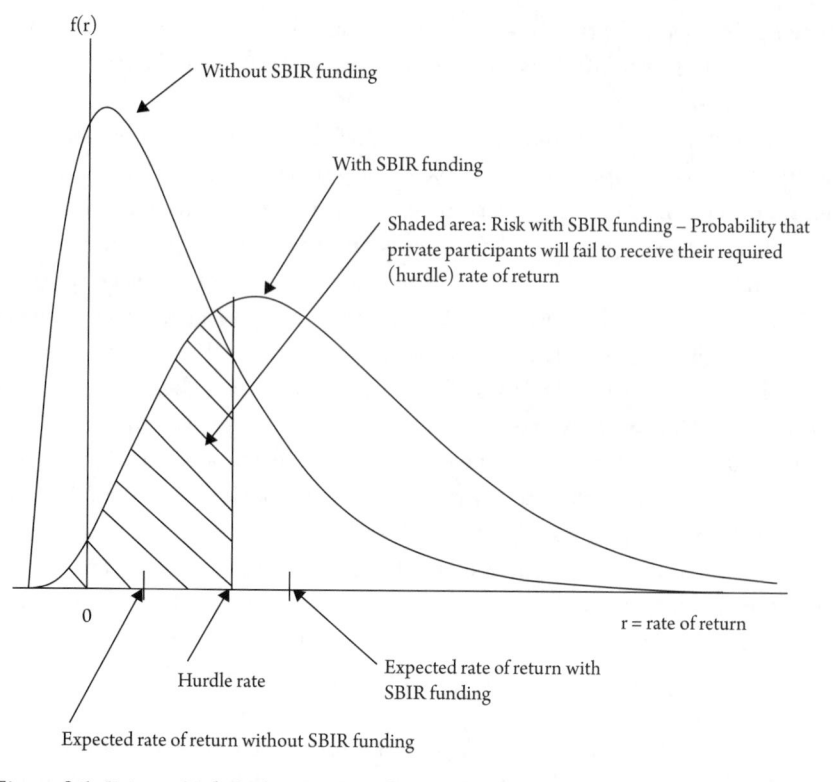

Figure 8.1 Private Risk Reduction Resulting from SBIR Funding.
Source: Based on Link and Scott 2010 and 2012.

why this is so, consider Figure 8.1. The figure is framed in terms of risk, hence the use of probability distributions and probabilities. However, the logic would be the same in the case of uncertainty; all that is needed is a relabeling of the vertical axis as the subjective likelihood of success and relabeling the probability distributions as subjective likelihood functions.

Figure 8.1 thus represents the reduction of technical and market risk due to receipt of an SBIR award. Consider first the firm's circumstances in the absence of SBIR funding. In that case, the probability distribution of the rate of return for the private firm's project will be the distribution on the left. As drawn, the private hurdle rate is to the right of the expected rate of return without SBIR funding, meaning that the private firm will not undertake this research because the firm will not receive its required rate of return.[4] The risk of the project for the firm is the probability of failure, that is, the probability that the rate of return is less than the firm's hurdle rate. Thus, the risk of the project is equal to the area under the "without SBIR" distribution that is to the left of the private hurdle rate.[5]

Now consider the effect of an SBIR award. For a given SBIR award, the expected rate of return associated with any particular outcome of the underlying stochastic process will be higher. Hence, an SBIR award will result in a rightward shift in the distribution of the rate of return for the private firm. Because of that rightward shift, the firm's expected private rate of return, as well as the variance in the rate of return, will increase.[6] And with that increase, the downside risk associated with undertaking R&D, illustrated in Figure 8.1 by the shaded region, will fall, hence making it more likely that the firm's expected private rate of return will exceed the firm's hurdle rate.[7,8]

Note, however, that SBIR funding will not increase the probability that the research will be successful, assuming that it were undertaken absent SBIR funding. But it will reduce private risk by increasing the expected private rate of return, which will be based on a smaller private outlay.[9] Hence, SBIR funding leverages the private firm's investment by a greater expected return and a greater variance in the distribution. That in turn increases the overall level of R&D activity by program participants.

Finally, although we will conclude that SBIR funding reduces risk—as defined operationally in terms of reducing the probability of a rate of return below the private hurdle rate—our analysis is in no way wed to any particular measure of risk or model of capital asset pricing with associated systematic and non-systematic risk. Instead, our treatment encompasses any and all such models because the relevant risk, however private firms perceive it, is captured in the private hurdle rate, and the distributions of returns are otherwise represented by their expected values. In describing the effect of SBIR funding on the distribution of private rates of return, we are describing an underlying reality that would be reflected in the private hurdle rate—as determined by some model—and in the expected value of the returns.

The Small Business Innovation Development Act as an Example of Public Sector Entrepreneurship

The relevant question to ask to determine if the Small Business Innovation Development Act, and the SBIR program in particular, meets our criterion for public sector entrepreneurship is whether the SBIR program is an innovative public policy that improves the social network for the affected parties operating in an uncertain economic environment, that is, whether it increases the number and quality of heterogeneous experiential ties for the affected party(s), thus resulting in those parties having an enhanced ability to identify and take advantage of heretofore unexploited opportunities.

Clearly, the SBIR program is innovative both in its focus on small business and in its structured approach to providing support and encouragement for R&D. Moreover, the effects of the SBIR program were at the time clearly uncertain. In addition, it is clear, as summarized in Table 8.2, that the SBIR program has resulted in improved social networks, even if the program—like the R&E tax credit—is not directly focused on enhancing such networks like the Bayh-Dole, Stevenson-Wydler, and Federal Technology Transfer Acts.

The SBIR program improves the social networks of affected firms in three ways. First, the program increases the number of small business entrepreneurial projects by expanding the research base of those firms. While this does not directly focus on enhancing an individual firm's social network, it increases the number of firms engaged in the R&D process. As a result, the degree to which social networks are exploited can be expected to increase in the aggregate. Second, the three-stage process of applications and grants implicitly provides the firm with guidance on how "to do" R&D by putting the firm in touch with others familiar with the R&D process, thus broadening the firm's social network. Finally, for some firms, experiential ties might be developed if the firm that receives an award partners with a university to conduct R&D, or if

Table 8.2 **Public Sector Entrepreneurship: The SBIR Program Portion of the Small Business Innovation Development Act of 1982**

Characteristics	Descriptor	Comment
Advancement of knowledge	High	The SBIR program expanded the R&D base—or in some instances, the program creates the R&D base—of small firms that receive an award, thus having the potential to advance the knowledge base of the firm and of society as new technologies diffuse through the economy.
Impact on technology and innovation	Long term	The R&D process is long, especially the basic research portion of R&D, thus any impact on technology and subsequently on innovation will be long term.
Targeted parties	Small firms	All small firms are eligible to apply for an SBIR award, subject to application criteria.
Heterogeneity of experiential ties	Moderate	Experiential ties might be developed if the small firm that receives an award partners with a university to conduct the R&D, or if the funded firm enters into research relationships with other firms after the fact.

the funded firm enters into research relationships with other firms after the fact. To the extent this occurs, the access to universities or other firms creates, though with uncertainty, an increased access to perspectives that may not exist within the firm. And with that increased access to a different perspective come the creative synergies and dynamics that can result in new opportunities being recognized and ways to exploit such opportunities for commercial gain being discovered. Likewise, for those in the university or the other firms, the increased ability to engage in the transfer of knowledge with the small business opens them up, again with uncertainty, to the potential of alternative perspectives as well.

Together, these mechanisms mean that the SBIR program can be expected to result in a greater level of opportunity recognition and exploitation overall. For the firm, this means a greater chance at commercial success. But more than that, it means advances in the economy's overall knowledge base and, as new technologies diffuse through the economy, advances for society as well.

Impact and Effectiveness of the SBIR Program

The extant empirical evidence regarding the impact of the SBIR program suggests that it is in fact a successful one. Allen et al. (2012) conducted a traditional evaluation study of the program. Based on project data from the National Research Council (NRC) database on SBIR projects,[10] their analysis suggests that the ratio of social benefits associated with products and processes commercialized from SBIR-funded projects (e.g., increases in consumer and producer surplus) to program costs far exceeds unity.

Regarding the effectiveness of the program, SBIR participants were asked as part of the NRC survey: "In your opinion, in the absence of this SBIR award, would your firm have undertaken this project?" Among the almost 1,300 firm responses received, over 70 percent responded "probably not" or "definitely not" to that question. Interestingly, this high percentage was approximately the same across the various sponsoring agencies (DoD, NIH, NASA, DoE, and NSF), as reported by Link and Scott (2012) (see Table 8.3).

The success of the SBIR program has spawned the establishment of state-level programs. For example, as Hardin et al. (forthcoming 2015) carefully document, 14 states have initiated Phase I matching grant programs. It is too early to document the overall success of these programs, but a preliminary analysis by Hardin et al. suggests that the North Carolina program is generating positive spillovers to the state.[11]

Table 8.3 Responses to the Counterfactual Question: "In your opinion, in the absence of this SBIR award, would your firm have undertaken this project?"

Percentage and number of the 593 DoD projects (in the random sample) that answered:

Answer	Percentage	Number
Definitely yes	3.04	18
Probably yes	9.61	57
Uncertain	17.71	105
Probably not	32.72	194
Definitely not	36.93	219
Sum	100.00	593

Percentage and number of the 338 NIH projects (in the random sample) that answered:

Answer	Percentage	Number
Definitely yes	5.03	17
Probably yes	7.69	26
Uncertain	13.61	46
Probably not	27.81	94
Definitely not	45.86	155
Sum	100.00	338

Percentage and number of the 111 NASA projects (in the random sample) that answered:

Answer	Percentage	Number
Definitely yes	2.70	3
Probably yes	15.32	17
Uncertain	14.41	16
Probably not	35.14	39
Definitely not	32.43	36
Sum	100.00	111

(continued)

Table 8.3 **(Continued)**

Percentage and number of the 114 DOE projects
(in the random sample) that answered:

Answer	Percentage	Number
Definitely yes	0.00	0
Probably yes	3.51	4
Uncertain	13.16	15
Probably not	44.74	51
Definitely not	38.60	44
Sum	100.00	114

Percentage and number of the 121 NSF projects
(in the random sample) that answered:

Answer	Percentage	Number
Definitely yes	3.31	4
Probably yes	12.40	15
Uncertain	18.18	22
Probably not	42.15	51
Definitely not	23.97	29
Sum	100.00	121

Note: Not all firms that were asked to complete the NRC project survey responded to this question.

Source: Based directly on Link and Scott 2012.

Summary

The Small Business Innovation Development Act—particularly the SBIR program, which stimulates technological innovation among small business and increases associated private sector commercialization—represents another example of public sector entrepreneurship, albeit, like the R&E tax credit, one less directly focused on social networks than are the Bayh-Dole, Stevenson-Wydler, and Federal Technology Transfer Acts. Initially passed in 1982, but modified and renewed several times since, the SBIR program has been instrumental in inducing large numbers of small businesses to take on R&D projects that they otherwise would not have, and of generating social benefits that far exceed the costs of the program.

9

The National Cooperative Research Act of 1984

The highest form of efficiency is the spontaneous cooperation
of a free people.
—Woodrow Wilson

Legislative Background

One important outcome of the White House Domestic Policy Review of Industrial Innovation, conducted in 1978 and 1979 at the beginning of the second productivity slowdown, was President Jimmy Carter's charge to the Department of Justice to clarify its position on research collaboration among firms. President Carter believed—and this was a bold and forward-looking view—that antitrust laws should not prevent cooperative activity aimed at innovation as long as competition is not harmed. The Department of Justice responded to President Carter's call through the publication of its *Antitrust Guide Concerning Research Joint Ventures* (U.S. Department of Justice 1980). In the *Guide* are important premises upon which the legislation leading to the passage of the National Cooperative Research Act of 1984 was implicitly based:

> Research itself presents a broad spectrum of activity, from pure basic research into fundamental principles, on the one hand, to development research focusing on promotional differentiation of a product or marketing issue on the other extreme. In general, basic research is undertaken with less predictability of outcome, and thus more risk, than developmental research. Moreover, *the outcomes of basic research are less likely to be appropriable and thus more likely to be widely diffused in the economy, with the possibility of there being the basis of future advance and competitive opportunity for all* [emphasis added].
>
> The intensity of antitrust concerns about joint research will vary along the research spectrum: less intense about pure basic research,

undertaken without ancillary restraints on use of the results, to more intense at the developmental end of the research spectrum, particularly if ancillary restraints are involved. A pure research joint venture with ancillary restraints has never been challenged by the Antitrust Division. ... Nevertheless ... concern has been expressed that valuable joint research efforts, particular in basic research, might be deterred by fear, possibly unwarranted, of exposure to antitrust attack.

In general, the closer the joint activity is to the basic end of the research spectrum——i.e., the further removed it is from substantial market effects and developmental issues—the more likely it is to be acceptable under the antitrust laws. (U.S. Department of Justice 1980, pp. 1–3)

Several bills were introduced in the 98th Congress that focused explicitly on R&D joint ventures. The Thurmond bill would have excused all R&D joint ventures from existing provisions of antitrust law related to any treble damages that could have been assessed in a successful lawsuit. The Glenn and Rodino bills went even further; they argued for a relaxation of all antitrust regulations that were serving as barriers to the formation of R&D joint ventures. The Mathias bill was still even more comprehensive; it included a proposal for sharing patent and royalty rights among cooperative ventures.

As noted in the House report about the proposed High Technology Research and Development Joint Ventures Act of 1983,

a number of indicators strongly suggest that the position of world technology leadership once firmly held by the United States is declining. The United States, only a decade ago, with only five percent of the world's population was generating about 75 percent of the world's technology. Now, the U.S. share has declined to about 50 percent and in another ten years, without fundamental changes in our Nation's technological policy ... the past trend would suggest that it may be down to only 30 percent. [In hearings,] many distinguished scientific and industry panels had recommended the need for some relaxation of current antitrust laws to encourage the formation of R&D joint ventures. ... The encouragement and fostering of joint research and development ventures are needed responses to the problem of declining U.S. productivity and international competitiveness. According to the testimony received during the Committee hearings, this legislation will provide for a significant increase in the efficiency associated with firms doing similar research and development and will also provide for more effective use of scarce technically trained personnel in the United States. (H. R. 3393)

In another House report, the Joint Research and Development Act of 1984 (H. R. 5041), the *supposed* [emphasis added] benefits of joint research and development were for the first time clearly articulated:

> Joint research and development, as our foreign competitors have learned, can be procompetitive. It can reduce duplication, promote the efficient use of scarce technical personnel, and help to achieve desirable economies of scale. ... [W]e must ensure to our U.S. industries the same economic opportunities as our competitors, to engage in joint research and development, if we are to compete in the world market and retain jobs in this country.

We emphasize the word *supposed* above for two reasons. First, at the time the legislation was proposed there was no systematic information available about the economic benefits of joint R&D. Second, and this is the more important reason—the word *supposed* underscores the uncertainty, as opposed to risk, associated with the outcome of these proposed policies, that is, the uncertainty associated with the expectations of the public sector entrepreneurship that was to follow.

These early initiatives culminated on October 11, 1984, with the passage of the National Cooperative Research Act (NCRA) of 1984, Public Law 98-462. The preamble to the law states that this Act will "promote research and development, encourage innovation, stimulate trade, and make necessary and appropriate modifications in the operation of the antitrust laws." The Act defined a "joint research and development venture" as

> any group of activities, including attempting to make, making, or performing a contract, by two or more persons for the purpose of—
> (A) theoretical analysis, experimentation, or systematic study of phenomena or observable facts,
> (B) the development or testing of basic engineering techniques,
> (C) the extension of investigative findings or theory of a scientific or technical nature into practical application for experimental and demonstration purposes, including the experimental production and testing of models, prototypes, equipment, materials, and processes,
> (D) the collection, exchange, and analysis of research information, or
> (E) any combination of the purposes specified in subparagraphs (A), (B), (C), and (D), and may include the establishment and operation of facilities for the conducting of research, the conducting of such venture on a protected and proprietary basis, and the prosecuting of applications for patents and the granting of licenses for the results of such venture.

The NCRA of 1984 created a registration process under which joint research and development ventures or, more simply, research joint ventures (RJVs) can voluntarily disclose their research intentions to the Department of Justice; all disclosures are made public in the *Federal Register*.[1]

RJVs gain two significant benefits from filing with the Department of Justice under the NCRA. One, if the venture were subjected to criminal or civil antitrust action, the courts would evaluate the alleged anticompetitive behavior under a rule of reason rather than presumptively ruling that the behavior constituted a per se violation of the antitrust law. For RJVs that have filed, the Act states:

> In any action under the antitrust laws ... the conduct of any person in making or performing a contract to carry out a joint research and development venture shall not be deemed illegal per se; such conduct shall be judged on the basis of its reasonableness, taking into account all relevant factors affecting competition, including, but not limited to, effects on competition in properly defined, relevant research and development markets.

And two, if the venture were found to fail a rule-of-reason analysis it would be subject to actual damages rather than treble damages.

The National Cooperative Research and Production Act (NCRPA) of 1993, Public Law 103-42, extended the safe harbor to RJVs involved in production as well as research. As background, the Act states:

> (1) Technological innovation and its profitable commercialization are critical components of the ability of the United States to raise the living standards of Americans and to compete in world markets; (2) cooperative arrangements among nonaffiliated businesses in the private sector are often essential for successful technological innovation; and (3) the antitrust laws may have been mistakenly perceived to inhibit procompetitive cooperative innovation arrangements, and so clarification serves a useful purpose in helping to promote such arrangements.

The "clarification" was to include, as an amendment to the NCRA, a safe harbor for research and production joint ventures rather than only R&D joint ventures.

Finally, the NCRA was amended in 2004 under the Standards Development Organization Advancement Act (SDOAA) of 2004, Public Law 108-237:[2]

> To encourage the development and promulgation of voluntary consensus standards by providing relief under the antitrust laws to standards

development organizations with respect to conduct engaged in for the purpose of developing voluntary consensus standards, and for other purposes.

An Economic Model of Cooperative R&D

Cooperation in R&D has both benefits and costs. Following Hagedoorn et al. (2000), who drew from the theoretical literature on cooperation R&D and related RJVs, the benefits include:[3]

- The opportunity for participants to capture knowledge spillovers from other members
- Reduced research costs due to a reduction in duplicative research
- Faster commercialization since the fundamental research stage is shortened
- The opportunity to develop industry-wide competitive vision

The costs include:

- A lack of appropriability since research results are shared among the participants
- Managerial tension, in some cases, as participants learn to trust each other and to work together

We present here a model of the cooperative R&D process based closely on Bozeman et al. (1986).[4] Rather than relying on a game theoretic approach, we employ a neoclassical, equilibrium approach most famously developed by Samuelson (1954) that illustrates in a straightforward manner the implications of free-riding versus cooperation. The maintained assumptions of our model are that R&D includes an investment into the production of technical knowledge, and that technical knowledge has the characteristics of a public good (Arrow 1962).

These assumptions are motivated by the observation that technical knowledge is not fully appropriated by the firm conducting the R&D and thus, over time, diffuses throughout the industry and the economy. Technical knowledge can either diffuse as information per se or as information embodied in new vintages of capital. In our model, we are implicitly treating R&D as a homogeneous input into the production of knowledge, though the activities broadly grouped under that rubric are in fact quite heterogeneous.

Research may be defined as the primary search for technical or scientific advancement; development is the translation of such advancement into product or process innovations. In the 1950s, the NSF fostered a more detailed breakdown: basic research, applied research, and development.[5] In practice, of course, industrial R&D is even more heterogeneous than these category-of-use labels imply, and not all R&D categories of use yield the kind of knowledge that can be characterized as a public good. The output from activities near the basic end of the R&D spectrum is the closest to a public good, the least appropriable, and thus the most likely to be widely diffused (Arrow 1962, Nelson 1959).

Suppose, then, that an industry is composed of two firms, A and B, each of whom is engaged in R&D. Let each firm have an endowment of resources (this endowment can be thought of as the firm's total R&D budget) that is used as an input into the R&D process. Assume further that these resources are allocated between two activities: development (i.e., the production of applied knowledge, a private good) and research (i.e., the production of basic or technical knowledge, a public good). With access to these two forms of knowledge, each firm then engages in production and marketing, thus generating profits.

Using Figure 9.1 to illustrate our model, let the tradeoff between the production of the applied component and the basic component of R&D be an identical constant so that, given a particular endowment, each firm's production possibilities curve can be illustrated by a straight line with the same slope. Thus, assuming that firm A has a larger endowment than firm B, the production possibilities curve for firm A can be represented by some line aa', and the production possibilities curve for firm B can be represented by some line bb'.

Assume that each firm seeks to maximize its profits and that each firm has the same set of iso-profit curves, represented in Figure 9.1 by the curves W, X, Y, and Z. Hence, firm A, were it the only firm in the industry, would maximize

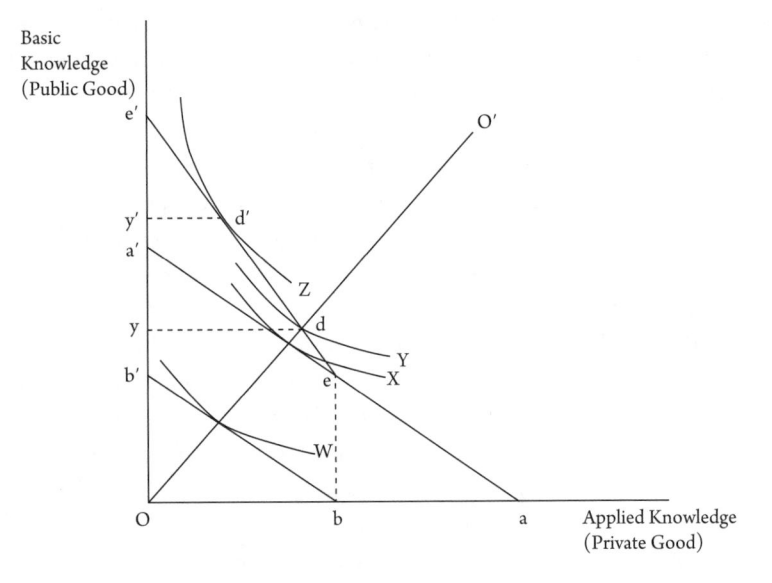

Figure 9.1 Two Firm Model of R&D Cooperation: The Collaborative Case

its profits where the iso-profit curve X is tangent to firm A's production possibilities curve aa'. Likewise, firm B, again assuming it were the only firm in the industry, would maximize its profits where the iso-profit curve W is tangent to firm B's production possibilities curve bb'. Hence, if we allow for the possibility of alternative endowment sizes, the collection of optimal investment choices across all possible endowments is defined by the ray OO'.

Of course there are two firms in the industry, not one, and because the purpose of this model is to determine the effect of R&D cooperation on the level of basic R&D produced, the question becomes how much basic knowledge will be produced if the firms make their R&D investment decisions independently versus collaboratively.

Consider first the case in which the firms act independently. In that case, each firm initially is essentially unaware that the other exists. Each will act as if it was the only firm in the industry (the case discussed above) and will therefore choose to produce that combination of applied and basic knowledge where its production possibilities curve (aa' or bb') intersects the locus of optimal investment choices OO'. However, after making this choice, each firm will find that it has access to more basic knowledge than it anticipated because of the unanticipated production of basic knowledge by the other firm. In essence, then, each firm will be free-riding on the basic knowledge production of the other. As a result, the R&D investment mix for each firm will lie above the optimal investment choice curve OO'. Thus each firm will, from a profit perspective, have too much basic knowledge relative to applied knowledge. Because this means profits are not as high as they might be, each firm will therefore reduce its production of basic knowledge and increase its production of applied knowledge to end up with a mix of basic and applied knowledge that does maximize profits. By definition, this mix must be located on the optimal investment choice curve OO'.

To determine where on OO' each firm will eventually be located, consider the characteristics of that optimal mix of basic and applied knowledge. Because basic knowledge is a public good, both firms will have access to the same amount of it. But given that basic knowledge must be the same for both firms, and given that both firms must be on the same optimal investment choice curve OO', it must be that both firms will also produce the same amount of applied knowledge.[6]

Given this condition, then, we can determine where on the OO' curve each firm will be located by considering all the possible combinations of basic and applied knowledge to which each firm will have access, assuming that both firms produce the same amount of applied knowledge. If both firms were to produce no applied knowledge (that is, each invests its entire endowment in the production of basic knowledge), the total amount of basic knowledge produced would be Oe' (= Oa' + Ob'), and each firm would have access to a mix of basic and applied knowledge denoted by point e'. Likewise, if both firms were to produce Ob of the numeraire good, each firm would have a mix of basic and applied knowledge denoted by point e. Given the constant tradeoff between the production of basic and applied knowledge, the set of basic-knowledge/applied-knowledge combinations that each firm would have access to will be defined by the line ee'.[7] And hence the ideal mix of basic and applied knowledge for each firm will be point d, where the line ee' intersects the line OO'.

It might be objected that point d cannot be the ideal mix of basic and applied knowledge because the iso-profit curve Y that goes through point d is not tangent to the line ee', that is, point d is not efficient. It is true that point d is not efficient. However, it will be the ideal for each firm because each firm is acting independently and therefore takes no account of the extra technical knowledge that the other firm produces and that (mysteriously) appears.[8] Hence the trade-off between the production of basic and applied knowledge will be reflected by the slope of each firm's original production possibilities curve (aa' or bb'), and the slope of the iso-profit curve Y at point d is exactly equal to that trade-off. We can conclude that in an industry of independently acting firms in which basic knowledge is a public good, each firm will free-ride off of all other firms and end up with identical amounts of both basic and applied knowledge even though their initial endowments are different.[9]

How, then, will R&D investment choices change if the firms collaborate in their R&D investment decisions? In such a case, each firm will be aware of the other firm's production of basic knowledge and so will realize that the effective production possibilities curve for each firm is in fact ee'. Each firm will therefore choose that mix of basic and applied knowledge production that is located on ee' and that maximizes profits. The ideal mix must be at some point d' where an iso-profit curve, labeled Z in Figure 9.1, is tangent to the cooperative production possibilities curve ee'. In other words, point d', which is the result of collaboration in the production of R&D, is efficient. At point d', both firms will have higher profits than at point d and the level of technical knowledge collaboratively produced by both firms will be higher (Oy' instead of Oy). Thus, both firms are better off if they engage in a RJV instead of free-riding off of each other's production of basic knowledge.

From a broader perspective, then, the total level of basic knowledge increases as a result of collaboration facilitated by, for example, the NCRA and its amendments, and this creates an incentive for firms engaged in R&D to collaborate on activities that are focused on the basic research end of the R&D spectrum. This conclusion follows for at least two reasons. First, because basic research has more public goods characteristics than applied research or development activities, an individual firm would not be able to fully appropriate the resulting basic knowledge if that research were conducted privately. In other words, the individual firm would recognize that other firms would free-ride on its research efforts and would therefore take appropriate (i.e., profit-maximizing) actions. Second, there are financial economies of scale associated with R&D in general, and it is not unreasonable to conjecture that, owing to the greater uncertainty of basic research, these financial economies will be even greater for R&D activities focused on basic research. As a result of these economies of scale and self-financing constraints that firms face for R&D, firms may be willing to share in those basic research costs. In our model above, the only cost sharing comes about through a sharing of the basic research production process so that each firm can reduce its endowment of basic research yet gain access to an increased amount of basic knowledge. Were we to incorporate economies of scale into our model, the conclusion that collaboration results in an increase in the total amount of basic knowledge and an increase in the profits of the individual firms would hold *a fortiori*. To the extent that cooperation takes place through R&D joint ventures as opposed to, say, consortia arrangements, the resulting social benefits may show up as increased productivity growth, given that basic research makes a primary contribution (Mansfield 1980, Link 1981).

In addition to the incentives established for R&D joint ventures in the NCRA and its amendments, how else might cooperative research arrangements be achieved? When public goods exist, beneficiaries do have an incentive to free-ride. One obvious solution is to make free-ridership (or non-cooperation) costly. A role for the public sector could be to make appropriate tax adjustments such that firms would have an incentive to launch cooperative research ventures.

Such a policy is worth considering when the firm sizes are sufficiently different. In terms of our model, firm size is determined by the size of the firm's endowment. But as Figure 9.2 reveals, when the firms are sufficiently

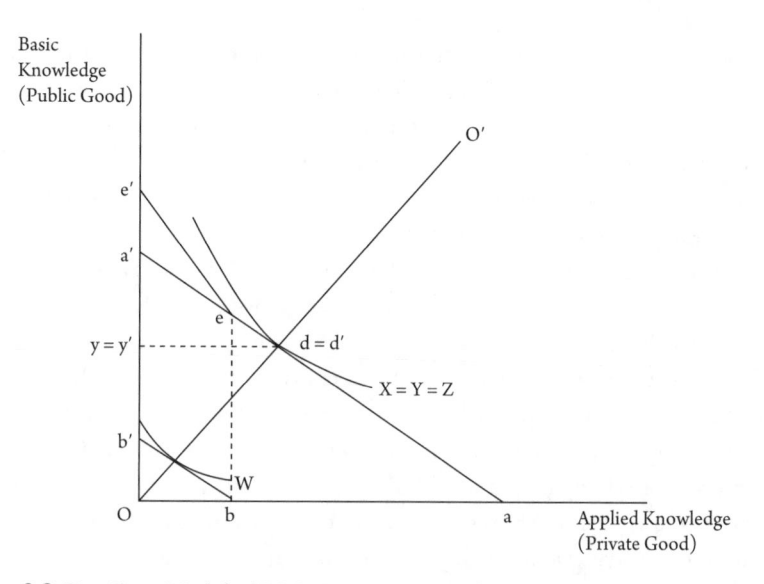

Figure 9.2 Two Firm Model of R&D Cooperation with Disparate Firm Sizes

disparate in size—that is, when Ob is smaller than the projection of point d onto the horizontal axis—the smaller firm may free-ride. Thus, in this case the non-collaborative and collaborative outcomes will be the same: the smaller firm will produce nothing but applied knowledge and will free-ride off the larger firm's production of basic knowledge. Although the larger firm may not like this outcome, it is nonetheless in its interest to produce where its individual production possibilities curve aa' intersects the ray OO'.

Thus, small firms in an industry with different-sized firms may have an incentive to free-ride, and the smaller the small firms, the greater the likelihood of this occurring. As a result, in an oligopolistic market with different-sized firms, R&D joint ventures may only emerge among the relatively larger firms. This implies that a tax incentive afforded to the relatively small firms should be disproportionately greater than that for the relatively larger firms in order to induce the optimal amount of R&D.

Examples of Research Collaborations

Semiconductor Research Corporation

One of the first formal research collaborations in the United States was the Semiconductor Research Corporation (SRC). Like many of the research collaborations that followed, the SRC was formed to meet industry-wide technological needs.

In 1961, the first integrated circuits (ICs) became commercially available, and by 1964, two million ICs had already been sold.[10] The application of ICs was economically and militarily important. Early support of IC development came from the U.S. Air Force, and ICs were used in the Minuteman missile in 1962.

Japanese companies gained 42 percent of the U.S. market for 16 kilobit DRAMs (memory devices) and converted Japan's IC trade balance with the United States from a negative $122 million in 1979 to a positive $40 million in 1980. The U.S. IC industry thus became painfully aware that its dominance was being seriously challenged and its strength in the semiconductor market was being compromised from a military point of view.

> In 1981, the concern with the U.S. position in the integrated circuit industry extended beyond the industry itself to those concerned with the economy and national defense. The economists were, as usual, somewhat vague but were beginning to view semiconductors as a key to successful competition. This view was and is still less focused than that of the Defense Department which had a clear opinion. It recognized integrated circuits as a key differentiating technology, an

important enabler of a military strategy based on having a technology edge. (Burger 1990, p. 19)

The press release for the creation of the SRC read as follows:

Palo Alto, CA, December 16, 1981—A major program to stimulate joint research in advanced semiconductor technology by industry and U.S. universities was announced today by the Semiconductor Industry Association (SIA).[11]

"The Semiconductor Research Cooperative (SRC) has been established by the SIA to encourage increased efforts by manufacturers and universities in long-term semiconductor research, and to add to the supply and quality of degreed professional people," said Robert N. Noyce, SIA chairman and Intel Corporation vice chairman.

"As semiconductor technology becomes more complex with VLSI (very large-scale integration), and more dependent on sophisticated processes, designs, technologies, packing and testing, there is a clear need to channel more funds to research," Noyce said. "We hope that shared-research programs will encourage a broader spectrum of participation and increased research activity."

"Despite its growth, the semiconductor industry still is in its early stages. New developments are coming at a rapid rate. Leadership in semiconductor research will determine market performance in the future. Although semiconductor industry research has been increasing, for a number of reasons total U.S. research in real dollars has been decreasing in the last few years. Cooperative research such as the SRC should help reverse this trend," continued Noyce.

Noyce cited such generic science-related fields as electron beam and x-ray technology, new semiconductor processes, materials science and computer-aided design techniques as areas which might qualify as joint research projects.

The SRC is composed of U.S.-based semiconductor manufacturers and both merchant and user firms. Foreign manufacturers are eligible for participation provided that their home nation permits similar access. Its members who participate in the research cooperative will provide funding, equipment and technical staff to universities and research centers to pursue research projects of importance to SRC members.

Erich Bloch, IBM vice president, technical personnel development, has been named chairman of the interim board of directors of the SRC. Bloch said the SRC will concentrate on research projects of from three to 10 years in length that would be difficult for a single manufacturer or university to attempt. Bloch noted that many SIA members had pledged support for the goals of SRC, including merchant semiconductor manufacturers and companies that manufacture and use internally large numbers of semiconductor devices such as computer and instrument firms.

The SRC, which is now operating as a committee, will be established as a subsidiary of the SIA. Other members of the SRC interim board include Gordon Bell, vice president, engineering, Digital Equipment Corp.; Charles C. Harwood, president, Signetics Corp.; William Howard, vice president, Motorola/Semiconductor Products Sector: Gordon Moore, chairman, Intel Corp.; Robert Price, president, Control Data Corp.; W.J. Sanders, III, president, chairman, and CEO, Advanced Micro Devices, Inc.; and Charles Sporck, president, National Semiconductor Corp.

Membership in the SRC will be available to all qualified semiconductor manufacturers upon incorporation, which is expected early in the first quarter of 1982.[12] (Burger 1990, p. 23)

At the June 12, 1981, meeting of the SIA Board, it was stated that

the SRC [consists] of U.S. corporations whose business is closely tied to semiconductor technology with the principle purpose being cooperation in the support, definition, and guidance of university-conducted basic research. Other expected benefits that were identified included: obtaining a clearer understanding of technology directions, opportunities, and problems will result from cooperative planning and provide increased relevancy to the university program, creating efforts above the critical thresholds required in certain research areas as a result of the increased resources, focusing national attention on industry's dedication to technological progress and thus attracting student and faculty talent to address industry needs, conserving resources by reducing unintended redundancy. (Burger 1990, p. 24)

Policymakers soon noticed the virtues of cooperative research both because such organizational structures had worked well in Japan and because the organizational success of the SRC demonstrated that cooperation among competitive firms at the fundamental research level was feasible.

SEMATECH

The SIA and the SRC began to explore the possibility of joint industry/government cooperation because the U.S. semiconductor industry continued to be in a precarious economic position.[13] During 1986, Japan overtook the United

States for the first time in terms of its share of the world semiconductor market. Japan had about 45 percent of the world market, and its share was increasing; the United States had about 42 percent, and its share was decreasing.

In January 1987, President Ronald Reagan recommended $50 million in matching federal funding for R&D related to semiconductor manufacturing, and this was to be part of the DoD's 1988 budget. But the president was not initially in favor of this action.

> The Reagan administration initially opposed an industry/govern-ment consortium, considering it inappropriate industrial policy. But Congress, concerned with what it considered to be the real prospect that the United States would cede the IC manufacturing industry to Japan, approved a bill creating SEMATECH, and President Reagan signed it into law. (van Atta and Slusarczuk 2012, pp. 54–55)

Soon thereafter, the SIA approved the formation of SEMATECH (SEmiconductor MAnufacturing TECHnology) and the construction of a world-class research facility in Austin, Texas. The founding members of SEMATECH were Advanced Micro Devices; AT&T; Digital Equipment Corporation; Harris Corporation; Hewlett-Packard Company; IBM Corporation; Intel Corporation; LSI Logic Corporation; Micron Technology, Inc.; Motorola, Inc.; National Semiconductor Corporation; Rockwell International Corporation; and Texas Instruments, Inc.

SEMATECH filed its joint venture with the Department of Justice on May 19, 1988. Noted in the filing was the following cryptic statement of the venture's objective:

> SEMATECH's area of planned activity is research and development related to advanced semiconductor manufacturing techniques that can be used by SEMATEC's [sic] members in their own manufacturing processes.[14]

In September 1987, Congress authorized $100 million in matching funding for SEMATECH. The consortium and its members have a mission to create a competitive advantage by working together to achieve leadership in the manu-facturing of semiconductors.

Other Examples

There are many other examples of early RJVs. Lee and Lee, for example, provide an excellent overview of the General Motors and Toyota joint venture in 1982:

> In January of 1979, 850,000 unsold Japanese cars had accumulated in the United States. When an oil shortage arose in 1979, gasoline prices

skyrocketed and the demand for smaller, more fuel-efficient cars followed. ... General Motors had several motives for entering into a joint venture with Toyota. First, G.M. wanted an additional subcompact vehicle at a competitive price. At that time, G.M.'s major entry in the subcompact field was the Chevette, an outdated car for which G.M. was losing $400 on every car sold. ... Toyota, on the other hand, was being pressured both by its own government and the U.S. government to invest in the United States. Believing that a manufacturing presence in the U.S. would eventually have to be established, Toyota felt that a joint venture with a leading U.S. company was a good start. ... With certain caveats, the joint venture between G.M. and Toyota has been a success. It has provided G.M. with a high quality car and has increased productivity at the Fremont plant. It has given G.M. first-hand insights into Toyota's technology and efficient management practices. On Toyota's side, Toyota has gained a manufacturing foothold in the U.S. at half the cost of its Japanese competitors who established their own plants. G.M. has also introduced Toyota to the American suppliers who were most likely to meet the strict quality and cost standards of Toyota. (Lee and Lee 1991, p. 348–349)

Trends and Patterns from *Federal Register* Filings of Research Joint Ventures

In 1994, in response to the perceived growth in RJVs based on reports from the Department of Justice about *Federal Register* filings, the NSF established the COoperative REsearch (CORE) database to begin to understand the fundamental characteristics of RJVs. The CORE database defines the RJV to be the unit of observation.[15]

Figure 9.3 shows the number of *Federal Register* filings per year in response to the NCRA of 1984 and its amendments. Clearly, the number of *Federal Register* filings increased through 1995, and the decline since then has been pronounced. Brod and Link (2001) show empirically that the trend in RJV filings is related to the business cycle. As the economy—as measured by an index of industrial production—weakens, firms tend to rely more on RJVs as a mechanism for conducting research.

Figure 9.4 shows the percentage of the filings per year that have a university as a research partner. Clearly, the pattern in the figure is not systematic. Baldwin and Link (1998) demonstrate that larger RJVs, measured in terms of membership size, are more likely to include a university as a research partner. This is also evident from the descriptive statistics in Table 9.1. We expand upon the entrepreneurial role of universities as research partners below.

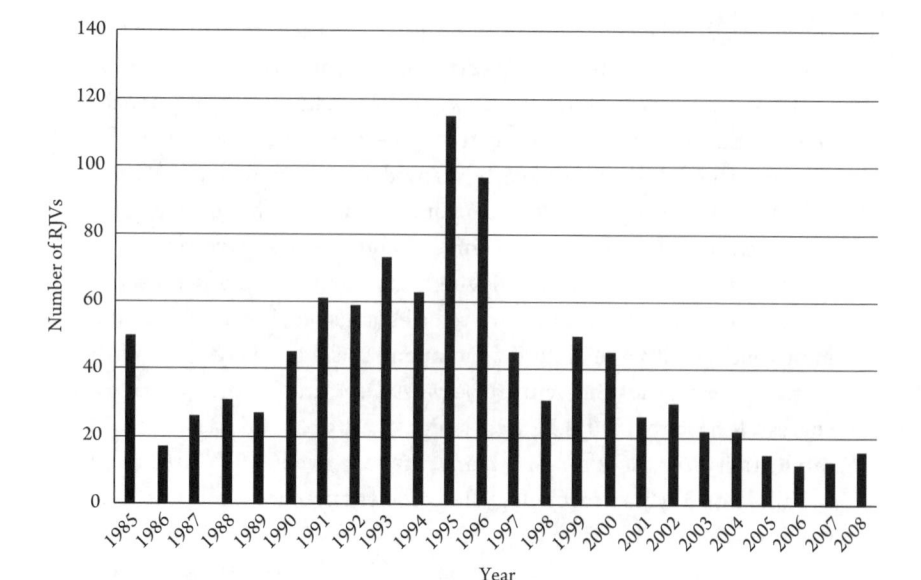

Figure 9.3 Trend in the Number of *Federal Register* Filings of New RJVS, by Year 1985–2008

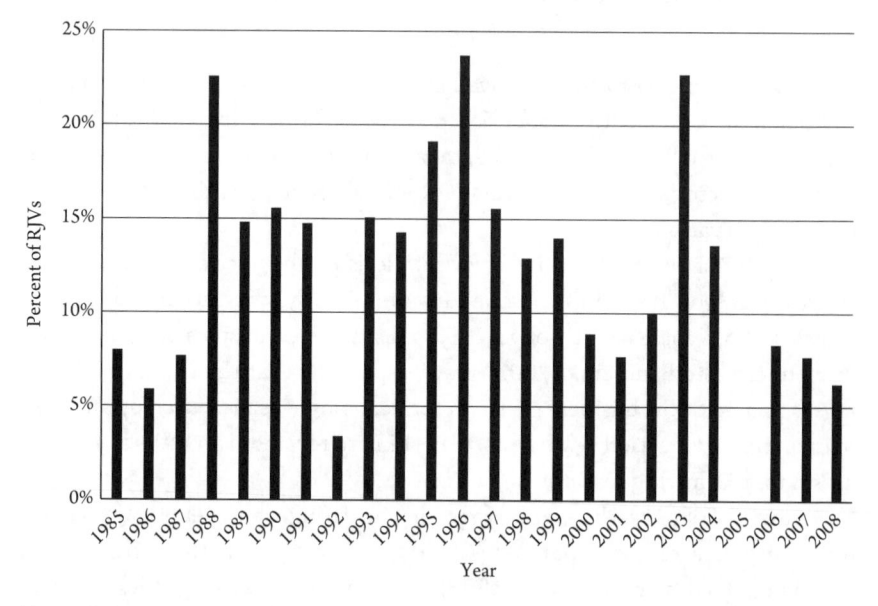

Figure 9.4 Percentage of *Federal Register* Filings of New RJVs with a University as a Research Partner, by Year 1985–2008

Table 9.1 **Membership Size of RJVs With and Without a University as a Research Partner, 1985–2008**

	RJVs With University (n = 139)	RJVs Without University (n = 852)
Mean membership size	33.3	9.7
Median membership size	9.0	4.0

The National Cooperative Research Act and Its Amendments as an Example of Public Sector Entrepreneurship

The relevant question to ask to determine if the NCRA, together with its amendments, meets our criterion for being an example of public sector entrepreneurship is whether the legislation is innovative public policy that improves the social network for the affected parties operating in an uncertain economic environment, that is, whether it increases the number and quality of heterogeneous experiential ties for the affected parties thus enhancing their ability to identify and use previously unexploited opportunities.

Clearly, the NCRA was an innovative public policy whose effects at the time were uncertain. Moreover, as summarized in Table 9.2, the NCRA does create a significant improvement in social networks.

More specifically, social networks consist of experiential ties arise from the firm's initial alliances—which could be with other firms, with universities, with government agencies, or with all of the above—and subsequent research collaborations. By redefining property rights (in particular, the scope and application of antitrust laws), the NCRA and its amendments reduced a major impediment to the formation of social networks by facilitating the formation of RJVs. As Figure 9.3 shows, the number of RJVs initially increased. Like the Bayh-Dole, Stevenson-Wydler, and Federal Technology Transfer Acts, the NCRA and its amendments represent an innovative policy that acted directly to stimulate the formation and exploitation of social networks. Whether the RJV is with another firm, a university, or a government agency, the general effect is the same: the ability to engage with others with different perspectives that enhances creativity. And with that synergy ultimately comes the creation and sharing of experiential as well as technical knowledge, which over time leads to increased innovation, productivity, and economic growth.

Table 9.2 **Public Sector Entrepreneurship: The National Cooperative Research Act and Its Amendments**

Characteristics	Descriptor	Comment
Advancement of knowledge	High	The NCRA and it amendments advanced knowledge through collaborative R&D, thus having the potential to advance the knowledge base of the collaborative organizations and of society as new technologies diffuse through the economy.
Impact on technology and innovation	Long term	The R&D process is long, especially the basic research portion, thus any impact on technology and subsequently on innovation will be long term.
Targeted parties	All research firms and other research organizations	All firms are eligible to file their RJV with the Department of Justice.
Heterogeneity of experiential ties	Significant	Experiential ties that enhance all collaborating research partner through knowledge sharing and cooperation in R&D.

Impact and Effectiveness of the National Cooperative Research Act and Its Amendments: The Special Role of Universities

As the trends and patterns from *Federal Register* filings discussed above show, it is not uncommon for RJVs to have a university as a research partner. Universities put faculty and students (particularly those in graduate school) with a variety of interests, knowledge, and experiences in touch with their research partners, thus increasing the number and quality of the heterogeneous experiential ties for both research partners and university students. This improvement in the social network for all parties in the face of the uncertain economic environment results in those universities and their partners having an enhanced ability to identify and utilize heretofore unexploited opportunities. To be sure, not all universities are public. But most are, and all focus on the general creation and promulgation of knowledge, a role that is fundamentally public (small "p") in nature. And thus university programs that seek to partner with firms in the private sector (itself an activity with an uncertain outcome) are special examples of public sector entrepreneurship.

As Hall et al. (2000, 2003) noted, the academic literature has identified two broad industry motivations for engaging in an industry-university research relationship. The first is access to complementary research activity and results. Academic research augments the capacity of businesses to solve complex problems. The second industry motivation is access to key university personnel. University motivations for partnering with industry seem to be financially based. Administration-based financial pressures for faculty to engage in applied commercial research with industry have long been growing.[16] However, there are drawbacks to university involvement with industry R&D, such as the diversion of faculty time and effort from teaching, the conflict between industrial trade secrecy and traditional academic openness, and the distorting effect of industry funding on the university budget allocation process (in particular, the tension induced when the distribution of resources is vastly unequal across departments and schools).

Regarding effectiveness of cooperation in R&D, Link and Rees (1990) estimated the rates of return to investments in R&D using a production function model (Link 1987, Link and Siegel 2003). Using data specific to New York State, Link and Rees found that the return to R&D among firms that partnered with a university was more than 2.5 times greater than the return to R&D among firms that did not have such a partnership. More specifically, the return to R&D among firms engaged in cooperative research with a university was 34.5 percent compared to a 13.2 percent return to R&D among those not cooperating with a university.

According to Schumpeter (1934), innovation can be described in several ways. Schumpeter spelled out a number of new combinations of resources and structures, including the creation of a new good or new quality of good, the creation of a new method of production, the opening of a new market, the capture of a new source of supply, and the new organization of industry. Over time the forces of these new combinations dissipate as new becomes part of old. This is the dynamic character of innovation, but as such it does not change the essence of the entrepreneurial function. "Everyone is an entrepreneur only when he actually 'carries out new combinations'" (Schumpeter 1934, p. 78), and he loses that character when his actions become old, or revert to the status quo.

Schumpeter also defined innovation by means of the production function. The production function "describes the way in which quantity of product varies if quantities of factors vary. If instead of quantities of factors, we vary the form of the function, we have an innovation" (1939, p. 62).

Schumpeter recognized that the knowledge supporting the innovation need not be new, although the combination of resources must. It may be that existing knowledge is used that has not been used before. He wrote:

> There has never been any time when the store of scientific knowledge has yielded all it could in the way of industrial improvement, and, on the other hand, it is not the knowledge that matters, but the successful solution of the task *sui generis* of putting an untried method into practice—there may be, and often is, no scientific novelty involved at all, and even if it be involved, this does not make any difference to the nature of the process. (1928, p. 378)

Successful innovation therefore requires an act of will, not intellect, he argued; successful innovation depends on leadership, not intelligence.

When firms initiate a research partnership with a university, or when a university initiates a research partnership with a firm, each is acting entrepreneurially as it systematically and purposely attempts to identify (i.e., to explore) and capture a new source of supply—knowledge. Each then uses (i.e., exploits) this new source systematically and purposely to create, among other things, a new method of production, be it a good or service or intellectual output. That new method of production can lead to a new market or industry organization.[17]

Here we build on our model of entrepreneurship and experiential ties to broaden the scope of interpretation about universities as research partners.[18] As noted above, university joint venture programs connect the variety of interests, knowledge, and experiences of its faculty and students with private sector firms, thereby increasing the number and quality of the heterogeneous experiential ties for both firms and university and thus enhancing the ability of both to identify heretofore unexploited opportunities and make use of them. This example of public sector entrepreneurship has been examined from a variety of perspectives by a number of scholars. But as our overview of selected, yet representative, elements of the extant literature on universities as research partners shows below, most scholars who have approached this important topic have done so in what we call a structure-conduct-performance paradigm, defined below (and we emphasize that we are loosely borrowing that term from Mason [1939] and Bain [1949]). We argue, however, that the literature should be viewed more broadly, within the intellectual thought of entrepreneurial activity as related to the creation and use of knowledge, or to innovation. As such, this literature has public policy implications.

A Paradigmatic Overview of the Literature

Industry-university relationships have been strengthening in industrialized nations for decades. The Council on Competitiveness recently noted this trend in the United States:

> Participants in the U.S. R&D enterprise will have to continue experimenting with different types of partnerships to respond to the economic constraints, competitive pressures and technological demands that are forcing adjustments across the board. ... [and in response] industry is increasingly relying on partnerships with universities. (1996, pp. 3–4)

A number of studies support this trend. For example, Link (1996c) showed that university participation in formal RJVs has increased steadily since the mid-1980s; Cohen et al. (1997) documented that the number of industry-university R&D centers increased by more than 60 percent during the 1980s; and a recent survey of U.S. science faculty by Morgan (1998) revealed that many desire even more partnership relationships with industry. Mowery and Teece contend that such growth in strategic alliances in R&D is indicative of a "broad restructuring of the U.S. national R&D system" (1996, p. 111).

According to Hall et al. (2000, 2003), little is known about the types of roles that universities play in such research partnerships or about the economic consequences associated with those roles.[19] What research there is on the topic of universities as research partners falls broadly into examinations of either *industry motivations* or of *university motivations* for engaging in an industry-university research relationship.

As Hall et al. (2000, 2003) noted, the literature has identified two broad industry motivations for engaging in an industry-university research relationship. The first is access to complementary research activity and research results.[20] Rosenberg and Nelson emphasized: "What university research most often does today is to stimulate and enhance the power of R&D done in industry, as contrasted with providing a substitute for it" (1994, p. 340). Pavitt (1998), based on his review of this literature, was more specific in this regard. He concluded that academic research augments the capacity of businesses to solve complex problems. The second industry motivation is access to key university personnel.[21]

University motivations for partnering with industry seem to be financially based. Because of financial pressures, university adminstrations have pressured faculty to engage in applied commercial research with industry are growing.[22] Zeckhauser, to repeat, was subtle when he referred to the supposed importance of industry-supported research to universities as he describes how such relationships might develop: "Information gifts [to industry] may be a part of [a university's] commercial courtship ritual" (1996, p. 12,746).

Along those same lines, Cohen et al. argued that "university administrators appear to be interested chiefly in the revenue generated by relationships with industry" (1997, p. 177). [23] They are also of the opinion that faculty, who are fundamental to making such relationships work,

> desire support, *per se*, because it contributes to their personal incomes [and] eminence ... primarily through foundation research that provides the building blocks for other research and therefore tends to be widely cited. (1997, p. 178)

However, several drawbacks to university involvement with industry have been identified, such as the diversion of faculty time and effort from teaching, the conflict between industrial trade secrecy and traditional academic openness, and the distorting effect of industry funding on the university budget allocation process (in particular, the tension induced when the distribution of resources is vastly unequal across departments and schools).

Table 9.3 summarizes selected, yet representative, recent empirical research related to universities as research partners. Defining "conduct" as partnering with a university and "structure" as those firm, university, or environmental characteristics that bring about partnering, then the structure → conduct literature can be summarized as follows.

To generalize, observing universities partnering with firms—conduct—is more likely in the following independent situations—structure:

- The firm is engaged in exploratory internal R&D (Bercovitz and Feldman 2007).
- The firm is mature and large (Stuart et al. 2007, Fontana et al. 2006).
- There is a lack of intellectual property issues between the firm and the university (Hall 2004, Hall et al. 2001).
- University faculty are male, with tenure, and are part of a university research center (Boardman and Corley 2008, Link et al. 2007).

Table 9.4 focuses on a conduct–performance paradigm where "performance" is defined in terms of the economic consequences of partnering with

Table 9.3 **Selected Literature on Universities as Research Partners: Structure → Conduct**

Author(s) (alphabetically)	Observations	Findings
Bercovitz and Feldman (2007)	Canadian R&D firms	Firms are more likely to establish university research relationships when internal R&D is exploratory.
Boardman and Corley (2008)	U.S. university faculty survey data	Likelihood of industry-university research collaboration is greater when university scientists are affiliated with an industry-liked university research center.
Fontana et al. (2006)	KNOW survey of EU firms	Larger firms are more likely to collaborate with public research organizations (i.e., universities).
Hall (2004)	Literature review	IP mechanisms affect the extent and scope of industry-university research relationships.
Hall et al. (2001)	Research projects funded by U.S. Advanced Technology Program (ATP)	When research results are expected to be less appropriable, IP issues prevent the industry-university partnership from taking place.
Link et al. (2007)	U.S. university faculty survey data	Male tenured faculty are more likely to engage in informal research relationships with industry.
Stuart et al. (2007)	U.S. biotechnology firms	Biotechnology firms upstream alliances with universities increase as firms mature.

Table 9.4 **Selected Literature on Universities as Research Partners: Conduct → Performance**

Author(s) (alphabetically)	Observations	Findings
Bozeman et al. (2008)	North Carolina nanotechnology firms	Lack of access to university faculty is a significant barrier to the growth of nanotechnology firms.
Cohen et al. (2002)	Carnegie Mellon survey of industry R&D firms	Key channels through which university research impacts industry R&D are indirect, including publications, conferences, and information relationships.
Hall et al. (2000, 2003)	Research projects funded by U.S. Advanced Technology Program (ATP)	Projects with universities as research partners are in areas involving "new" science and are thus experience more difficultly and delay; universities contribute to basic research awareness and thus help to ensure the project's successful completion.
Hertzfeld et al. (2006)	U.S. firms involved in RJVs	Industry learns through prior partnership experiences with universities how to overcome IP problems.
Kodama (2008)	Research firms in TAMA cluster region of Japan	No relationship between university research collaboration and firm size of firm profitability.
Link (2005)	U.S. RJVs	Upward trend in the percent of RJVs with U.S. university as a research member
Link and Rees (1990)	Interview data from U.S. research firms	Productivity of R&D increases when a university is involved, especially in smaller firms.
Link and Ruhm (2008)	U.S. Small Business Innovation Research (SBIR) program projects funded by NIH	Probability of commercialization greater in those projects with university involvement in the research.
Link and Scott (2005)	U.S., RJVs	Larger RJVs are more likely to include university as research partner.
Link and Scott (2007)	Literature review on university research parks	Growth of university research parks, which is one indicator of intent of universities to partner with industry in research, is a post-WWII and it continued into the 1980s and then has been sporadic but positive.

a university. The conduct → performance literature can be summarized as follows:

Given a university-industry research partnership, it is likely that the following attributes—performance—will be observed:

- There will be two-way flows of knowledge through publication and conferences, and through the formation of research joint ventures (Cohen et al. 2002, Link 2005, Link and Scott 2005, Hertzfeld et al. 2006).
- Firm R&D will be more successful (Link and Rees 1990, Hall et al. 2000, 2003, Kodama 2008).
- University research parks will grow, as will attendant industries (Link and Scott 2007, Bozeman et al. 2008).

A Model of University-with-Business Collaborative Research Partnerships[24]

To understand the complexities of the role universities play in facilitating knowledge transmission to private sector enterprises that results in economic growth, begin by considering the nature of private sector collaboration between firms. Firms engage in collaborative R&D because they believe it will enhance their ability to earn profits. Suppose then, that engaging in a collaborative research venture with other firms increases the revenues a firm can expect to earn in its output market because of the increased synergies that come from widening the firm's social network. But there are diminishing returns to that revenue stream, so that—as Figure 9.5 represents—the marginal revenue associated with increasing the number of research partners is a declining function of the total number of partners.

The decline in marginal revenue associated with increasing the number of research partners occurs for at least two reasons: An increase in the number of research partners increases the probability that among the firm's collaborators will be some who compete with firm. An increase in the number of research partners also reduces the time it takes before the knowledge generated by the shared research spreads to non-collaborating, competitor firms.

Firms that engage in collaborative research also incur R&D costs. Assume that those costs rise with the number of collaborative partners and do so at an accelerating rate (see again Figure 9.5) for two reasons. First, with an increase in the number of collaborators, there will be an increase in the scale of R&D; while there may be some initial economies of scale at first, diminishing returns are likely to be present in the end. Second, as the number of collaborators increases, so does the risk that some of those partners may attempt to manipulate the group's activities for their own private benefit or even free-ride. Such

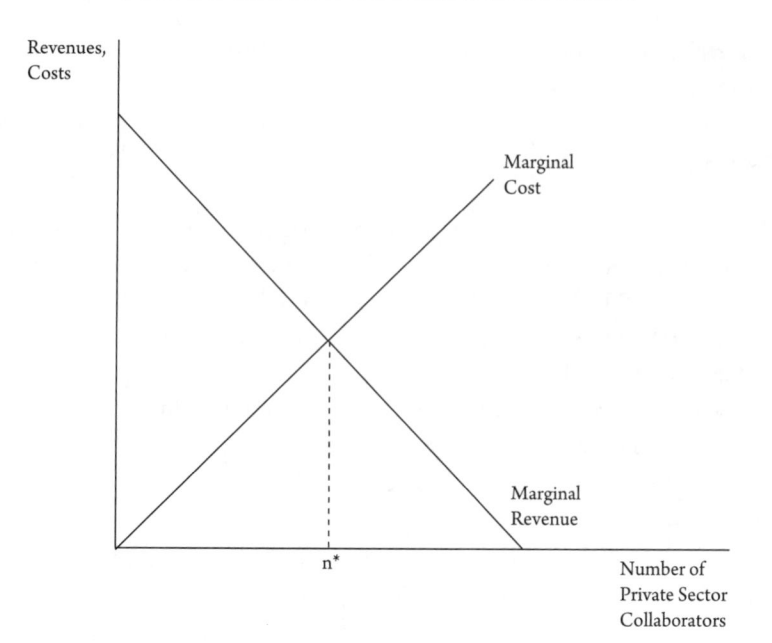

Figure 9.5 Private Sector Business Enterprise Collaboration

activities will drive up the firm's cost of maintaining and monitoring its partnerships in order to protect itself.

Given this pattern of revenues and costs associated with taking on an
increasing number of private sector research partners, the ideal number
of partners will be, as Figure 9.5 illustrates, such that for the last partner
added, the marginal revenue associated with that partner equals the marginal cost associated with that same partner. While this structure is a general one, it glosses over what may be important differences between firms.
The knowledge spillover theory of entrepreneurship (see, e.g., Acs et al. 2009,
Braunerhjelm et al. 2010) argues there is a significant difference between
incumbent firms and startup entrepreneurs, and this difference results in
incumbent firms generally preferring a higher number of R&D partners
than will startup entrepreneurs. Incumbent firms engage in R&D to generate marginal improvements in knowledge that they can exploit; startup
entrepreneurs are typically individuals who only recently exited from an
incumbent firm and whose focus is on the exploitation of the total knowledge set that they have taken with them. Moreover, startup entrepreneurs
may perceive the loss of appropriation associated with having R&D partners
as a greater threat than will incumbent firms, both because the entrepreneurs are more susceptible to such risks and because they are unlikely to
have the infrastructure and negotiating leverage to protect themselves from
such loss of appropriation. Thus, startup entrepreneurs will have lower,

steeper marginal revenue functions than incumbent firms. Hence, they will prefer a smaller number of private sector R&D partners.

For the private sector firm, whether an incumbent or a startup, the decision to collaborate with a university ultimately depends on whether profits are higher or lower as a result of that collaboration. Interestingly, whether a firm that chooses to collaborate with a university views the university as a substitute or a complement for private sector collaboration will depend on the relative change in the firm's R&D costs and revenues that come about as a result of that university collaboration.

To understand this, begin by considering how collaborating with a university affects a firm. In brief, a university can increase the firm's economies of technological scope, reduce the firm's ability to appropriate revenues, and change the firm's cost of engaging in R&D:

- *Increase a firm's economies of scope*: At a minimum, a university acts much like another private sector firm. Thus, it can contribute to the firm's social network and provide greater access to research capital and other knowledge spillovers—all of these effects can be expected to increase the firm's revenues. Interestingly, however, the startup entrepreneur will view a university as a somewhat safer partner to the extent the university is perceived as less of a competitive threat.

  But of course, a university is more than just another private sector firm; it also embodies unique human and technical capital that might not be available in the private sector or, if available, at a much higher cost.[25] And access to such unique capital increases the research synergies that come from being able to explore a broader spectrum of research issues and to view research questions from a different perspective. Particularly for startup entrepreneurs whose stock of human and especially physical capital is likely to be low compared to incumbent firms, this benefit is potentially of great significance.

  The university also may act as a facilitator for firm-to-firm synergies. By providing physical facilities for collaboration and joint research; by sponsoring seminars, conferences, workshops, and receptions; and by generally acting as matchmaker and objective chaperone, a university can increase the quality of interactions among those firms.[26] But while this may benefit startup entrepreneurs, particularly if it provides those enterprises with a safer environment in which to develop trust with other private sector enterprises, it nonetheless contains the risk of reducing the firm's ability to appropriate the benefits of its research. On the whole, then, the university affords firms with some ability to earn greater revenue both from their direct interaction with the university and from the increased value of their collaboration with other business enterprises.

- *Reduction in the firm's ability to appropriate revenue:* The presence of a university also reduces the ability of collaborating firms to appropriate for private gain the output of their shared research. The reward structure for researchers in a university is primarily based on publications (Link 1996c). As a result, there will be limited interest on the part of university researchers to collaborate with firms if they cannot use such collaboration to generate publications. Moreover, university missions typically include providing general benefits to society in the form of increased knowledge. They tend to focus more on basic research than do businesses, and the commercial value of basic research is by nature difficult to appropriate. For these reasons, collaborating with a university reduces the ability of firms to appropriate the increased revenue those firms get from collaborating with a university and with other firms.

- *Change in a firm's R&D costs:* Finally, collaboration with a university will affect a firm's R&D costs, although the direction of change is not clear. On the one hand, the presence of a university might be expected to reduce the firm's R&D costs because (1) a university may not require full compensation for the R&D production costs it incurs as a collaborator owing to the infrastructural nature of university research; (2) a university in its role as an "honest broker" can reduce various monitoring and transaction costs incurred by the firm with which it collaborates and thereby reduce the chance of the R&D process being manipulated to the benefit of a subset of collaborating firms; and (3) a university may cover the cost of interactions among firms by providing physical facilities for meetings and joint research, as well as sponsoring seminars, conferences, workshops, and receptions. On the other hand, a firm's R&D costs may rise as a result of collaborating with a university because of the additional costs associated with university requirements (including a possible fee) or with added lobbying and reporting costs associated with participating in a bureaucratic or political process.[27]

The net effect of all these factors is complex, but the bottom line can be summarized by Figure 9.6. In brief, the incentive to collaborate with a university depends on how R&D costs and revenues change:

- If collaboration with the university results in revenues rising and R&D costs falling, revenues rising proportionately more than R&D costs rise, or revenues falling proportionately less than R&D costs fall, then business enterprises that are relatively more active in private sector R&D collaborative activity (particularly incumbent firms) will choose to collaborate with the university. (Regions 2 and 4 in Figure 9.6.)

- If collaboration with the university results in higher revenues, then firms that are relatively less active in private sector R&D collaborative activity

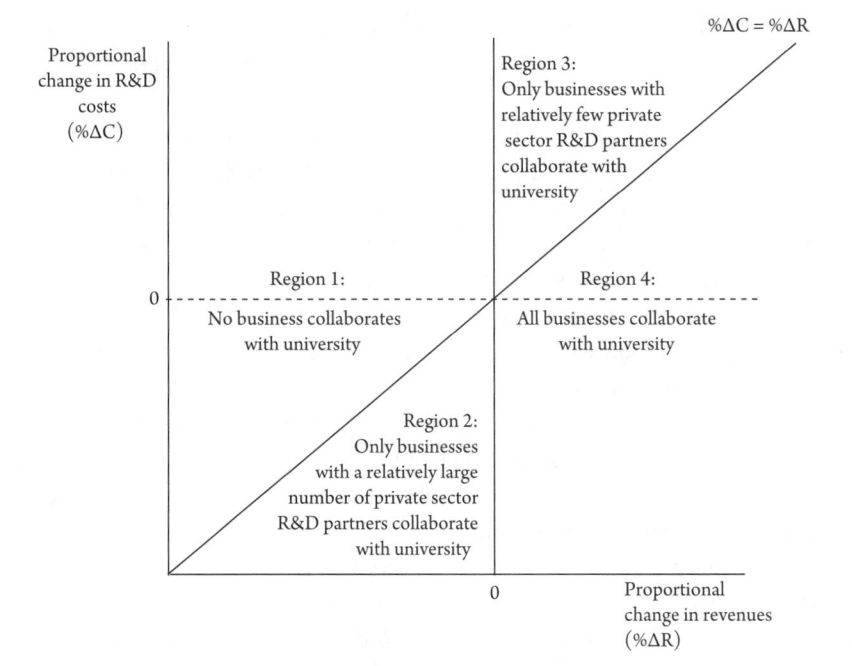

Figure 9.6 Which Business Enterprises Collaborate with the University?

(particularly startup entrepreneurs) will choose to collaborate with the university. (Regions 3 and 4 in Figure 9.6)

For those firms that choose to collaborate with the university, whether those firms treat the university as a substitute for or complement to private sector collaboration will depend on the relative change in R&D costs versus the relative change in revenues:

- If R&D costs rise proportionately more than revenues rise, university collaboration will be a substitute for private sector R&D collaboration and the number of private sector R&D collaborators will fall. (Region 3 in Figure 9.6)
- If revenues rise while R&D costs fall, or rise proportionately more than R&D costs rise, or fall proportionately less than R&D costs fall, university collaboration will be a complement for private sector R&D collaboration and the number of private sector R&D collaborators will rise. (Regions 2 and 4 in Figure 9.6)

Finally, the degree to which firms collaborate with the university and the effect of that collaboration with the university on the level of collaboration with other firms will depend not just on firm behavior but also on choices that the university makes regarding the collaborative R&D program it establishes.

And those choices depend in turn on what the university's objectives are, what the cost of delivering the collaborative research program are, and how that program is paid for.

Consider first the cost of delivering a university collaborative research program. As noted above, the university increases the profits of a collaborating firm by providing some combination of enhanced economies of technological scope and possible reduced costs sufficient to overcome any loss in appropriability and possible increased costs. If, as we would argue, the cost of providing enhanced economies of technological scope rises at an increasing rate, and the cost of providing reduced R&D costs to a collaborating firm rises in the same manner, then a university's costs will be characterized by a rising marginal cost as it attempts to provide firms with increased revenue and/or reduced R&D costs. These rising marginal costs are illustrated in Figure 9.7 by the iso-cost curves B_0, B_1, and B_2 such that total costs are zero along the iso-cost curve B_0 and increase as the university moves from B_0 to B_1 to B_2. Note also that the value of the university's program to participating firms increases with the cost of the program. Thus, point A represents the minimal possible program, that is, a program of no net cost to the university and for which there are no enhanced economies of scope and no change in the R&D cost function for firms that collaborate with the university.

What program a university chooses to operate will depend on the university's objectives and what funding arrangements exist. Based on our

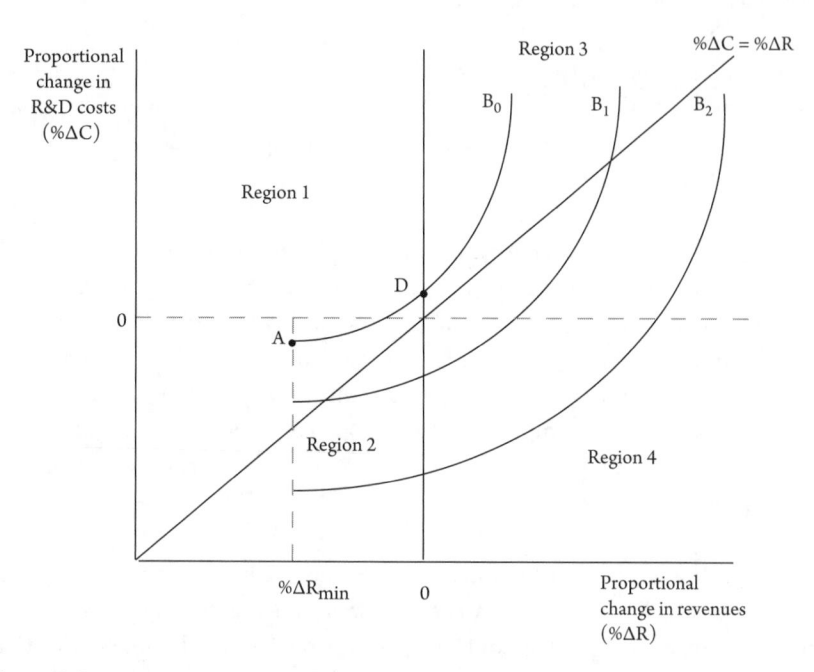

Figure 9.7 University Supply of Collaboration

experience that universities typically expand programs when presented with increased funding, university motivations are most likely viewed as those of a budget-maximizing bureaucrat.[28] A university would prefer if possible to run a program with a budget located on an iso-budget curve as high as possible. If the budget were high enough, this would also mean that the program could be located in region 4 and therefore could stimulate increased collaboration among private sector firms rather than act as a substitute for such activity.[29] But that means that the university must find a source of revenue to support such a program that does not come from the firms that participate in the program.[30]

Thus, if a university seeks to engage in collaborative R&D with both incumbent firms and startup entrepreneurs in a way that stimulates collaborative R&D among those private sector firms, it needs to structure its collaborative research program so that firm revenues increase and firm R&D costs rise by a smaller proportion, if they rise at all (and a fall would be better). Such a structure is consistent with both firm and university interests but is only likely to be feasible if a university is subsidized to cover the cost of such public-private collaborative research partnerships. In the absence of such support, a university will have to cover its costs through a fee charged to participating firms and that will result in the university more likely being seen as a substitute rather than a complement to private sector collaborative R&D and an unattractive partner for many firms.

Summary

The NCRA and its amendments, which relaxed the applicability and enforcement of antitrust laws, reduced a major impediment to the formation of social networks in the form of RJVs and stands as a significant and successful example of public sector entrepreneurship. Passed in 1984, the Act resulted in the creation of hundreds of RJVs. Like the Bayh-Dole, Stevenson-Wydler, and Federal Technology Transfer Acts, the NCRA and its amendments represent an innovative policy that directly stimulated the formation and exploitation of social networks and hence the ability of RJV participants to engage with others with different perspectives; enhance entrepreneurial creativity; and ultimately increase the level of innovation, productivity, and economic growth.

The Omnibus Trade and Competitiveness Act of 1988

I go for all sharing the privileges of the government who assist
in bearing its burdens.

—Abraham Lincoln

Legislative Background

The Advanced Technology Program (ATP) was established within the National
Institute of Standards and Technology (NIST) through the Omnibus Trade and
Competitiveness Act of 1988, Public Law 100-418:

> There is established in the [National Institute of Standards and
> Technology] an Advanced Technology Program (hereafter in this
> Act referred to as the Program) for the purpose of assisting United
> States businesses in creating and applying the generic technology
> and research results necessary to (1) commercialize significant new
> scientific discoveries and technologies rapidly; and (2) refine manu-
> facturing technologies. ... The Program focuses on improving the
> competitive position of the United States and its businesses, gives
> preference to discoveries and to technologies that have great eco-
> nomic potential, and avoids providing undue advantage to specific
> companies. [T]he Program ... may (1) aid United States joint research
> and development ventures ... including those involving collab-
> orative technology demonstration projects which develop and test
> prototype equipment and processes, through (A) provision of orga-
> nizational and technical advice; and (B) participation in such joint
> ventures.

This charge was reinforced through the American Technology Preeminence Act of 1991, Public Law 102-245:

The Congress finds that—(A) technological innovation and its profitable inclusion in commercial products are critical components of the ability of the United States to raise the living standards of Americans and to compete in world markets; (B) maintaining viable United States-based high technology industries is vital to both the national security and the economic well-being of the United States; (C) the Department of Commerce has reported that the United States is losing or losing badly, relative to Japan and Europe, in many important emerging technologies and risks losing much of the $350,000,000,000 United States market and $1,000,000,000,000 world market expected to develop by the year 2000 for products based on emerging technologies; (D) it is in the national interest for the Federal Government to encourage and, in selected cases, provide limited financial assistance to industry-led private sector efforts to increase research and development in economically critical areas of technology; (E) joint ventures are a particularly effective and appropriate way to pool resources to conduct research that no single company is likely to undertake but which will create new generic technologies that will benefit an entire industry and the welfare of the Nation; (F) it is vital that industry within the United States attain a leadership role and capability in development, design, and manufacturing in fields such as high-resolution information systems, advanced manufacturing, and advanced materials; and (G) the Advanced Technology Program ... is the appropriate vehicle for the United States Government to provide limited assistance to joint development within the United States of new high technology capabilities in fields such as high-resolution information systems, advanced manufacturing technology, and advanced materials, and can help encourage United States industry to work together on problems of mutual concern.

More specifically, at least in terms of how ATP interpreted these charges:

The goal of the ATP is to benefit the U.S. economy by cost-sharing research with industry to foster new, innovative technologies. The ATP invests in risky, challenging technologies that have the potential for a big pay-off for the nation's economy. These technologies create opportunities for new, world-class products, services and industrial processes, benefiting not just the ATP participants, but other companies and industries and ultimately consumers and taxpayers as well.

> By reducing the early-stage R&D risks for individual companies, the
> ATP enables industry to pursue promising technologies which other-
> wise would be ignored or developed too slowly to compete in rapidly
> changing world markets.[1]

Beginning with its first Congressional appropriation in fiscal year 1990, ATP
funded basic and applied research rather than product development. Through
its cost sharing with industry, ATP invested in risky technologies that were
thought to have the potential for spillover benefits to the economy but because
of the risks and knowledge externalities were unlikely to be funded exclusively
by the private sector.

Appropriations to ATP increased over time from $10 million in 1990 to a
peak level of $341 million in 1995. However, funding decreased in 1996 to
$221 million, and thereafter averaged about $200 million per year until 2004,
when it fell to just under $150 million.

Over the 17-year period from 1991 through 2007, ATP funded (via a series
of competitions) 824 individual research projects and RJVs chosen from 7,530
proposals that involved over 1,600 organizations. ATP awards totaled over
$2.4 billion, with industry contributing an equal amount through matching
research funds. ATP's annual awards are shown in Figure 10.1. No new awards
were made in 2005 and 2006.

The ATP was eliminated with President Bush's signing of the America
COMPETES Act of 2007, Public Law 110-69. America COMPETES was a complex piece of legislation that arose out of a concern that U.S. science and technology, especially in manufacturing, continued to be weak with little prospect

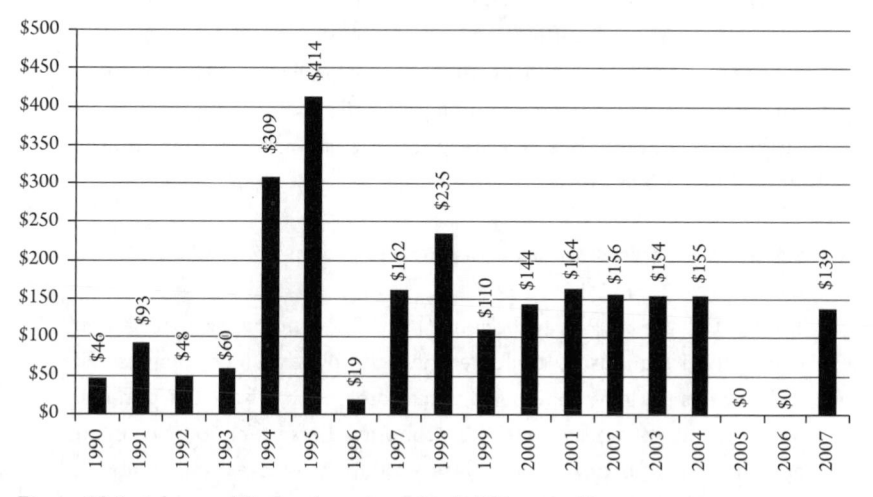

Figure 10.1 Advanced Technology Awards, $Millions by Year.

Source: www.atp.nist.gov/eao/atp_funding.htm

for improvement. Among the Act's many provisions was charging the Office of Science and Technology Policy (OSTP), which advises the president from within the Executive Office of the President, to (1) provide the federal government with a strategic plan every five years on how best to support advanced manufacturing R&D, and (2) support STEM educational and job-training programs.

The Lack of an Economic Argument for the Advanced Technology Program

The mission of ATP is, on several levels, like that of the Defense Advanced Research Projects Agency (DARPA), a bipartisan favored child of Congress. ATP funded "challenging technologies that have the potential for a big pay-off for the nation's economy."[2] Yet, as noted above, Congressional support for ATP waned after 1995, and ATP was eliminated in 2007.

Tassey effectively argued that "because ATP was focused on supporting economic growth rather than a specific social mission, such as national defense or health care, the program has been the focus of intense, interminable debate" (2007b, p. 285). Tassey's argument is reflective of a more general issue for any public sector entrepreneurial effort. In the private sector, entrepreneurial efforts are ultimately owned by the entrepreneur, who looks to satisfying a customer base in order to garner entrepreneurial returns. So too, public sector entrepreneurs (e.g., bureaucrats, legislators, or other elected officials) need a constituent base of individuals who benefit from their actions and as a result provide them with returns. In the case of the ATP, the benefits were sufficiently diffused that there was no well-defined constituency to provide the political returns to Congress, which played the role of the entrepreneur.

Connected to this lack of a well-defined constituency for ATP—and perhaps there was a reason why there was no well-defined constituency—was the inability of ATP or its entrepreneurial sponsors to articulate a strong rationale for the program's activities. The general argument for programs that seek to stimulate private sector innovative activity is that they correct a market failure. In ATP's case, this approach would have seemed to fit well, because the program's focus on the development of enabling technologies is at least implicitly based on correcting a market failure. Market failure, especially technological market failure, is based on the argument that the market (i.e., the private sector) underinvests (i.e., fails), from society's perspective, in R&D and the development of knowledge-based technologies with public good characteristics. The underinvestment results from the private sector's inability to capture or appropriate benefits associated with its investments.[3] However, ATP and its sponsors did not sufficiently demonstrate that the technology development it funded had public good characteristics that were beneficial to specific constituency groups.

In short, the ultimate demise of ATP might reasonably be attributed to the program being too diffused and lacking a focused rationale, and this led to the failure of a constituency group to provide the necessary political support to keep the program running.[4]

The Omnibus Trade and Competitiveness Act of 1988 as an Example of Public Sector Entrepreneurship

The relevant question to ask to determine if the Omnibus Trade and Competitiveness Act, and particularly the ATP, meet our criterion for being examples of public sector entrepreneurship is to ask whether they are innovative public policies that improve the social network for the affected parties operating in an uncertain economic environment. In other words, do they increase the number and quality of heterogeneous experiential ties for the affected parties, thus enhancing those parties' ability to identify and utilize previously unexploited opportunities.

Clearly, the Omnibus Trade and Competiveness Act embodied an innovative approach to stimulating the economy, and its effects at the time were just as clearly uncertain. And, Table 10.1 summarizes, it did create improvements in social networks.

Like all of the policy initiatives described in the previous chapters, the Omnibus Trade and Competiveness Act represents an innovative policy that acted directly to stimulate the formation and exploitation of social networks. ATP in particular was charged with fostering the creation and application of generic technology for commercial success through financial, organizational, and technical support for joint research and development ventures and collaborative technology demonstration projects. Such collaborative R&D is by definition about putting together and exploiting private sector entrepreneurial social networks. Whether the joint venture is with another firm, a university, or a government agency, the benefit of such network exploitation comes from the ability to engage with others with different perspectives to enhance creativity. And with that synergy ultimately comes the creation and sharing of knowledge that results over time in increased innovation, productivity, and economic growth. Thus the Omnibus Trade and Competitiveness Act, especially through its ATP, provided support for private sector firms to expand and exploit their social networks more fully.

Table 10.1 **Public Sector Entrepreneurship: The Omnibus Trade and Competitiveness Act**

Characteristics	Descriptor	Comment
Advancement of knowledge	High	Firm R&D and RJVs advance knowledge through own R&D and collaborative R&D, thus having the potential to advance the knowledge base of the collaborative organizations and of society as new technologies diffuse through the economy.
Impact on technology and innovation	Long term	The R&D process is long, whether performed individually or collectively. Thus, any impact on technology and subsequently on innovation will be long term.
Targeted parties	All research firms and parties that are involved in RJVs	It is not unusual for an ATP-funded research joint venture to have a university as a research partner.
Heterogeneity of experiential ties	Significant	Experiential ties that enhance all collaborating research partner through knowledge sharing and cooperation in the research joint venture.

Impact and Effectiveness of the Omnibus Trade and Competitiveness Act of 1988

Assessing the impact and effectiveness of the Omnibus Trade and Competiveness Act is a difficult task. On the one hand, there are numerous economic impact assessments and evaluations, conducted by ATP, that showed positive net social benefits associated with its investments. On the other hand, the program was terminated. So, is it reasonable to ask if the Act has social value, and from whose perspective?

To glean a fuller appreciation for the impact of the Omnibus Trade and Competitiveness Act, recall from above the language of the Act itself:

> The Congress finds that ... joint ventures are a particularly effective and appropriate way to pool resources to conduct research that

> no single company is likely to undertake but which will create new generic technologies that will benefit an entire industry and the welfare of the Nation.

and

> The Advanced Technology Program . . . is the appropriate vehicle for the United States Government to provide limited assistance to joint development within the United States of new high technology capabilities.

The fact that numerous economic impact assessments and evaluations conducted by ATP showed that the net social benefits associated with its funded research conducted through RJVs are positive underscores the economic importance of cooperative research as initiated through the NCRA of 1984. (One of these studies is summarized in the appendix to this chapter.) Moreover, the Act also implicitly reinforced the NCRA and its subsequent amendments. Recall from Chapter 9 that the NCRA established a path through which firms could engage in cooperative R&D. RJVs were indemnified from certain antitrust violations if they followed simple registration procedures.

The demise of ATP, then, should not be seen as an indictment of its effectiveness. In many respects, the Act can be seen in broader terms as an intermediate step in a long sequence of public sector entrepreneurial policies that began with the Bayh-Dole and Stevenson-Wydler Acts and continues to this day. The particular problems with ATP, as analyzed above, stem more from its lack of focus on a particular and supportive constituency rather than from the quality of the ATP and its other provisions. The demise of the Omnibus Trade and Competitiveness Act was not a rejection of the general purpose and approach embodied in that Act. Indeed, in many ways, the America COMPETES Act, which replaced the Omnibus Trade and Competitiveness Act in 2007, represents not so much a per se rejection of the ATP portion but rather an entrepreneurial reformulation to provide greater focus and engender the necessary constituent support.

Summary

The Omnibus Trade and Competiveness Act of 1988—like the Bayh-Dole Act, the Stevenson-Wydler Act, the Federal Technology Transfer Act, and the NCRA—represents an important and valuable example of public sector entrepreneurship. It directly stimulated the formation and exploitation of private sector social networks using financial, organizational, and technical support for joint research and development ventures. Empirical evidence shows that these efforts were of significant economic benefit not only to the firms involved but to the U.S. economy in general. The fact that Congress ceased to find ATP effective should not be seen as an indictment of the quality of the program or of the Act itself. Rather, its demise was the result of a more general reformulation of federal governmental policies focused on stimulating innovation and economic growth.

Appendix

Examples of Economic Impact and Assessment Studies Commissioned by the Advanced Technology Program

A complete listing of ATP's economic impact and assessment studies can be found through its website.[5] One example is abstracted below.

DNA Diagnostics

Since 1993, the ATP has provided technical and financial support for 42 Tools for DNA Diagnostics projects, [6] most of which were competitively funded under a focused program established to drive innovation in the biotechnology sector.

When the focused program was launched, the scientific and medical community's understanding of molecular biology and genomics was increasing rapidly, as was the accumulation of genetic data. But tools had yet to be developed to efficiently acquire that information or make efficient use of the enormous potential it held for medical science.

Advances in molecular diagnostics technologies would permit scientists to conduct more robust tests and analyses for disease susceptibility in humans, plants, and animals; forensics testing; disease identification; and drug effects studies; among other biotechnology applications.

ATP contracted with RTI International to perform an independent assessment of its Tools for DNA Diagnostics projects. This report reviews eight such projects, three of which are presented in two in-depth case studies.

The first case study is the Affymetrix-Molecular Dynamics MIND Development project—the largest in ATP's history—which led to advances in DNA microarray technologies and the development of the first high-throughput capillary array DNA sequencer. The case study chronicles how ATP-sponsored research accelerated the scientific community's adoption of microarray technologies, the Human Genome Project, and innovations in DNA sequencing.

The second case study reviews two projects at Molecular Tool (later known as Orchid Cellmark) and their contributions to rapid genetic analysis testing.

Qualitative analyses of the remaining five projects contribute to a broader understanding of the market, scientific, and public health impacts of the Tools for DNA Diagnostics project portfolio.

The analysis covers the period from the first project start date in 1993 through the last project end date in 2006. Resources and time were not available to investigate all 42 projects; therefore, the benefits quantified in the two case studies were compared with the costs of all 42 projects to provide a set of conservative, lower-bound performance measures. The following measures reflect realized benefits that accrued through 2005:

- Net present value of net public benefits, using a 7-percent discount rate (1995 base year and real 2005 dollars): $119.7 million.
- Internal rate of return: 28 percent.
- Benefit-to-cost ratio: 1.90.

PART III

THE PUBLIC SECTOR ENTREPRENEURSHIP PERSPECTIVE

Past is Prologue

The past is but the beginning of a beginning, and all that is and has been is but the twilight of the dawn.
—Herbert George Wells

New frontiers of the mind are before us, and if they are pioneered with the same vision, boldness, and drive with which we have waged this war we can create a fuller and more fruitful employment and a fuller and more fruitful life.
—President Franklin D. Roosevelt

Policy Background

On November 17, 1944, President Franklin D. Roosevelt wrote to Vannevar Bush, director of the Office of Scientific Research and Development. In this letter, President Roosevelt wrote:

The Office of Scientific Research and Development, of which you are the Director, represents a unique experiment of team-work and cooperation in coordinating scientific research and in applying existing scientific knowledge to the solution of the technical problems paramount in war. Its work has been conducted in the utmost secrecy and carried on without public recognition of any kind; but its tangible results can be found in the communiques coming in from the battlefronts all over the world. Someday the full story of its achievements can be told.

There is, however, no reason why the lessons to be found in this experiment cannot be profitably employed in times of peace. The information, the techniques, and the research experience developed by the Office of Scientific Research and Development and by the thousands of scientists in the universities and in private industry, should be used in the days of peace ahead for the improvement of the national health, the creation of new enterprises bringing new jobs, and the betterment of the national standard of living.

It is with that objective in mind that I would like to have your recommendations on the following four major points:

First: What can be done, consistent with military security, and with the prior approval of the military authorities, to make known to the world as soon as possible the contributions which have been made during our war effort to scientific knowledge? The diffusion of such knowledge should help us stimulate new enterprises, provide jobs for our returning servicemen and other workers, and make possible great strides for the improvement of the national well-being.

Second: With particular reference to the war of science against disease, what can be done now to organize a program for continuing in the future the work which has been done in medicine and related sciences? The fact that the annual deaths in this country from one or two diseases alone are far in excess of the total number of lives lost by us in battle during this war should make us conscious of the duty we owe future generations.

Third: What can the Government do now and in the future to aid research activities by public and private organizations? The proper roles of public and of private research, and their interrelation, should be carefully considered.

Fourth: Can an effective program be proposed for discovering and developing scientific talent in American youth so that the continuing future of scientific research in this country may be assured on a level comparable to what has been done during the war? New frontiers of the mind are before us, and if they are pioneered with the same vision, boldness, and drive with which we have waged this war we can create a fuller and more fruitful employment and a fuller and more fruitful life.

I hope that, after such consultation as you may deem advisable with your associates and others, you can let me have your considered judgment on these matters as soon as convenient—reporting on each when you are ready, rather than waiting for completion of your studies in all. (Bush 1945, pp. 3–4)

Bush submitted his report, *Science—the Endless Frontier*, on July 25, 1945, to President Harry S. Truman.[1] In his letter of transmittal, Bush wrote, perhaps in response to President Roosevelt's claim about pioneering the new frontiers of the mind:

The pioneer spirit is still vigorous within this nation. Science offers a largely unexplored hinterland for the pioneer who has the tools for his task. The rewards of such exploration both for the Nation and the individual are great. Scientific progress is one essential key to our security as a nation, to our better health, to more jobs, to a higher standard of living, and to our cultural progress. (Bush 1945, p. 2)

Science—the Endless Frontier: A Precursor to Public Sector Entrepreneurship

Bush's report was remarkably prescient in its view of technology and innovation policy. In laying out his vision and recommendations for future technology and innovation policy, he argued that the key to future development of new technologies and related innovations is focusing on developing and enhancing experiential ties among researchers. He stressed that it is through knowledge flows among participants in the process of research that innovation takes place. Although arrived at through a different path, this is essentially the same argument that we have made (with less elegance than Bush's original work) in our theory of entrepreneurship in Chapter 3:

> Of course, the cost of searching will also depend on other factors, most notably the effectiveness of the entrepreneur's social network which we assume is a positive function of the heterogeneity of the entrepreneur's social ties and past experiences. While the entrepreneur's social network may include individuals with various types of engineering and scientific knowledge, as well as knowledge of the entrepreneurial process, it will also include individuals with knowledge of seemingly disparate areas of knowledge. Indeed, it is precisely the variety, and even incongruity, of ideas that gives rise to the creativity that underlies the innovation process.

It was precisely this argument that was used as the touchstone for evaluating the degree to which the six technology and innovation policy initiatives that we set forth in the previous chapters of this book could be considered examples of public sector entrepreneurship.

Table 11.1 provides a closer examination of these six initiatives in light of the policy recommendations in Bush's *Science—the Endless Frontier* by directly comparing the policy objectives of each initiative with Bush's own analysis. Despite the nearly 40-year gap in time between *Endless Frontier* and these initiatives, the similarities remain striking.

Table 11.1 **A Comparison between Technology and Innovation Policies that Represent Public Sector Entrepreneurship and Science—the Endless Frontier**

Legislation	*Targeted Parties*	*Policy Objective*	*Policy Statement*	*Relationship to Science—the Endless Frontier*
University and Small Business Patent Procedure Act of 1980 (known as the Bayh-Dole Act of 1980)	Universities	Technology transfer	"It is the policy and objective of the Congress to use the patent system to promote the utilization of inventions arising from federally supported research or development"	"Progress . . . depends upon a flow of new scientific knowledge. New products, new industries, and more jobs require continuous additions to knowledge of the laws of nature, and the application of that knowledge to practical purposes." (p. 5)
				"How do we increase . . . scientific capital? [W]e must strengthen the centers of basic research which are principally the colleges, universities, and research institutes. These institutions provide the environment which is most conducive to the creation of new scientific knowledge and least under pressure for immediate, tangible results. With some notable exceptions, most research in industry and Government involves application of existing scientific knowledge to practical problems. It is only the colleges, universities, and a few research institutes that devote most of their research efforts to expanding the frontiers of knowledge." (p. 6)
				"It has been basic United States policy that Government should foster the opening of new frontiers. . . . [S]cientific progress is, and must be, of vital interest to Government. Without scientific progress the national health would deteriorate; without scientific progress we could not hope for improvement in our standard of living or for an increased number of jobs for our citizens; and without scientific progress we could not have maintained our liberties against tyranny." (p. 11)

"The publicly and privately supported colleges, universities, and research institutes are the centers of basic research. They are the well-springs of knowledge and understanding. As long as they are vigorous and healthy and their scientists are free to pursue the truth wherever it may lead, there will be a flow of new scientific knowledge to those who can apply it to practical problems in Government, in industry, or elsewhere." (p. 12)

"Basic research leads to new knowledge. It provides scientific capital. It creates the fund from which the practical applications of knowledge must be drawn. New products and new processes do not appear full-grown. They are founded on new principles and new conceptions, which in turn are painstakingly developed by research in the purest realms of science. Today, it is truer than ever that basic research is the pacemaker of technological progress. . . . Industry is generally inhibited by preconceived goals, by its own clearly defined standards, and by the constant pressure of commercial necessity. Satisfactory progress in basic science seldom occurs under conditions prevailing in the normal industrial laboratory. There are some notable exceptions, it is true, but even in such cases it is rarely possible to match the universities in respect to the freedom which is so important to scientific discovery." (p. 19)

(continued)

Table 11.1 (Continued)

Legislation	Targeted Parties	Policy Objective	Policy Statement	Relationship to *Science—the Endless Frontier*
Stevenson-Wydler Technology Innovation Act of 1980 (known as the Stevenson-Wydler Act of 1980)	National laboratories and other research organizations through CRADAs	Technology transfer	"It is the continuing responsibility of the Federal Government to ensure the full use of the results of the Nation's Federal investment in research and development. To this end the Federal Government shall strive where appropriate to transfer Federally owned or originated technology to State and local governments and to the private sector."	*Although Bush was referring to military materials and devices developed during World War II, the concept of technology transfer from national laboratories is applicable today as it was then:* "A broad dissemination of scientific information upon which further advances can readily be made furnishes a sounder foundation … than a policy of restriction which would impede our own progress." (p. 29)
Economic Recovery Tax Act of 1981 (relevant section known as the R&E tax credit of 1980)	Firms conducting R&D that can benefit from tax credits	Additional R&D investments	"Congress concluded that a substantial tax credit for incremental research and experimental expenditures was needed to overcome the reluctance of many ongoing companies to bear the significant costs of staffing and supplies, and certain equipment expenses such as computer charges, which must be incurred to initiate or expand research programs in a trade or business."	"The most important ways in which the Government can promote industrial research [is] to provide suitable incentives to industry to conduct research." (p. 7) "One of the most important factors affecting the amount of industrial research is the income-tax law. Government action in respect to this subject will affect the rate of technical progress in industry. Uncertainties as to the attitude of the Bureau of Internal Revenue regarding the deduction of research and development expenses are a deterrent to research expenditure. These uncertainties arise from lack of clarity of the tax law as to the proper treatment of such costs. The Internal Revenue Code should be amended to remove present uncertainties in regard to the deductibility of research and development expenditures as current charges against net income." (p. 21)

Act	Applicability	Activity	Purpose/objectives	Commentary
Small Business Innovation Development Act of 1982 (referenced herein in terms of the SBIR program)	Small firms (< 500 employees) with or without R&D technology	Conduct R&D and commercialize agency-relevant technology	"(1) to stimulate technological innovation; (2) to use small business to meet Federal research and development needs; (3) to foster and encourage participation by minority and disadvantaged persons in technological innovation; and (4) to increase private sector commercialization innovations derived from Federal research and development."	"The benefits of basic research do not reach all industries equally or at the same speed. Some small enterprises never receive any of the benefits. It has been suggested that the benefits might be better utilized if 'research clinics' for such enterprises were to be established. Businessmen would thus be able to make more use of research than they now do. This proposal is certainly worthy of further study." (p. 21)
National Cooperative Research Act of 1984 (referred to herein as NCRA)	Firms of all sizes and their research partners (which could be a university or government agency)	Reduced redundancy in and the cost of R&D, especially in basic research	"Joint research and development, as our foreign competitors have learned, can be procompetitive. It can reduce duplication, promote the efficient use of scarce technical personnel, and help to achieve desirable economies of scale. ... [W]e must ensure to our U.S. industries the same economic opportunities as our competitors, to engage in joint research and development, if we are to compete in the world market and retain jobs in this country."	Although Bush was referring to academic freedom at universities, he did realize the joint benefits of cooperative research. "Cooperative research performed for industry in universities can be expected to increase in the future to the advantage of both parties concerned." (p. 91)

(continued)

Table 11.1 (Continued)

Legislation	Targeted Parties	Policy Objective	Policy Statement	Relationship to *Science—the Endless Frontier*
Omnibus Trade and Competitiveness Act of 1988 (referenced herein in terms of ATP)	Firms all of sizes conducting technologies, often through joint research ventures, to promote economic growth	Subsidize R&D aimed at generic technologies, and its businesses, gives preference to discoveries and to technologies that have great economic potential, and avoids providing undue advantage to specific companies.	"The Program focuses on improving the competitive position of the United States focused R&D	"It has been basic United States policy that Government should foster the opening of new frontiers. . . . [S]cientific progress is, and must be, of vital interest to Government. Without scientific progress the national health would deteriorate; without scientific progress we could not hope for improvement in our standard of living or for an increased number of jobs for our citizens; and without scientific progress we could not have maintained our liberties against tyranny." (p. 11)

Table 11.1 is self-contained and self-explanatory. The table shows how directly the recommendations of Bush are linked to the themes of this book:

- The development and enhancement of experiential ties among researchers by stressing that knowledge flows among participants in the process of research.
- The importance of new knowledge as the mother's milk of innovation.
- The critical role that uncertainty plays in the firm's decision whether to engage in the process of innovation.
- The importance of continually (re)creating and maintaining a system of knowledge creation and innovation.
- The fundamental value of innovation to economic, social, and political prosperity.

Summary

The prescience of Vannevar Bush in his 1945 report *Science—the Endless Frontier* for laying out the essence of public sector entrepreneurship is remarkable both in its detail and its scope. While the degree to which his work is the foundation from which Congress began more than three decades later remains an open question,[2] it is clear that his work provides a clear vision from the perspective of a policy practitioner of what public sector entrepreneurship is, what its objectives are, and how it should function.

Concluding Observations

Others apart sat on a hill retired,
In thoughts more elevate, and reasoned high
Of Providence, foreknowledge, will, and fate,
Fixed fate, free will, foreknowledge absolute,
And found no end, in wand'ring mazes lost.
—John Milton

Public sector entrepreneurship refers to innovative public policy initiatives that generate greater economic prosperity by transforming a status-quo economic environment into one that is more conducive to economic units engaging in creative activities in the face of uncertainty. In today's economic environment, public sector entrepreneurship affects that transformation primarily by increasing the effectiveness of social networks, that is, by increasing the heterogeneity of experiential ties among economic units and the ability of those same economic units to exploit (i.e., learn from) such diversity. Through policy initiatives that are characterized by public sector entrepreneurship, there will be more development of new technology and hence more innovation throughout the economy.

The primary focus of our concept of public sector entrepreneurship has been on six U.S. technology and innovation policies that were initiated in response to the productivity slowdown of the 1970s:

- Bayh-Dole Act of 1980 (Chapter 5)
- Stevenson-Wydler Act of 1980 (Chapter 6)
- R&E Tax Credit of 1981 (Chapter 7)
- Small Business Innovation Development Act of 1982 (Chapter 8)
- National Cooperative Research Act of 1984 (Chapter 9)
- Omnibus Trade and Competitiveness Act of 1988 (Chapter 10)

We have argued that these policies are valid examples of public sector entrepreneurship, and accordingly we have related our theory of public sector entrepreneurship to related topics in the remaining chapters.

Because the application of our conceptualization of public sector entrepreneurship rests with these policies, we summarize our arguments in Table 12.1.

While these policies vary in terms of the degree to which they advance knowledge, whom they target, and the speed with which the policy is likely to generate effects, they all increase the heterogeneity of a firm's experiential ties, which are the essence of a firm's social network. There has, to be sure, been some variation in the experience with each policy, and indeed the child of one of the policies—the Omnibus Trade and Competitiveness Act's ATP—was eliminated in recent years. Just as the object of all these acts is the enhancement of the uncertain process of private sector entrepreneurial innovation, so too the acts themselves have taken place in an uncertain economic and political environment. With that uncertainty comes non-measurable chances of success or failure.

In Chapter 1 we suggested that it would be ideal to be able to present in parallel one technology or innovation policy that is entrepreneurial and another that is not, and to then demonstrate that the entrepreneurial policy is more efficient and effective than the non-entrepreneurial policy, thus making the case that it is important for the public sector to act entrepreneurially when it comes to the promulgation of policy. Information does not exist to allow for such a counterfactual experiment. However, we conclude this book with what we believe approaches a second-best illustration.

Recall that we motivated our discussion of the technology and innovation polices discussed in this book in terms of a public sector response to the productivity slowdown in the 1970s, all illustrated again here in Figure 12.1, which was originally presented as Figure 4.1.

We offer the following information to substantiate our view of public sector entrepreneurship, especially the contention that, through policy initiatives that are characterized by public sector entrepreneurship, there will be more development of new technology and hence more innovation throughout the economy. If this is true, one might expect that the productivity of private sector investments in R&D during the period of time prior to the initiation of the six policies in question would be less than after those policies had been in effect.

Building on the conclusions in Chapter 4's appendix, TFP can be expressed as a linear function of the proportion of GDP dedicated to R&D (see the appendix to this chapter for the derivation):

$$\text{TFP} = \lambda + \rho(\text{RD}/\text{Q}). \tag{12.1}$$

Table 12.1 **Summary of U.S. Technology and Innovation Policies that Represent Public Sector Entrepreneurship**

Public Sector Entrepreneurship Characteristics	Bayh–Dole Act of 1980	Stevenson-Wydler Act of 1980	R&E Tax Credit of 1981	Small Business Innovation Development Act of 1982	National Cooperative Research Act of 1984	Omnibus Trade and Competitiveness Act of 1988
Advancement of knowledge	Low	Low	High	High	High	High
Impact on technology and innovation	Immediate	Immediate	Long term	Long term	Long term	Long term
Targeted parties	Universities Private sector firms	Federal laboratories Private sector firms	All firms	Small firms	All research firms and other research organizations	All research firms and parties that are involved in RJVs
Heterogeneity of experiential ties	Significant	Significant	Marginal to moderate	Moderate	Significant	Significant

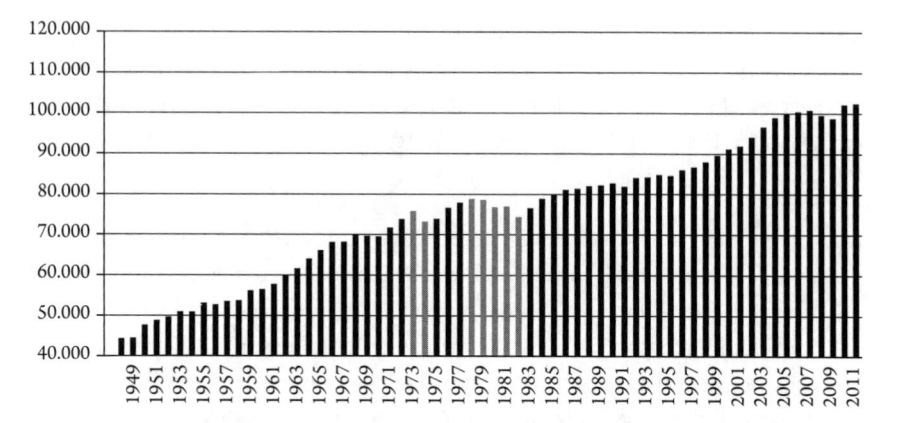

Figure 12.1 U.S. Total Factor Productivity Index, 1948–2011 (2005 = 100)

where RD is aggregate R&D expenditures, Q is GDP, λ is the nation's disembodied growth rate, and ρ is the rate of return on R&D investments. Using
equation (12.1), we estimated the average rate of return earned on R&D
investments economy wide using the TFP data that underlie Figure 12.1, and
data on national R&D (RD) and GDP (Q). The result was a rate of return to
R&D investments over the period 1953–2009, of 21.5 percent.[1] However, on
re-estimation, by dividing the sample into two periods—before 1980 and from
1980 onward—the rate of return to R&D was 7.1 percent in the pre-public
sector entrepreneurship period and 32.8 percent in the public sector entrepreneurship period.

Although measuring the efficacy of public policies in effect in an uncertain economic environment is fraught with difficulties that suggest caution
with any empirical assessment, these results provide a remarkable first judgment on the performance of public sector entrepreneurship over the past
three decades.[2]

It is commonly held by scientists that one should not believe any theory
without evidence. We strongly agree, but we would add to that rule the exhorta-
tion that one should not trust any evidence without theory. Theory does not
exist in a vacuum, and data do not speak for themselves. It is for that reason
that we have presented both theoretical models and empirical evidence to argue
that policy initiatives that are characterized by public sector entrepreneurship
result in greater development of new technology and hence more innovation
throughout the economy. While public sector entrepreneurship, like its private
sector counterpart, is often a messy process that has no guarantee of success, we
argue that there is sufficient evidence after more than three decades to justify
the value of public sector entrepreneurship.

The difficulty, of course, is that the world does not stand still. Particularly in
an increasingly competitive (and, we might add, entrepreneurial) global economy,

continued economic success depends on continuing to engage in innovative public sector entrepreneurship. And while there is, as we have reported, evidence of the success of such an approach, it nonetheless requires a certain national courage to push forward in the face of uncertainty. But, as Vannevar Bush noted:

> The pioneer spirit is still vigorous within this nation. Science offers a largely unexplored hinterland for the pioneer who has the tools for his task. The rewards of such exploration both for the Nation and the individual are great. Scientific progress is one essential key to our security as a nation, to our better health, to more jobs, to a higher standard of living, and to our cultural progress. (Bush 1945, p. 2)

Appendix

R&D and Total Factor Productivity Relationship

The academic model underlying the relationship between R&D and TFP follows from the model in the appendix in Chapter 4. Assume a generalizable production function applicable to the ith firm, i^{th} industry, i^{th} sector, or the ith country, written as:

$$Q_i = A_i F(K_i, L_i, T_i) \qquad (A12.1)$$

where Q represents output. In equation (A12.1), A is a neutral disembodied shift factor. The stock of physical capital and labor are K and L, respectively. The stock of technical capital available to the unit of observation, i, hereafter referred to as the firm for simplicity, is represented as T.

Let T represent the ith firm's internal or self-financed previous R&D expenditures, RD, as

$$T_i = \Sigma a_{i,j} RD_{i,t-j}, \qquad (A12.2)$$

where the ith firm's accumulation weights, a_j, reflect the influence of a j-period distributed lag and obsolescence rate of R&D.

Assuming a Cobb-Douglas production function, it follows from (A.1) that

$$Q = A_0 e^{\lambda t} K^\alpha L^\beta T^\gamma, \qquad (A12.3)$$

where A_0 is a constant; λ is a disembodied rate of growth parameter; and α, β, and γ are output elasticities. Constant returns to scale are assumed; that is, $(\alpha + \beta + \gamma = 1)$.

Assuming K, L, and T are all functions of time, t, and letting $X' = dX/dt$, the growth rate of output is

$$Q'/Q = \lambda + \alpha K'/K + \beta L'/L + \gamma T'/T. \tag{A12.4}$$

An index of residually measured TFP is defined as

$$\text{TFP} = Q'/Q - \alpha K'/K - \beta L'/L = \lambda + \gamma T'/T. \tag{A12.5}$$

The parameter, γ, in equation (A.3) is the output elasticity of technical capital:

$$\gamma = (\partial Q/\partial T)\cdot(T/Q). \tag{A12.6}$$

Substituting the right-hand side of equation (A12.6) into equation (A12.5), and rearranging terms, yields

$$\text{TFP} = \lambda + \rho(T'/Q), \tag{A12.7}$$

where $\rho = (\partial Q/\partial T)$. From equation (A12.7), ρ is the marginal product of technical capital and T' is the firm's net private investment in the stock of technical capital.

If it is assumed that the stock of R&D-based technical capital does not depreciate, or if it does depreciate. it does so very slowly, then T' is reasonably approximated by the flow of self-financed R&D expenditures in a given period of time, RD:[3]

$$\text{TFP} = \lambda + \rho(\text{RD}/Q). \tag{A12.8}$$

NOTES

Chapter 1

1. Throughout intellectual history as we know it, the entrepreneur has worn many faces and played many roles. Thus, a single and clear definition of an entrepreneur, or of entrepreneurship in the sense of what an entrepreneur does, is a matter of debate. As Hébert and Link (1988, 2006b, 2009) have carefully chronicled, an entrepreneur has been thought of over time as the person who assumes the risk associated with uncertainty, the person who supplies financial capital, an innovator, a decision-maker, an industrial leader, a manager or superintendent, an organizer and coordinator of economic resources, the owner of an enterprise, an employer of factors of production, a contractor, an arbitrageur, and an allocator of resources among alternative uses. We expand on these points of view in Chapter 2.
2. We are of course aware of the rich literature on social entrepreneurship.
3. We leave aside issues of corruption and illegal aggrandizement.
4. Sahni et al. (2013, p. 27) offer compelling examples of breakthrough innovations in the public sector: "Leaders inside the public sector are slowly learning to pursue ... major breakthroughs without the benefit of the profit motives that drive entrepreneurs elsewhere."
5. We think of science, the precursor to technology, as the search for new knowledge; the search is based on observed facts and truths; science begins with known starting conditions and searches for unknown end results. Science policy is, however, a topic for discussion at another time.
6. It should be noted that there are two early tantalizing references to public sector entrepreneurship, though without using that phrase. In the late 1700s, Bentham in his work on prison reform described what we call indirect public sector entrepreneurship, that is, innovative public policies that would change the private sector market environment and thereby induce increased, and in his mind desirable, private sector entrepreneurial behavior (Hébert and Link 2006b). And in the 1940s, Schumpeter (1934) essentially describes what Schnellenbach (2007) rightly calls a political entrepreneurial activity—a form of direct public sector entrepreneurial behavior, though Schumpeter does not name it as such. However, it does not appear that either comment led others to develop the notion of public sector entrepreneurship more fully.
7. Table 1.1 presents a chronological summary of the attempts to define public sector entrepreneurship. Because the concept of public sector entrepreneurship was developed for the most part independently in the academic disciplines of economics, management, and public administration/political science, we group entries by those disciplines. For each article or book listed, we provide a brief description of who the author considered the public sector entrepreneur to be, along with the author's view as to the motivation of that

person. We also note whether the author considered innovation or Knightian uncertainty to be essential elements in that characterization. Finally, we have also noted whether the author considered public sector entrepreneurship as acting directly (that is, through the expenditure and service mechanisms of government) and/or indirectly (that is, by altering the private sector market environment to induce desirable behaviors on the part of private sector entrepreneurs).

8. Schneider et al. (1995, p. 119) found that "about 15 percent of the communities we surveyed had a pro-growth entrepreneur and almost 60 percent of the entrepreneurs in our sample advocated pro-growth policies of some kind."

9. While not perfect, the analogy to the biological distinction between genotype and phenotype is instructive. An organism's genotype is defined by its genetic code and hence, by inference, by the fundamental rules of its behavior. An organism's phenotype is defined by its outward appearance and actual behaviors. Thus, private sector entrepreneurs and public sector entrepreneurs can be viewed as sharing the same genotype but having different phenotypes. See Lewontin (2011) for a fuller examination of the distinction between genotype and phenotype from a biological and philosophical perspective.

10. We do not exclude the possibility that some public sector entrepreneurial policies may be directed toward institutional reform of government itself to make it more economically productive.

11. Among that broad range of polices are those that result in a well-developed system of property rights and contract law, access to fully functioning capital markets, and effective systems of education. However, such policies, while instrumental to the functioning of private sector entrepreneurial activities, do not directly affect that which is essentially entrepreneurial. Moreover, in developed economies, such policies are generally already present. Hence in terms of future policies, the biggest gain will come from increasing the effectiveness of social networks.

12. See the appendix in this chapter.

13. Cells B and C might be unrealistic situations. It might not be possible for there to be uncertainty in the implementation of the status quo—cell B. One might be able to envision the application of a status-quo policy to a situation in which it had never previously been applied. Likewise, it might not be possible for there to be an absence of uncertainty in the implementation of an innovative policy. By the fact that the policy action is innovative, there must be some degree of uncertainty, along with perhaps measurable risk, in terms of its outcomes.

14. Whereas *Government as Entrepreneurship* focused heuristically on technology-oriented public sector agencies and programs, this book focuses on technology and innovation polices from the perspective of a theory of public sector entrepreneurship.

15. See www.whitehouse.gov/economy/business/startup-america.

16. That is, the long-run Phillips curve will be vertical.

Chapter 2

1. An earlier version of this chapter is in Hébert and Link (2006a), and that reference draws from Hébert and Link (1988).

2. From a macroeconomic perspective, this supply-side view of entrepreneurship emphasized that entrepreneurial activities shift the AgS curve in Figure 1.3 to the right, thus increasing aggregate economic activity and lowering aggregate prices and inflation.

3. The term *entrepreneur* is a word of French origin that does not appear often in the pre-history of economics. Its common, though imprecise, use in the 18th century is one who undertakes a project, a manufacturer, a master builder. An earlier form of the word, *entrepredeur*, appears as early as the 14th century (Hoselitz 1960). Throughout the sixteenth and seventeenth centuries, the most frequent usage of the term connoted a government contractor, usually of military fortifications or public works.

4. After Cantillon's death, economic analysis in France was dominated by a group of writers who called themselves *Les Economistes*. As the term *economist* became more general in

use, however, historians began to refer to this particular group of French writers using the term *Physiocrats* (the term *physiocracy* means rule of nature). Its leader was François Quesnay.

5. From a macroeconomic perspective, this demand side view of entrepreneurship emphasized that entrepreneurial activities shift the AgD curve in Figure 3.1 to the right, thus increasing aggregate economic activity and increasing inflation.

6. This approach is not unique to Weber. See, for example, Knight (1921) and Schumpeter (1934).

7. Paradoxically, the role of the entrepreneur in standard microeconomic theory remains virtually nonexistent. Baumol (2006) offers some insights into why this omission persists.

8. Schumpeter was in fact quite explicit that risk-bearing was not an essential characteristic of the entrepreneur: "As it is the carrying out of new combinations that constitutes the entrepreneur, it is not necessary that he should be permanently connected with an individual firm; ... our concept is narrower than the traditional one in that it does not include all heads of firms or managers or industrialists who may operate an established business. ... Nevertheless I maintain that ... [my] definition does no more than formulate with greater precision what the traditional doctrine really means to convey. In the first place our definition agrees with the usual one on the fundamental point of distinguishing between 'entrepreneurs' and 'capitalists' irrespective of whether the latter are regarded as owners of money, claims to money, or material goods.... It also settles the question whether the ordinary shareholder as such is an entrepreneur, and disposes of the conception of the entrepreneur as risk bearer (1934, p. 75)." It is not clear whether this rejection of the entrepreneur as risk-bearer was due to his misunderstanding of Knight's distinction between risk and uncertainty, or to a more fundamental disagreement.

Chapter 3

1. An earlier mathematical version of this theory is in Leyden et al. (2014).

2. See Chapter 2 for Knight's place in the intellectual development of the characterization of entrepreneurship.

3. Knight (1921) also observed that through experience, the entrepreneur might bundle experiences to form what evolves into the entrepreneur's subjective probability estimates.

4. Nelson and Winter (1977) argued that the approach of treating innovation within a neoclassical equilibrium production context, even if couched in terms of known risks, risk aversion, and so on, misses the point. The problem of understanding innovation and entrepreneurship is fundamentally about uncertainty and not about definable risk. Thus, any analysis that seeks to provide real insight and guidance must accept a "diversity and disequilibrium of choices" (p. 47), that is, an analysis in which decisions ex ante cannot be evaluated as being correct or incorrect.

5. This distinction between knowledge and economic knowledge is foundational to the knowledge spillover theory of entrepreneurship (Acs et al. 2009, Audretsch and Lehmann 2005, Braunerhjelm et al. 2010).

6. Our notion of the entrepreneur's search for knowledge parallels what some scholars have referred to as the social dimension of context (e.g., Hoang and Antoncic 2003, Welter 2011, Zahra and Wright 2011). It is also related to the concept of creative cognition that exists in the psychology literature (e.g., Ward et al. 1999, Shalley and Perry-Smith 2008). Relatedly, Formica (2013, p. 9) writes about millennial generation innovations: "The new age of knowledge is generating an important understanding of the value that derives from innovation, the process by which knowledge is translated into action. Shared knowledge and collective intelligence are replacing the three traditional pillars of value creation: land, work and capital. ... In the age of knowledge, the main source of value creation resides in the hyper-mobility of knowledge, which both controls access to opportunities and determines the rate of progress."

7. See Chapter 1 for a more in-depth analysis of the nature of public sector entrepreneurship and why it manifests itself indirectly rather than directly through the creation of government programs.

8. Nelson and Winter (1977, pp. 52–53) described this set of heuristics that essentially embody an R&D search strategy as a "set of procedures for identifying, screening, and honing in on promising ways to get to [an] objective." The ability of the entrepreneur to search within and across sources of knowledge is determined by the size and heterogeneity of his effective networks; the greater the heterogeneity of social ties and past experiences, the more creative will be the entrepreneur.

9. The model in this chapter differs from the model in Leyden et al. (2014) primarily in an extension and refinement of the treatment of probability and likelihood in the face of uncertainty. There has also been a change in notation to facilitate the exposition in this chapter.

10. The combination of inputs to generate a desired innovation parallels Schumpeter's (1939) discussion of the entrepreneur who varies the form of the production function to achieve an innovation.

11. Both because the exploration process is an uncertain one and because the entrepreneur may believe that there is more than one combination of inputs that will result in success, one cannot—at least in formal terms—speak in terms of probabilities, subjective or not; thus, the use of the term *subjective likelihood* of an input combination being successful has meaning. Instead of speaking in terms of likelihoods or probabilities, Shackle (1979) argued that knowledge only allows the individual—the entrepreneur in our case—to rule out some combination as being not possible with varying degrees of confidence. Shackle labeled this judgment with the word *disbelief* and argued that disbelief is quantifiable and therefore can serve as a guide to the individual in making choices. We have chosen to use the term *subjective likelihood* because, in our estimation, it is more likely to be familiar to the reader and therefore understood. See Cowan (2003) for an overview of Shackle's work and the connection of it to the entrepreneurship literature.

12. It is important to note here the different perspective of the capital market regarding the chance that the entrepreneur will succeed. For the entrepreneur, the focus is on finding a combination of inputs that will yield success. Because there is likely to be more than one input combination associated with success, and because the entrepreneur knows that he does not know the entire universe of possibilities, one cannot speak in terms of probabilities, which in terms of formal theory must sum to one across all possibilities. Thus, the entrepreneur thinks in terms of the less constrained notion of likelihoods. For the capital market, in contrast, the focus is not on possible input combinations that might be successful. Instead, it is on the entrepreneur and whether that entrepreneur will be successful. The universe of possibilities is then the set of all entrepreneurs who come to the capital market for financial support. That set is known empirically, and so through the analysis of past successes and failures of entrepreneurs using statistical models and portfolio theory, the capital market constructs a probability of success. Relatedly, see Knight (1921) for a general discussion on how fundamental uncertainty is converted to risk through logical analysis, empirical research, and the bundling of individually uncertain circumstances into collections whose collective behavior is, at least probabilistically, knowable.

13. Indeed, as we noted in Chapter 2, Knight (1921) argued that it is precisely this difference of opinion between the entrepreneur and the market that gives rise to the potential for entrepreneurial return in the first place. In a somewhat different context, the knowledge spillover theory of entrepreneurship (Acs et al. 2009, Audretsch and Lehmann 2005, Braunerhjelm, et al. 2010) embodies the notion of a difference of opinion in its notion of a knowledge filter that is used to explain why entrepreneurial activity in the private sector is more prevalent in small, start-up enterprises than in larger, well established firms.

14. To be sure, the capital market's knowledge base, K, or even that of a private equity owner, does have an impact on the availability of private equity and thus on the level of entrepreneurial activity. But that knowledge base, which focuses on the end value, V, of the innovation were it to be achieved and on the empirical estimation of the chances of success

based on portfolio theory, is fundamentally of a different character from the accumulated knowledge (e.g., engineering and scientific knowledge, knowledge of the entrepreneurial process, etc.) that might be of use to the entrepreneur.

15. These sources might take a variety of forms. Within the educational community, this might be achieved through pairing disparate areas of study or focusing collectively on science, technology, engineering, and mathematics (i.e., STEM education). Outside of the educational community, this might be achieved by facilitating entrepreneurial teams with heterogeneous backgrounds, and such might be referred to as entrepreneurial joint ventures. Social networks have also been found to be important for an activity that combines innovation and entrepreneurship. For example, three key academic studies of academic entrepreneurship—Lockett et al. (2003), Niclaou and Birley (2003), and Mustar et al. (2006)—report that a key determinant of a university's ability to generate startups is the vastness of its academic social networks. These papers build on earlier quantitative and qualitative studies conducted by prominent sociologists and economists, and several of their former graduate students and postdocs on the importance of social networks in academic entrepreneurship (e.g., Powell et al. 1996, Zucker and Darby 2001, Owen-Smith and Powell 2001 and 2003).

16. Strictly speaking, it is sufficient to characterize public sector entrepreneurship simply as public policies that affect the private sector entrepreneurial innovation process, that is, the transformation of knowledge into economic knowledge, through the enhancement of entrepreneurial social networks since the object of such policies are by definition focused on opportunity identification and exploitation in an uncertain economic environment; any public policy that focuses on achieving that end in an uncertain environment is itself an act of opportunity identification and exploitation in an uncertain economic environment. We have chosen to keep the redundant language "Public sector entrepreneurship focuses on the development of *innovative public policies* that affect the private sector entrepreneurial innovation process" to highlight the fact that the DNA of the public sector entrepreneur is the same as the DNA of the private sector entrepreneur.

17. See Hébert and Link (2009) for their synthesis of the extant literature and their argument that what unifies a divergent literature is the notion that the entrepreneur is one who perceives opportunity and has the ability to act on that perception.

18. The historical discussion in this chapter draws directly from Link (1995, 2002), and Leyden and Link (2013).

19. North Carolina State College of Agriculture and Engineering of the University of North Carolina at Raleigh became North Carolina State University in 1965.

20. Although, as the history of the park shows, many individuals took credit for the park idea especially after its success was inevitable. See Link (1995).

21. See the discussion in Chapter 1 concerning Table 1.1, and particularly footnote 7, for a discussion of indirect versus direct public sector entrepreneurship. As we note in the section "Defining Public Sector Entrepreneurship" in Chapter 1, we are persuaded by the argument in Klein et al. (2009) that there are significant institutional and cultural impediments to the use of direct forms of public sector entrepreneurial policy.

22. This is an important statement, and one that at the time was often overlooked and misunderstood by non-academicians. The universities saw themselves as magnets to attract research companies to the area, not as participants in those companies' research efforts.

23. A competing conceptualization of the entrepreneur, most notably advocated by Adam Smith (1976), argued that the entrepreneur was the person who supplied capital (Smith used the word "adventurer"). But as the behavior of Karl Robbins indicates, his role as capitalist was limited and seemingly focused on managing his exposure to what he saw as risk, not uncertainty, through the process of investment diversification. When that attempt to diversify fell through, he removed himself from the Research Triangle Park development process. In short, his interest was not focused on the exploitation of an uncertain, innovative opportunity and therefore he was not, we would argue, an entrepreneur, at least with respect to the Research Triangle Park development process.

Chapter 4

1. The U.S. Bureau of Labor Statistics refers to TFP as multifactor productivity (MFP).
2. See http://www.bls.gov/mfp/mprtech.htm.
3. In 1990, the Technology Administration within the U.S. Department of Commerce documented in retrospect the U.S. position in world markets in emerging technologies. Compared to Japan, the United States lagged in advanced materials, advanced semiconductor devices, digital imaging technology, high-density energy storage, and optoelectronics. The United States was even with Japan in superconductors, and it was ahead of Japan in artificial intelligence, biotechnology, flexible computer-integrated manufacturing, high-performance computing, medical devices and diagnostics, and sensor technology. With respect to Europe, the United States was behind in digital imaging technology—even in flexible computer-integrated manufacturing—and superconductors, and ahead in advanced materials, advanced semiconductor devices, artificial intelligence, biotechnology, high-density data storage, high-performance computing, medical devices and diagnostics, optoelectronics, and sensor technology.

   With respect to trends, the United States was, to use the Technology Administration's terms, *losing badly* against Japan in advanced materials, biotechnology, digital imaging technology, and superconductors; and *losing* in advanced semiconductor devices, high-density data storage, high-performance computing, medical devices and diagnostics, optoelectronics, and sensor technology. The United States was doing much better relative to Europe. It was *losing badly* only in digital imaging technology and flexible computer-integrated manufacturing, and it was *losing* in medical devices and diagnostics.
4. The notion of direct versus indirect impact on R&D should not be confused with our discussion in earlier chapters of the distinction between direct and indirect public sector entrepreneurship. Each legislative initiative described in Table 4.1 is an example of indirect public sector entrepreneurship, that is, public sector entrepreneurship that focuses on changing the economic environment in which enterprises operate rather than establishing governmental agencies that attempt to directly alter productivity. Within the category of indirect public sector entrepreneurship, however, one can design policies that work by directly impacting the environment in which R&D decisions are made, as do the R&E Tax Credit of 1981, the Small Business Innovation Development Act of 1982, and the Omnibus Trade and Competitiveness Act of 1988; or indirectly by altering other aspects of the economic environment but that indirectly result in effects on R&D, as do the Bayh-Dole Act of 1980, the Stevenson-Wydler Act of 1980, and the National Cooperative Research Act of 1984.
5. An earlier version of this section was in Link and Scott (2009, 2012).
6. For a more complete discussion of production functions, see Link (1987) and Link and Siegel (2003).
7. The output elasticities α and β are generally estimated, respectively, by the shares of physical capital and labor in output.

Chapter 5

1. A natural reading of the U.S. Constitution—which authorizes Congress "to promote the progress of science and useful arts, by securing for limited times to authors and inventors the exclusive right to their respective writings and discoveries" (§8, clause 8)—suggests that the Founders intended copyrights and patents to be held by private parties. While there can be disputes as to who legally should be considered to be an author or inventor when such innovative activity is funded by others, Senator Bayh's observation, "It is not government's responsibility—or indeed, the right of government—to assume the commercialization function," would seem to meet the natural intent of the Founders.
2. In recent years, many TTOs have been renamed to offices of innovation and commercialization to emphasize that they are involved in not only getting the technology out the door but also in seeing it put to use.

3. There is a distinction between spinoffs and startups. Startups are companies created by licensing an early stage invention to an independent entrepreneur, who is not necessarily a university faculty member, with the goal of developing the company around the growth and commercialization of the technology. Spinoffs are new companies formed by individuals (i.e., faculty members) related to the university or university research park to develop a technology that was discovered in, and is transferred from, the parent organization.

4. A review of the university technology transfer literature is in Bradley et al. (2013a).

5. The Bayh-Dole Act is codified in 35 USC 200–212 and implemented by 37 CFR 401: "The *contractor* will disclose each subject invention to the *Federal Agency* within two months after the inventor discloses it in writing to *contractor* personnel responsible for patent matters. The disclosure to the agency shall be in the form of a written report and shall identify the *contract* under which the invention was made and the inventor(s). It shall be sufficiently complete in technical detail to convey a clear understanding to the extent known at the time of the disclosure, of the nature, purpose, operation, and the physical, chemical, biological or electrical characteristics of the invention."

6. We characterize the advancement of knowledge associated with the Bayh-Dole Act as low. This is not intended to characterize the per se knowledge embodied in the transferred technology as low but rather to emphasize that the Act did not itself advance the state of knowledge but rather the transfer of existing knowledge. Certainly, the transfer of existing knowledge might leverage the advancement of next-generation knowledge, but that would represent a second-level effect of the Bayh-Dole Act. This argument also holds for the Stevenson-Wydler Act discussed in Chapter 6.

7. A similar introductory table is in each of the following policy chapters.

8. Berman (2012) points out, correctly in our opinion, that there are many reasons other than the Bayh-Dole Act for the increase in university patenting that occurred before as well as after the passage of the Act. For example, there was in the late 1960s a change in intellectual property practices at the Department of Health, Education, and Welfare (HEW) to waive title to HEW. As a result, university research funded by the National Institutes of Health (NIH) allowed universities to retain the rights to the results of their research. And coincidental to the Bayh-Dole Act, the 1980 Diamond *v.* Chakrabarty Supreme Court decision to allow microorganisms to be patented had an impact on the overall patenting trend. Lastly, the establishment of the Court of Appeals for the Federal Circuit (CAFC) in 1982 also had an impact because there was now a home for patent appeals.

9. This September 2009 document was updated and released again in February 2011.

10. Partners in this cooperative effort included the Department of Energy along with the Economic Development Administration, the Department of Agriculture, the Environmental Protection Agency, the National Science Foundation, the National Institute of Standards and Technology, and the Patent and Trademark Office.

11. The six organizations that received funding included the Iowa Innovation Network i6 Green Project in Ames; the Proof of Concept Center for Green Chemistry Scale-up in Holland, Michigan; the iGreen New England Partnership; the Igniting Innovation (I2) Cleantech Acceleration Network in Orlando, Florida; the Louisiana Tech Proof of Concept Center in Ruston; and the Washington State Clean Energy Partnership Project.

12. An earlier version of this section is in Bradley et al. (2013b).

13. EERE (2011) views PoCCs within a broader context than a university infrastructure, and thus defines PoCCs as institutions that "support all aspects of the entrepreneurship process, from assisting with technology feasibility and business plan development, to providing access to early-stage capital and mentors to offer critical guidance to innovators. Centers allow emerging technologies to mature and demonstrate their market potential, making them more attractive to investors and helping entrepreneurs turn their idea or technology into a business." See http://www1.eere.energy.gov/financing/news_detail.html?news_id=16,787.

14. See Rasmussen and Sørheim 2012 for a discussion of PoCCs from a public sector perspective of bridging the funding gaps for university spinoffs.

15. Some might take issue with the centers that we have subjectively classified as PoCCs. If this is the case, it underscores that an accepted definition of a PoCC is evolving.
16. The underlying information came from the AUTM data; we retained AUTM's use of the term startup.
17. This expanded view of the technology transfer process draws on Bradley et al. (2013a) and the references therein.
18. Codified in 35 USC 206, the Bayh-Dole Act requires the Secretary of Commerce to produce a standard patent rights clause (SPRC). Section 37 CFR 401.14, the SPRC is the contractual means by which federal agencies manage patent rights in funding agreements. Under sub-section (f)(2) of the SPRC, the university requires a written agreement from its research employees to protect the federal government's interests. When research is conducted by a university scientist and an invention is made under the SPRC, the university may elect to retain title, assign its interest under the SPRC, or decline to retain title.

    If the university retains title, it can prevent the federal funding agency from requesting title from the university's scientist. Essentially, the university stands in for the federal agency to undertake the objectives of using patenting to promote the utilization of federally funded inventions under Bayh-Dole.

    If the university declines to retain title, the federal agency may request title under (f)(2) and file patent applications, request title under (f)(2) and let invention enter public domain, or allow the inventors to retain title, subject to 27 CFR 401.9 (after consulting with university).
19. See http://creativecommons.org/about.
20. See http://greenxchange.cc/info/about.
21. See http://www.sustainabilityconsortium.org/smrs/.

Chapter 6

1. Public Law 96-480 was passed on October 21, 1980.
2. The only exception was for the National Aeronautics and Space Administration (Schacht 2009b).
3. An often overlooked clause in the Bayh-Dole Act implies that the impact of the Bayh-Dole legislation should also encompass national laboratories that are government owned, contractor operated (GOCO). Specifically, the legislation stated that the contractor of a "Government owned research or production facility [may] elect to retain title to any subject invention." The Department of Energy (DOE) fought such an interpretation of the Bayh-Dole Act for a number of years, arguing—correctly, according to Walterscheid (1990)—that this interpretation changed the long-standing DOE patent policy originally established under the Atomic Energy Act of 1954 as amended and Section 9 of the Federal Nonnuclear Energy Research and Development Act of 1974.
4. Public Law 99-502 was passed on October 20, 1986. The Federal Technology Transfer Act allowed the director of any government-owned, government-operated (GOGO) laboratory to enter into a Cooperative Research and Development Agreement (CRADA) with industry or with universities for the transfer of federally owned or federally originated technologies. Government-owned and contractor-operated (GOCO) laboratories were granted the authority to enter into CRADA agreements under the 1990 Defense Authorization Act, Public Law 101-189 (Schacht 2009b).
5. The Federal Laboratory Consortium (FLC) was established with the assistance of the Department of Defense in the early 1970s for the purpose of coordinating the transfer of technology to local and state governments. The Federal Technology Transfer Act provided a Congressional mandate for these activities. See Schacht (2009b) for greater institutional detail.
6. This description draws directly from Papadakis and Link (1997).
7. This description also draws directly from Papadakis and Link (1997).

8. See the discussion in the section "The Bayh-Dole Act as an Example of Public Sector Entrepreneurship" in Chapter 5 for an explanation for why the transfer of existing knowledge is consistent with our characterization of public sector entrepreneurship.

9. There are two related academic studies of post-1980 patenting at federal laboratories. Jaffe et al. (1998) examined patenting activity at NASA and found that it increased in the 1980s without any decline in patent quality, measured in terms of citations. Jaffe and Lerner (2001) studied patenting in selected DOE laboratories and also found that it had increased since the early 1980s and by the early1990s was on par, per dollar of R&D, with universities. A case can be made that patents are only one of several dimensions to characterize the impact of the Stevenson-Wydler Act. However, to the best of our knowledge, no data have been assembled on the number of technology transfers or the license fees generated. Certainly, such an undertaking might reasonably be on the future research agenda of scholars.

10. In addition to the current 2,800 employees at NIST, there are about 1,800 visiting scientists and 1,400 affiliated field agents.

11. This early history draws directly from Ullrich (1999) and Sullivan (2010), as previously summarized in Link et al. (2011). See also Westwick (2003).

12. *Sandia* means "watermelon" in Spanish. The mountains east of Albuquerque are called the Sandia Mountains because they take on a color similar to the inside of a watermelon in the afternoon sun. See http://www.sandia.gov/about/history/faq/faq8.html.

13. See http://www.sandia.gov/about/history/faq/faq8.html.

14. See http://www.sandia.gov/mission/.

15. Until 1993, Sandia was managed by AT&T. AT&T assumed management responsibilities from the University of California at the request of President Harry Truman.

16. This early history draws from Link and Link (2009); see also Link et al. (2011). A standard is a prescribed set of rules, conditions, or requirements concerning definitions of terms; classification of components; specification of materials, their performance, and their operations; delineation of procedures; and measurement of quantity and quality in describing materials, products, systems, services, or practices.

17. Public Law 100-418 was passed on August 23, 1988.

18. These data were graciously provided by Sandia and NIST. No lag between R&D spending and patent application underlies the $R&D data in Figures 6.1 and 6.2. The following discussion regarding these figures draws directly from Link et al. (2011).

19. Sandia's production activities began in 1993 when it was assigned responsibility for the production of neutron tubes and neutron generators (see http://www.sandia.gov/media/neutron.htm). Previously, these weapons elements were produced at the Pinellas Plant in Florida, which is part of DOE's weapon's complex (see http://www.em.doe.gov/bemr/BEMRSites/pipl.aspx). Production began in 1996. More recently, in 2007, Sandia opened the 400,000-square-foot Microsystems Engineering Sciences and Applications (MESA) Complex to produce functional, robust, integrated microsystems (see http://www.sandia.gov/SAI/Manufacturingmaterials.htm).

20. This finding has implications for the future study of patenting activity at federal laboratories. In particular, documenting pre- and post-Stevenson-Wydler patenting trends may present an incomplete picture of how the laboratory has embraced the mandate of the act, unless resources allocated to these activities and any change in the mission of the laboratory are fully understood and taken into account statistically.

21. This historical overview is based on National Academies (2007).

22. As an example, the National Additive Manufacturing Innovation Institute (NAMII), based in Youngstown, Ohio, is a public/private partnership with member organizations from industry, academia, government, and workforce development resources all collaborating with a singular, shared vision. NAMII's goal is to transition additive manufacturing technology to the mainstream U.S. manufacturing sector and create an adaptive workforce capable of not only meeting industry needs but also increasing domestic manufacturing competitiveness. NAMII is organized and managed by the National Center for Defense Manufacturing and Machining (NCDMM), which brings a background steeped

in experience within the defense, additive, and general manufacturing industries, and a proven track record of developing and deploying manufacturing innovation. NAMII is a national asset significantly different than traditional research institutes. See http://namii.org/about.

Chapter 7

1. There is a distinction, from a NSF-reporting tax-credit perspective, between R&D and R&E expenditures. R&E expenditures are somewhat more narrowly defined to include all costs incident to development. R&E does not include ordinary testing or inspection of materials or products for quality control of those for efficiency studies, etc. R&E, in a sense, is the experimental portion of R&D. That said, in practice it is often difficult to distinguish one category from the other, and the National Science Board (2012) often uses the terms synonymously.

2. Under Section 174, businesses are not allowed to expense R&E-related equipment. Such equipment must be depreciated. However, the Economic Recovery and Tax Act of 1981 (ERTA) provided for a faster depreciation of R&E capital assets than other business capital assets.

3. An excellent primer on the legislative history of the R&E tax credit, and especially on the mechanics of the credit, is Guenther (2013).

4. See also Bozeman and Link (1985).

5. Recall the quoted passage above from the Joint Committee on Taxation (1981, p. 119):

   Congress concluded that a substantial tax credit for incremental research and experimental expenditures was needed to overcome the reluctance of many ongoing companies to bear the significant costs of staffing and supplies, and certain equipment expenses such as computer charges, which must be incurred to initiate or expand research programs in a trade or business. While such costs have characteristics of investment activity, the relationships between expenditures for research and subsequent earnings often are less directly identifiable, and many businesses have been reluctant to allocate scarce investment funds for uncertain rewards.

6. Definitionally,

   Basic research: The objective of basic research is to gain more comprehensive knowledge or understanding of the subject under study without specific applications in mind. Although basic research may not have specific applications as its goal, it can be directed in fields of present or potential interest. This is often the case with basic research performed by industry or mission-driven federal agencies. Applied research: The objective of applied research is to gain knowledge or understanding to meet a specific, recognized need. In industry, applied research includes investigations to discover new scientific knowledge that has specific commercial objectives with respect to products, processes, or services. Development: Development is the systematic use of the knowledge or understanding gained from research directed toward the production of useful materials, devices, systems, or methods, including the design and development of prototypes and processes. (National Science Board 2012, p. 4–55).

7. An early study on international comparisons was Leyden and Link (1993).

8. Atkinson's identification of problems determining the base level of R&D (for the purpose of implementing an incremental R&E tax credit) is more than a problem of data collection. As noted in Chapter 2 (especially in our discussion of Schumpeter), the determination of any base level of R&D will be colored by the entrepreneur's perception of future risks and uncertainties, and these risks and uncertainties will include the prospects for public policy changes (types, size, duration, etc.). Thus, the choice of R&D in the absence of an R&E tax credit may still be influenced by entrepreneurial anticipation of the possibility of such a credit (particularly if public discussion of such a credit has taken place over long

periods of time), and therefore it is not clear how one should define (not to mention measure) a base level of R&D.

Chapter 8

1. The following discussion on the legislative background draws directly from Link and Scott (2012, 2013).

2. This section draws directly from Link and Scott (2012, 2013).

3. As noted in Chapter 2, it is precisely this exposure to uncertainty that gives rise to entrepreneurial returns. See our model of entrepreneurship in Chapter 3 for an in-depth treatment of how the entrepreneur deals with problems of uncertainty.

4. Note that the expected rate of return does not necessarily correspond to the greatest frequency or probability density because the distribution of rates of return need not be symmetric.

5. This notion of downside risk is consistent with Shackle's (1979) analysis of decision making under uncertainty. For those used to thinking of the variance of the distribution as the measure of risk, this notion of downside risk—which is the probability of a rate of return less than the hurdle rate—might seem unusual. But the nature of the firm's problem is what is important. Variance measures of risk are based on the notion that the firm is concerned with the possibility that outcomes can differ from the expected outcome. But in the case of a firm deciding whether to engage in research, the concern is whether the research project will result in success or failure.

6. As Link and Scott (2010, 2012) explain, to capture the idea of limited liability for investors, we bound their return below by zero. Thus, the rate of return can be quite negative when the return falls below the amount invested, but because the return is bounded below at zero, the rate of return is bounded below by (–100 percent). The expected private rate of return with SBIR support is $r = $ [return—(total project cost—SBIR funding)]/[total project cost—SBIR funding]. Let $Z = $ (total project cost—SBIR funding). Then, $r = $ (return—Z)/$Z = $ [(return/Z)—1]. The variance of r is $[(1/Z)^2 \text{ Var(return)}]$, and it is a general proposition that as SBIR funding increases (and hence Z decreases) the variance in the private rate of return increases (since $(1/Z)$ gets larger). It is also a general proposition that the expected private rate of return = $E[(\text{return})/Z]—1]$ must increase for the same reason. Further, neither the expected social rate of return nor the variance in the social rate of return change at all. The social cost is the same, and the social return is the same.

7. We use a definition of risk that is focused on the operational concern with the downside outcomes for an investment. The shortfalls of the private expected outcomes from society's expected returns reflect appropriability problems. There are several related technological and market factors that will cause private firms to appropriate less return and to face greater risk than society faces. These factors underlie what Arrow 1962 identified as the non-exclusivity and public good characteristics of investments in the creation of knowledge. The private firm's incomplete appropriation of social returns in the context of technical and market risk can make risk in its operational sense unacceptably large for the private firm considering an investment. Operationally and with reference to Figure 8.1, Tassey (1992, 1997, 2003, 2005), for example, defined risk as the probability that a project's rate of return falls below a required, private rate of return or private hurdle rate (as opposed to simply deviating from an expected return). As illustrated in Link and Scott (2001), for many socially desirable investments, the private firm faces an unacceptably large probability of a rate of return that falls short of its private hurdle rate. Yet, from society's perspective, the probability of a rate of return that is less than the social hurdle rate is sufficiently small that the project is still worthwhile.

8. SBIR funding need not affect the firm's private hurdle rate; that rate is set by corporate policy in most cases. Conceivably, because the operational measure of risk falls, the hurdle rate might fall as well in the presence of SBIR funding, and the simulative effect of SBIR funding would hold *a fortiori*.

9. Also, in general it is possible that, apart from the funding itself, the support and guidance of the SBIR program will lower the probability of low returns.

10. The Small Business Reauthorization Act of 2000 mandated that, among other things, the National Research Council (NRC) conduct "an evaluation of the economic benefits achieved by the SBIR program [and make recommendations to Congress for] improvements to the SBIR program." As part of its study of the SBIR program, the NRC conducted an extensive and balanced survey in 2005 of 6,408 project based on a population of 11,214 projects completed from Phase II awards made between 1992 and 2001 by five agencies: DoD, NIH, NASA, DoE, and NSF. The random sample resulting from the NRC survey included 1,878 projects. It was assumed, as part of the NRC's sampling methodology, that Phase II awards made in 2001 would be completed by 2005.

11. Relatedly, in 2007, North Carolina established the North Carolina Green Business Fund to make research grants to small companies to encourage the growth of the State's green economy. According to Hall (2014), the net social benefits attributable to this program are positive.

Chapter 9

1. An excellent and readable summary of the NCRA is Wright (1986).

2. Congress recognized the importance of technical standards developed by voluntary consensus standards bodies to our national economy by enacting the National Technology Transfer and Advancement Act of 1995, Public Law 104-113.

3. See also Combs and Link (2003) for an analysis of these theoretical benefits and costs.

4. The model in Bozeman et al. (1986) is based on Buchanan (1968) that was later extended by Jeremias and Zardkoohi (1976).

5. For the history of the definitional categories of R&D, as reported by the National Science Foundation, see Link (1996b). Detailed definitions of basic research, applied research, and development are in chapter 7.

6. The conclusion that both firms will end up with an identical mix of basic and applied knowledge if they act independently follows from the public good nature of basic knowledge if both firms have the same technology for conducting R&D, the same profit function, and endowments that are sufficiently similar. In terms of Figure 9.1, endowments will be sufficiently similar if the smaller firm's maximum possible production of applied knowledge Ob is greater than the projection of point d onto the horizontal axis. If the two firms have different R&D production processes, different profit functions, and/or endowments that are not sufficiently similar, they may not produce the same amount of applied knowledge. They will, however, still have access to the same amount of basic knowledge. See our discussion below on what happens if endowments are not similar enough,

7. Note that because the production of technical knowledge is effectively shared, the marginal cost of a unit of basic knowledge (in terms of foregone units of applied knowledge) for each firm will be half of what it would be were each firm the only firm in the industry. Thus, the ee' line is twice as steep as the original production possibility curves.

8. This inefficient and yet individually ideal outcome is simply a graphical version of the familiar outcome of a prisoner's dilemma game.

9. It can be show that increasing the number of firms does not in general change this conclusion. See Bozeman et al. (1986).

10. Much of the history of the SRC that follows is based on Burger (1990) and Link (1996a, 2006).

11. The Semiconductor Industry Association was formed in 1977 to collect and assemble reliable information on the industry and to develop mechanisms for addressing industry issues with the federal government.

12. At the June 10, 1981, meeting of the SIA, the following statement was released for the creation of the SRC: "Environment—U.S. semiconductor industry growth potential is high, requires large capital, is facing intense Japanese R&D competition, and needs more and better trained manpower. U.S. technology lead is vanishing. Purpose and objectives— Maintain U.S. technology leadership by focused and long-term university research that

also adds to quantity and quality of professional manpower. Implement with broad cooperative support from industry. Why the SRC?—Research is critical to growth, innovation, competitiveness, and productivity; and leads to market leadership. Because competition is intensifying, industry must cooperate to obtain critical mass. It must share costs and risks. Other research funding is decreasing. What is the SRC?—Cooperative activity for upgrading: 1) uncoordinated and struggling efforts of universities, 2) research in materials, processes, tools, design, reliability, 3) semiconductor curricula, and 4) industry interactions." (Burger 1990, p. 24)

13. Much of this discussion about SEMATECH comes from Link (1996a, 2006), and Link et al. (1996).

14. The quote comes from filing number 98 in the *Federal Register*, May 19, 1988, p. 17987.

15. From 1994 through 2008, the CORE database resided at the University of North Carolina at Greensboro. It was updated annually by Link and continues to be distributed on request.

16. Zeckhauser was subtle when he referred to the supposed importance of industry-supported research to universities as he describes how such relationships might develop: "Information gifts [to industry] may be a part of [a university's] commercial courtship ritual." (1996, p. 12,746)

17. Bercovitz and Feldman (2007), building on the conceptual advances of Pisano (1991) and Chesbrough (2003), talk about exploration and exploitation in the context of upstream university research alliances.

18. An earlier version of this material was in Link and Wessner (2011).

19. Hall's (2004) subsequent emphasis on industry-university research partnerships in the United States is on intellectual property. See also the role of intellectual property protection mechanisms (Hertzfeld et al. 2006).

20. Cohen et al. (1997) provide a selective review of this literature, emphasizing the studies that have documented that university research enhances firms' sales, R&D productivity, and patenting activity. See Blumenthal et al. (1986), Jaffe (1989), Adams (1990), Berman (1990), Feller (1990), Mansfield (1991, 1992), Van de Ven (1993), Bonaccorsi and Piccaluga (1994), Klevorick et al. (1994), Zucker et al. (1994), Henderson et al. (1995), Mansfield and Lee (1996), Zeckhauser (1996), Campbell (1997), and Baldwin and Link (1998). Cockburn and Henderson (1997) show that it was important for innovative pharmaceutical firms to maintain ties to universities. Hall et al. (2000, 2003) suggest that perhaps such research ties with universities increase the absorptive capacity, in the sense of Cohen and Leventhal (1990), of the innovative firms.

21. See Leyden and Link (1992) and Burnham (1997). Link (1995) documented that one reason for the growth of Research Triangle Park (North Carolina) was the desire of industrial research firms to locate near the triangle universities (University of North Carolina in Chapel Hill, North Carolina State University in Raleigh, and Duke University in Durham).

22. See Berman (1990), Feller (1990), Henderson et al. (1995), and Siegel et al. (1999).

23. Siegel et al. (1999) document that university administrators consider licensing and royalty revenues from industry as an important output from university technology transfer offices.

24. This section is based on Leyden and Link (2013).

25. There are, of course, markets for human and technical capital, but the nature of R&D in a business enterprise is likely to be more focused on the development side and therefore more applied and proprietary, while the nature of R&D in a university is likely to be more focused on the research side.

26. Bozeman et al. (2008) and Leyden et al. (2008) demonstrate this point.

27. See Baldwin and Link (1998) and Leyden and Link (1999) for empirical analyses based on the latter two effects—a reduction in appropriability and a (reduction) in business enterprise research costs.

28. See Coates and Humphreys (2002) and Coates et al. (2004) for background research that provides support for this argument.

29. Our analysis assumes that the university program exists in isolation. However, we recognize that university objectives are likely more complex with multiple objectives and the

possibility for fungibility in the funding of multiple programs. Åstebro and Bazzazian (2011), for example, note the potential conflict between university efforts to support local startups and university desire for licensing revenue, and Ehrenberg et al. (1993) provides evidence of universities using revenues from one program to subsidize others. To the extent universities treat the revenues of various programs as fungible, a research program with somewhat higher costs (on the iso-cost curve B_1 for example) might be possible without a grant. Initial work on a more sophisticated model of university objectives suggests that the relative salience to the university of its various programs determines the degree to which funding in one program is used to subsidize others.

30. Business enterprise support for universities, to the extent it is motivated by profit considerations, is subsumed within the structure of this model. However, business support for universities may also be motivated by more uncertain, dynamic, and longer-term considerations such as the development and maintenance of relationships, access to future graduates, etc.

Chapter 10

1. See http://www.atp.nist.gov/atp/imp_fact.htm.
2. See http://www.atp.nist.gov/atp/imp_fact.htm.
3. Following Arrow (1962, p. 609), there are three sources of market failure that characterize R&D or any knowledge-based inventive or innovative activity: indivisiblities, inappropriability, and uncertainty.
4. For an example of a more detailed analysis of the role well-defined constituency groups play in determining the structure of government programs, see Leyden's (1992) analysis of intergovernmental grants structures.
5. http://www.atp.nist.gov/eao/eao_pubs.htm
6. This study was conducted by O'Connor et al. (2007). See http://www.atp.nist.gov/eao/gcr06-898.pdf

Chapter 11

1. President Roosevelt passed on April 12, 1945.
2. We are reminded of John Maynard Keynes's observation in the last chapter of his *General Theory*: "Practical men, who believe themselves to be quite exempt from any intellectual influences, are usually the slaves of some defunct economist" (Keynes 2011, p. 36).

Chapter 12

1. The data on R&D and GDP came from the National Science Board (2012).
2. Relatedly, although in our opinion a second-best effort to examine the efficacy of the technology and innovation policies discussed herein, Bozeman and Link (2014) have shown that the level of aggregate annual R&D investments increased during the 1980–2011 period compared to the 1953–1979 period.
3. Empirical estimates of ρ from equation (A12.8) have been interpreted as an estimate of the marginal rate of return to investments in R&D.

REFERENCES

The most beautiful thing we can experience is the mysterious. It is the source of all true art and science.

—Albert Einstein

Acs, Zoltan J., Pontus Braunerhjelm, David B. Audretsch, and Bo Carlsson (2009). "The Knowledge Spillover Theory of Entrepreneurship," *Small Business Economics* 32: 15–30.

Adams, James D. (1990). "Fundamental Stocks of Knowledge and Productivity Growth," *Journal of Political Economy* 98: 673–702.

Allen, Stuart D., Stephen K. Layson, and Albert N. Link (2012). "Public Gains from Entrepreneurial Research: Inferences about the Economic Value of Public Support of the Small Business Innovation Research Program," *Research Evaluation* 21: 105–112.

Alvarez, Sharon A., and Jay B. Barney (2005). "How Do Entrepreneurs Organize Firms under Conditions of Uncertainty?," *Journal of Management* 31: 776–793.

Alvarez, Sharon A., and Lowell W. Busenitz (2001). "The Entrepreneurship of Resource-Based Theory," *Journal of Management* 27: 755–775.

Arrow, Kenneth J. (1962). "Economic Welfare and the Allocation of Resources for Invention," in *The Rate and Direction of Inventive Activity*, edited by R. R. Nelson. Princeton, NJ: Princeton University Press, pp. 609–626.

Åstebro, Thomas B., and Navid Bazzazian (2011). "Universities, Entrepreneurship and Local Economic Development," in *Handbook of Research on Entrepreneurship and Regional Development*, edited by M. Fritsch. New York: Edward Elgar, pp. 252–333.

Atkinson, Robert D. (2007). "Expanding the R&E Tax Credit to Drive Innovation, Competitiveness and Prosperity," *Journal of Technology Transfer* 32: 617–628.

Audretsch, David B., and Erik E. Lehmann (2005). "Does the Knowledge Spillover Theory of Entrepreneurship Hold for Regions?" *Research Policy* 34: 1191–1202.

Auerswald, Philip E., and Louis M. Branscomb (2003). "Valleys of Death and Darwinian Seas: Financing the Invention to Innovation Transition in the United States," *Journal of Technology Transfer* 28: 227–239.

Bain, Joe S. (1949). "Price and Production Policies," in *A Survey of Contemporary Economics*, edited by H. S. Ellis. Philadelphia: The Blakiston Company, pp. 129–173.

Baldwin, William L., and Albert N. Link (1998). "Universities as Research Joint Venture Partners: Does Size of Venture Matter?" *International Journal of Technology Management* 15: 895–913.

Baudeau, Nicolas ([1767] 1910). *Premiere introduction a la philosophie economique*, translated by A. Dubois. Paris: P. Geuthner.

Baumol, William J. (2006). "Textbook Entrepreneurship: Comment on Johanssen," *Econ Journal Watch* 3: 133–136.

Bellone, Carl J., and George Frederick Goerl (1992). "Reconciling Public Entrepreneurship and Democracy," *Public Administration Review* 52: 130–134.

Bentham, Jeremy (1952). *Jeremy Bentham's Economic Writings*, edited by W. Stark. London: Allen and Unwin.

Bentham, Jeremy ([1838–1843] 1962). *The Works of Jeremy Bentham*, edited by J. Bowring. New York: Russell and Russell.

Bentham, Jeremy ([1787] 2004). *Defence of Usury*. New York: Kessinger Publishing Company.

Berman, Elizabeth Popp (2012). *Creating the Market University*. Princeton, NJ: Princeton University Press.

Berman, Evan M. (1990). "The Economic Impact of Industry-Funded University R&D," *Research Policy* 19: 349–355.

Bernier, Luc, and Taïib Hafsi (2007). "The Changing Nature of Public Entrepreneurship," *Public Administration Review* 67: 488–503.

Bercovitz, Janet E. L., and Maryann P. Feldman (2007). "Fishing Upstream: Firm Innovation Strategy and University Research Alliances," *Research Policy* 36: 930–948.

Blumenthal, David, Michael E. Gluck, Karen S. Lewis, Michael A. Stoto, and David Wise (1986). "University Industry Research Relationships in Biotechnology: Implications for the University," *Science* 232: 1361–1366.

Boardman, P. Craig, and Elizabeth A. Corley (2008). "University Research Centers and the Composition of Research Collaborations," *Research Policy* 37: 900–913.

Bonaccorsi, Andrea, and Andrea Piccaluga (1994). "A Theoretical Framework for the Evaluation of University-Industry Relationships," *R&D Management* 24: 229–247.

Boyett, Inger (1997). "The Public Sector Entrepreneur—A Definition," *International Journal of Entrepreneurial Behaviour and Research* 3: 77–92.

Bozeman, Barry, John Hardin, and Albert N. Link (2008). "Barriers to the Diffusion of Nanotechnology," *Economics of Innovation and New Technology* 17: 751–753.

Bozeman, Barry, and Albert N. Link (1984). "Tax Incentives for R&D: A Critical Evaluation," *Research Policy* 13: 21–31.

Bozeman, Barry, and Albert N. Link (1985). "Public Support for Private R&D: The Case of the Research Tax Credit," *Journal of Policy Analysis and Management* 4: 370–382.

Bozeman, Barry, and Albert N. Link (2014). "Toward an Assessment of Impacts from U.S. Technology and Innovation Policies." University of North Carolina mimeograph.

Bozeman, Barry, Albert N. Link, and Asghar Zardkoohi (1986). "An Economic Analysis of R&D Joint Ventures," *Managerial and Decision Economics* 7: 263–266.

Bradley, Samantha R., Christopher S. Hayter, and Albert N. Link (2013a). "Models and Methods of University Technology Transfer," *Foundations and Trends in Entrepreneurship* 9: 365–570.

Bradley, Samantha R., Christopher S. Hayter, and Albert N. Link (2013b). "Proof of Concept Centers in the United States: An Exploratory Look," *Journal of Technology Transfer* 38: 349–381

Braunerhjelm, Pontus, Zoltan J. Acs, David B. Audretsch, and Bo Carlsson (2010). "The Missing Link: Knowledge Diffusion and Entrepreneurship in Endogenous Growth," *Small Business Economics* 34: 105–125.

Brod, Andrew C., and Albert N. Link (2001). "Trends in Cooperative Research Activity," in *Innovation Policy in the Knowledge-Based Economy*, edited by M. Feldman and A. Link. Norwell, MA: Kluwer Academic Publishers, pp. 105–120.

Buchanan, James M. (1968). *The Demand and Supply of Public Goods*. Chicago: Rand McNally.

Burger, Robert M. (1990). "Cooperative Research: The New Paradigm." Research Triangle Park, NC: Semiconductor Research Corporation (Unpublished manuscript).

Burnham, James B. (1997). "Evaluating Industry/University Research Linkages," *Research-Technology Management* 40: 52–55.

Bush, Vannevar (1945). *Science—the Endless Frontier*. Washington, DC: Office of Scientific Research and Development.

Campbell, Teresa Isabelle Daza (1997). "Public Policy for the 21st Century: Addressing Potential Conflicts in University-Industry Collaboration," *The Review of Higher Education* 20: 357–379.

Cantillon, Richard ([1755] 1931). *Essai sur la nature du commerce en general*, edited and translated by H. Higgs. London: Macmillan.

Carlin, Edward A. (1956), "Schumpeter's Constructed Type—The Entrepreneur," *Kyklos* 9: 27–43.

Casson, Mark (1982). *The Entrepreneur: An Economic Theory*. Oxford: Martin Robinson.

Casson, Mark (2003). *The Entrepreneur: An Economic Theory* (2nd edition). Cheltenham, UK: Edward Elgar.

Chesbrough, Henry (2003). *Open Innovation: The New Imperative for Creating and Profiting from Technology*. Boston: Harvard Business School Publishing.

Coates, Dennis, and Brad R. Humphreys (2002). "The Supply of University Enrollments: University Administrators as Utility Maximizing Bureaucrats," *Public Choice* 110: 365–392.

Coates, Dennis, Brad R. Humphreys, and Michelle A. Vachris (2004). "More Evidence that University Administrators Are Utility Maximizing Bureaucrats," *Economics of Governance* 5: 77–101.

Cockburn, Iain, and Rebecca Henderson (1997). "Public-Private Interaction and the Productivity of Pharmaceutical Research," NBER Working Paper 6018.

Cohen, Wesley M., Richard Florida, Lucien Randazzese, and John Walsh (1997). "Industry and the Academy: Uneasy Partners in the Cause of Technological Advance," in *Challenge to the University*, edited by R. Noll. Washington, DC: Brookings Institution Press, pp. 171–200.

Cohen, Wesley M., and Daniel A. Leventhal (1990). "The Implications of Spillovers for R&D and Technology Advance," in *Advanced in Applied Micro-Economics*, edited by V. K. Smith and A. N. Link. Greenwich, CT: JAI Press, pp. 29–46.

Cohen, Wesley M., Richard R. Nelson, and John P. Walsh (2002). "Links and Impacts: The Influence of Public Research on Industrial R&D," *Management Science* 48: 1–23.

Combs, Kathryn, and Albert N. Link (2003). "Innovation Policy in Search of an Economic Foundation: The Case of Research Partnerships in the United States," *Technology Analysis and Strategic Management* 15: 177–187.

Council on Competitiveness (1996). *Endless Frontiers, Limited Resources: U.S. R&D Policy for Competitiveness*. Washington, DC: Council on Competitiveness.

Council of Economic Advisers (annual). *Economic Report of the President*. Washington, DC: U.S. Government Printing Office.

Cowan, Tyler (2003). "Entrepreneurship, Austrian Economics, and the Quarrel between Philosophy and Poetry," *The Review of Austrian Economics* 16: 5–23.

EERE (2011). "Obama Administration Announces Launch of i6 Green Challenge to Promote Clean Energy Innovation and Economic Growth," *EERE News*, http://apps1.eere.energy.gov/news/progress_alerts.cfm/pa_id=503.

Ehrenberg, Ronald. G., Daniel I. Rees, and Dominic J. Brewer (1993). "How Would Universities Respond to Increased Federal Support for Graduate Students?" in *Studies of Supply and Demand in Higher Education*, edited by C. Clotfelter and M. Rothschild. Chicago: University of Chicago Press, pp. 183–210.

Etzkowitz, Henry (2003). "Innovation in Innovation: The Triple Helix of University-Government-Industry Relations," *Social Science Information* 42: 293–337.

Executive Office of the President (1994). *Science in the National Interest*. Washington, DC: Office of Science and Technology Policy.

Executive Office of the President (1998). *Science and Technology: Shaping the Twenty-First Century*. Washington, DC: Office of Science and Technology Policy.

Executive Office of the President (2009). *A Strategy for American Innovation: Driving Towards Sustainable Growth and Quality Jobs*. Washington, DC: Executive Office of the President.

Executive Office of the President (2012). *A National Strategic Plan for Advanced Manufacturing*. Washington, DC: Office of Science and Technology Policy.

Feller, Irwin (1990). "Universities as Engines of R&D-Based Economic Growth: They Think They Can," *Research Policy* 19: 349–355.

Fontana, Roberto, Aldo Geuna, and Mireille Matt (2006). "Factors Affecting University-Industry R&D Projects: The Importance of Searching, Screening and Signaling," *Research Policy* 35: 309–323.

Formica, Piero (2013). *Stories of Innovation for the Millennial Generation: The Lynceus Long View.* New York: Palgrave-Macmillan.

Gulbranson, Christine A., and David B. Audretsch (2008). "Proof of Concept Centers: Accelerating the Commercialization of University Innovation," *Journal of Technology Transfer* 33: 249–258.

Guenther, Gary (2013). "Research Tax Credit: Current Law, Legislation in the 113th Congress, and Policy Issues," Washington, DC: Congressional Research Service.

Hagedoorn, John, Albert N. Link, and Nicholas S. Vonortas (2000). "Research Partnerships," *Research Policy* 29: 567–586.

Halévy, Elie (1955). *The Growth of Philosophic Radicalism,* translated by M. Morris. Boston: Beacon Press.

Hall, Bronwyn H. (2004). "University-Industry Research Partnerships in the United States," in *Rethinking Science Systems and Innovation Policies,* edited by J. Contzen, D. Gibson, and M. V. Heitor. West Lafayette, IN: Purdue University Press, pp. 1–31.

Hall, Bronwyn H., Albert N. Link, and John T. Scott (2000). "Universities as Research Partners," NBER Working Paper 7643.

Hall, Bronwyn H., Albert N. Link, and John T. Scott (2001). "Barriers Inhibiting Industry from Partnering with Universities: Evidence from the Advanced Technology Program," *Journal of Technology Transfer* 26: 87–98.

Hall, Bronwyn H., Albert N. Link, and John T. Scott (2003). "Universities as Research Partners," *Review of Economics and Statistics* 85: 485–491.

Hall, Bronwyn H., and John van Reenen (2000). "How Effective are Fiscal Incentives for R&D? A Review of the Evidence," *Research Policy* 29: 449–469.

Hall, Michael J. (2014). *State Support of Sustainability Innovation in Small Firms: North Carolina's Green Business Fund.* Doctoral dissertation, University of North Carolina at Greensboro.

Hardin, John, Lauren Lanahan, and Lukas C. Brun (forthcoming 2015). "Assessing State-level Science and Technology Policies: North Carolina's Experience with SBIR State Matching Grants," in *Oxford Handbook of Local Competitiveness,* edited by D. B. Audretsch, A. N. Link, and M. Walshok. New York: Oxford University Press.

Hébert, Robert F., and Albert N. Link (1988). *The Entrepreneur: Mainstream Views and Radical Critiques* (2nd edition). New York: Praeger.

Hébert, Robert F., and Albert N. Link (2006a). "The Entrepreneur as Innovator," *Journal of Technology Transfer* 31, 589–597.

Hébert, Robert F., and Albert N. Link (2006b). "Historical Perspectives on the Entrepreneur," *Foundations and Trends in Entrepreneurship* 2: 461–408.

Hébert, Robert F., and Albert N. Link (2009). *A History of Entrepreneurship.* London: Routledge.

Henderson, Rebecca, Adam B. Jaffe, and Manuel Trajtenberg (1995). "Universities as a Source of Commercial Technology: A Detailed Analysis of University Patenting 1965–1988," NBER Working Paper No. 5068.

Hertzfeld, Henry R., Albert N. Link, and Nicholas S. Vonortas (2006). "Intellectual Property Protection Mechanisms in Research Partnerships," *Research Policy* 35: 825–838.

Hisrich, Robert D., and Amir Al-Dabbagh (2013). *Governpreneurship: Establishing a Thriving Entrepreneurial Spirit in Government.* Cheltenham, UK: Elgar.

Hoang, Ha, and Bostjan Antoncic (2003). "Network-Based Research in Entrepreneurship," *Journal of Business Venturing* 18: 165–187.

Holcombe, Randall G. (2002). "Political Entrepreneurship and the Democratic Allocation of Economic Resources," *Review of Austrian Economics* 15: 143–159.

Hoselitz, Bert F. (1960). "The Early History of Entrepreneurial Theory," in *Essays in Economic Thought: Aristotle to Marshall,* edited by J. J. Spengler and W. R. Allen. Chicago: Rand McNally, pp. 234–257.

Hughes, Jonathan (1991). "Public Sector Entrepreneurship," in *Favorites of Fortune: Technology, Growth, and Economic Development since the Industrial Revolution,* edited by P. Higonnet, D. D. Landes, and H. Rosovsky. Cambridge, MA: Harvard University Press, pp. 297–321.

Jaffe, Adam. (1989). "Real Effects of Academic Research," *American Economic Review* 79: 957–978.

Jaffe, Adam B., and Josh Lerner (2001). "Reinventing Public R&D: Patent Policy and the Commercialization of National Laboratory Technologies," *RAND Journal of Economics* 32: 167–198.

Jaffe, Adam B., Michael S. Fogarty, and Bruce A. Banks (1998). "Evidence from Patents and Patent Citations on the Impact of NASA and Other Federal Labs on Commercial Innovation," *Journal of Industrial Economics* 46: 183–205.

Jeremias, Ronald, and Asghar Zardkoohi (1976). "Distributional Implications of Independent Adjustments in an Economy with Public Goods," *Economic Inquiry* 14: 305–308.

Joint Committee on Taxation (1981). "General Explanation of the Economic Recovery Tax Act of 1981." Washington, DC: U.S. Congress.

Jones, Philip (1978). "The Appeal of the Political Entrepreneur," *British Journal of Political Science* 8: 498–504.

Kanbur, S. M. (1980). "A Note on Risk-Taking, Entrepreneurship, and Schumpeter," *History of Political Economy* 12: 489–498.

Kerr, Clark (2001). *The Uses of the University.* Cambridge, MA: Harvard University Press.

Keynes, John Maynard ([1936] 2011). *The General Theory of Employment, Interest and Money* [Kindle edition].

Kingdon, John W. (1984). *Agenda, Alternatives, and Public Policies.* New York: Longman.

Kirchheimer, Donna W. (1989). "Public Entrepreneurship and Sub-National Government," *Polity* 22: 108–122.

Kirzner, Israel M. (1973). *Competition and Entrepreneurship.* Chicago: University of Chicago Press.

Klein, Peter G., Joseph T. Mahoney, Anita M. McGahan, and Christos N. Pitelis (2009). "Toward a Theory of Public Entrepreneurship." Working paper 09-0106, College of Business, University of Illinois at Urbana-Champaign, http://www.business.illinois.edu/Working_Papers/papers/09-0106.pdf.

Klein, Peter G., Joseph T. Mahoney, Anita M. McGahan, and Christos N. Pitelis (2011). "Resources, Capabilities, and Routines in Public Organization." Working paper 11-0101, College of Business, University of Illinois at Urbana-Champaign, http://www.business.illinois.edu/Working_Papers/papers/11-0101.pdf.

Klevorick, Alvin K., Richard C. Levin, Richard R. Nelson, and Stanley G. Winter (1994). "On the Sources and Significance of Interindustry Differences in Technological Opportunities," *Research Policy* 24: 195–206.

Knight, Frank H. (1921). *Risk, Uncertainty, and Profit.* Boston: Houghton Mifflin.

Knight, Frank H. (1951). *The Economic Organization.* New York: Augustus M. Kelley.

Kodama, Toshihiro (2008). "The Role of Intermediation and Absorptive Capacity in Facilitating University-Industry Linkages: An Empirical Study of TAMA in Japan," *Research Policy* 37: 1224–1240.

Lee, Michelle K., and Marvis K. Lee (1991). "High Technology Consortia: A Panacea for America's Technological Competitiveness Problems?" *Berkeley Technology Law Journal* 6: 335–372.

Lewontin, Richard (2011). "The Genotype/Phenotype Distinction," in *The Stanford Encyclopedia of Philosophy*, edited by N. Zalta. Retrieved from http://plato.stanford.edu/archives/sum2011/entries/genotype-phenotype/.

Leyden, Dennis P. (1992). "Donor Determined Intergovernmental Grants Structure," *Public Finance Quarterly* 20: 321–37.

Leyden, Dennis P. and Albert N. Link (1992). *Government's Role in Innovation*, Norwell, Mass.: Kluwer Academic Publishers.

Leyden, Dennis P. and Albert N. Link (1993). "Tax Policies Affecting R&D: An International Comparison," *Technovation* 13: 17–25.

Leyden, Dennis P. and Albert N. Link (1999). "Federal Laboratories as Research Partnerships," *International Journal of Industrial Organization* 17: 575–592.

Leyden, Dennis P. and Albert N. Link (2013). Knowledge Spillovers, Collective Entrepreneurship, and Economic Growth: The Role of Universities," *Small Business Economics: An Entrepreneurship Journal* 41: 797–817.

Leyden, Dennis P., Albert N. Link, and Donald S. Siegel S. (2008). "A Theoretical and Empirical Analysis of the Decision to Locate on a University Research Park," *IEEE Transactions on Engineering Management* 55: 23–28.

Leyden, Dennis P., Albert N. Link, and Donald S. Siegel (2014). "A Theoretical Analysis of the Role of Social Networks in Entrepreneurship," *Research Policy* 43: 1157-1163. DOI: 10.1016/j.respol.2014.04.010.

Link, Albert N. (1981). "Basic Research and Productivity Increase in Manufacturing: Additional Evidence," *American Economic Review* 71: 1111–1112.

Link, Albert N. (1987). *Technological Change and Productivity Growth*, Chur, Switzerland: Harwood Academic Publishers.

Link, Albert N. (1995). *A Generosity of Spirit: The Early History of the Research Triangle Park*, Research Triangle Park: Research Triangle Foundation of North Carolina.

Link, Albert N. (1996a). *Evaluating Public Sector Research and Development*, New York: Praeger Publishers.

Link, Albert N. (1996b). "On the Classification of R&D," *Research Policy* 25: 397–401.

Link, Albert N. (1996c). "Research Joint Ventures: Patterns from *Federal Register* Filings," *Review of Industrial Organization* 11: 617–628.

Link, Albert N. (1999). "Public/Private Partnerships in the United States," *Industry and Innovation* 6: 191–217.

Link, Albert N. (2002). *From Seed to Harvest: The Growth of the Research Triangle Park*, Research Triangle Park: Research Triangle Foundation of North Carolina.

Link, Albert N. (2005). "Research Joint Ventures in the United States: A Descriptive Analysis," in *Essays in Honor of Edwin Mansfield: The Economics of R&D, Innovation, and Technological Change*, edited by A. N. Link and F. M. Scherer. Norwell, MA: Springer, pp. 187–193.

Link, Albert N. (2006). *Public/Private Partnerships: Innovation Strategies and Policy Alternatives*, New York: Springer.

Link, Albert N. and Jamie R. Link (2009). *Government as Entrepreneur*, New York: Oxford University Press.

Link, Albert N. and John Rees (1990). "Firm Size, University-Based Research, and the Returns to R&D," *Small Business Economics* 2: 25–31.

Link, Albert N. and Christopher J. Ruhm (2008). "Bringing Science to Market: Commercializing from NIH SBIR Awards," NBER Working Paper 14057.

Link, Albert N., Christopher J. Ruhm, and Donald S. Siegel (2013). "Private Equity and the Innovation Strategies of Entrepreneurial Firms: Empirical Evidence from the Small Business Innovation Research Program, *Managerial and Decision Economics*. DOI: 10.1002/mde.2648.

Link, Albert N. and John T. Scott (2001). "Public/Private Partnerships: Stimulating Competition in a Dynamic Market," *International Journal of Industrial Organization* 19: 763–794.

Link, Albert N. and John T. Scott (2005). "Universities as Partners in U.S. Research Joint Ventures," *Research Policy* 34: 385–393.

Link, Albert N. and John T. Scott (2007). "The Economics of University Research Parks," *Oxford Review of Economic Policy* 23: 661–674.

Link, Albert N. and John T. Scott (2009). *Public Goods, Public Gains: Calculating the Social Benefits of Public R&D*, New York: Oxford University Press.

Link, Albert N. and John T. Scott (2010). "Government as Entrepreneur: Evaluating the Commercialization Success of SBIR Projects," *Research Policy* 39: 589–601.

Link, Albert N. and John T. Scott (2012). *Employment Growth from Public Support of Innovation in Small Firms*, Kalamazoo, MI: W.E. Upjohn Institute for Employment Research.

Link, Albert N. and John T. Scott (2013). *Bending the Arc of Innovation: Public Support of R&D in Small, Entrepreneurial Firms*, New York: Palgrave Macmillan.

Link, Albert N. and Donald S. Siegel (2003). *Technological Change and Economic Performance*, London: Routledge.

Link, Albert N., Donald S. Siegel, and Barry Bozeman (2007). "An Empirical Analysis of the Propensity of Academics to Engage in Informal Technology Transfer," *Industrial and Corporate Change* 16: 641–655.

Link, Albert N., Donald S. Siegel, and David D. Van Fleet (2011). "Public Science and Public Innovation: Assessing the Relationship between Patenting at U.S. National Laboratories and the Bayh-Dole Act," *Research Policy* 40: 1094–1099.

Link, Albert N., David J. Teece, and William Finan (1996). "Estimating the Benefits from Collaboration: The Case of SEMATECH," *Review of Industrial Organization* 13: 737–751.

Link, Albert N. and Charles W. Wessner (2011). "Universities as Research Partners: Entrepreneurial Explorations and Exploitations," in *Handbook of Research on Innovation and Entrepreneurship*, edited by D. Audretsch. London: Edward Elgar Publishing, pp. 290–299.

Loasby, Brian J. (2002). "The Organizational Basis of Cognition and the Cognitive Basis of Organization," in *The Economics of Choice, Change and Organization: Essays in Honor of Richard M. Cyert*, edited by M. Augier and J. G. March. Cheltenham, U.K.: Edward Elgar, pp. 147–167.

Lockett, Andy, Mike Wright, and Stephen Franklin (2003). "Technology Transfer and Universities' Spin-Out Strategies," *Small Business Economics* 20: 185–200.

Machlup, Fritz (1980). *Knowledge and Knowledge Production*, Princeton: Princeton University Press.

Mansfield, Edwin (1980). "Basic Research and Productivity Increase in Manufacturing," *American Economic Review* 70: 863–873.

Mansfield, Edwin (1991). "Academic Research and Industrial Innovation," *Research Policy* 20: 1–12.

Mansfield, Edwin (1992). "Academic Research and Industrial Innovation: A Further Note," *Research Policy* 21: 295–296.

Mansfield, Edwin and Jeong-Yeon Lee (1996). "The Modern University: Contributor to Industrial Innovation and Recipient of Industrial R&D Support," *Research Policy* 25: 1047–1058.

Martin, Stephen and John T. Scott (2000). "The Nature of Innovation Market Failure and the Design of Public Support for Private Innovation," *Research Policy* 29: 437–447.

Mason, Edward S. (1939). "Price and Production Policies of Large Scale Enterprises," *American Economic Review* 29: 61–74.

Maia, Catarina and João Claro (2013). "The Role of a Proof of Concept Center in a University Ecosystem: An Exploratory Study," *Journal of Technology Transfer* 38: 641–650.

Miller, David J. and Zoltan J. Acs (2013). "Technology Commercialization on Campus: Twentieth Century Frameworks and Twenty-First Century Blind Spots," *Annals of Regional Science* 50: 407–423.

Moon, Myung J. (1999). "The Pursuit of Managerial Entrepreneurship: Does Organization Matter?" *Public Administration Review* 59: 31–43.

Morgan, Robert P. (1998). "University Research Contributions to Industry: The Faculty View," in *Trends in Industrial Innovation: Industry Perspectives and Policy Implications*, edited by P. D. Blair and R. A. Frosch. Research Triangle Park, NC: Sigma Xi, The Scientific Research Society, pp. 163–170.

Morris, Michael H. and Foard F. Jones (1999). "Entrepreneurship in Established Organizations: The Case of the Public Sector." *Entrepreneurship Theory & Practice* 24: 71–91.

Mowery, David C. (2001). "Using Cooperative Research and Development Agreements as S&T Indicators: What Do We Have and What Would We Like?" in *Strategic Research Partnerships: Proceedings from an NSF Workshop*, edited by J. E. Jankowski, A. N. Link, and N. S. Vonortas. Arlington, VA: National Science Foundation, pp. 93–112.

Mowery, David C. and David J. Teece (1996). "Strategic Alliances and Industrial Research," in *Engines of Innovation: U.S. Industrial Research at the End of an Era*, edited by R. S. Rosenbloom and W. J. Spender. Boston: Harvard Business School Publishing, pp. 111–130.

Munger, Michael C. (2000). *Analyzing Policy*. New York: W. W. Norton.

Mustar, Phillippe, Marie Renault, Massimo G. Colombo, Evila Piva, Margarida Fontes, Andy Lockett, Mike Wright, Bart Clarysse, and Nathalie Moray (2006). "Conceptualising the

Heterogeneity of Research-based Spin-offs: A Multi-dimensional Taxonomy," *Research Policy* 35: 289–308.

Nabseth, Lars and George F. Ray (1974). *The Diffusion of New Industrial Processes: An International Study*. New York: Cambridge University Press.

National Academies (2007). *Rising Above the Gathering Storm: Energizing and Employing America for a Brighter Economic Future*, Washington, DC: National Academies Press.

National Science Board (2012). *Science and Engineering Indicators 2012*, Arlington, VA: National Science Foundation.

Nelson, Richard R. (1959). "The Simple Economics of Basic Scientific Research," *Journal of Political Economy* 67: 297–306.

Nelson, Richard R. and Sidney G. Winter (1977). "In Search of Useful Theory of Innovation," *Research Policy* 6: 36–76.

Niclaou, Nicos and Sue Birley (2003). "Social Networks in Organizational Emergence: The University Spinout Phenomenon," *Management Science* 49:1702–1725.

Oakerson, Ronald J. and Roger B. Parks (1988). "Citizen Voice and Public Entrepreneurship: The Organizational Dynamic of a Complex Metropolitan County," *Publius: The Journal of Federalism* 18: 91–112.

O'Connor, Alan, Brent Rowe, Michael Gallaher, Joel Sevinsky, and Dallas Wood (2007). *Economic Impact of ATP's Contributions to DNA Diagnostics Technologies*, Gaithersburg, MD: National Institute of Standards and Technology.

Office of Technology Policy (1996a). *Effective Partnering: A Report to Congress on Federal Technology Partnerships*, Washington, DC: U.S. Department of Commerce.

Office of Technology Assessment (1996b). "The Effectiveness of Research and Experimentation Tax Credits," Washington, DC: U.S. Congress, Office of Technology Assessment.

Organisation for Economic Co-operation and Development, (OECD, 2010). *R&D Tax Incentives and Government Foregone Tax Revenue: A Cross-Country Comparison*, Paris: OECD.

Osborne, David and Ted Gaebler (1992). *Reinventing Government: How the Entrepreneurial Spirit is Transforming the Public Sector*, New York: Addison-Wesley.

Ostrom, Elinor (1964). "Public Entrepreneurship: A Case Study in Ground Water Basin Management," University of California, Los Angeles, CA, (unpublished Ph.D. dissertation).

Ostrom, Elinor (2005). "Unlocking Public Entrepreneurship and Public Economies," Working Paper DP2005/01, World Institute for Development Economic Research (UNU-WIDER).

Owen-Smith, Jason and Walter W. Powell (2001). "To Patent or Not: Faculty Decisions and Institutional Success at Technology Transfer," *Journal of Technology Transfer* 26: 99–114.

Owen-Smith, Jason and Walter W. Powell (2003). "The Expanding Role of University Patenting in the Life Sciences: Assessing the Importance of Experience and Connectivity," *Research Policy* 32: 1695–1711.

Padt, Frans J. G. and Albert E. Luloff (2011). "A Critical Review of a Managerial Approach to 'Green' Community Planning in the Rural USA and the Netherlands," *Journal of Environmental Planning and Management* 54: 445–56.

Papadakis, Maria and Albert N. Link (1997). "Measuring the *Unmeasurable*: Cost-Benefit Analysis for New Business Start-ups and Scientific Research Transfers," *Evaluation and Program Planning* 20: 91–102.

Papandreou, Andreas G. (1943). "The Location and Scope of the Entrepreneurial Function." Ph.D. thesis. Harvard University.

Pavitt, Keith (1998). "The Social Shaping of the National Science Base," *Research Policy* 27: 793–305.

Pisano, Gary (1991). "The Governance of Innovation: Vertical Integration and Collaborative Arrangements in the Biotechnology Industry," *Research Policy* 20: 237–249.

Powell, Walter W., Kenneth W. Koput, and Laurel Smith-Doerr (1996). "Inter-organizational Collaboration and the Locus of Innovation: Networks of Learning in Biotechnology," *Administrative Science Quarterly* 41: 116–45

President's Council of Advisors on Science and Technology (PCAST) (2011). *Ensuring American Leadership in Advanced Manufacturing*, Washington, DC: Office of Technology Policy.

President's Council of Advisors on Science and Technology (PCAST) (2012). *Capturing Domestic Advantage in Advanced Manufacturing*, Washington, DC: Office of Technology Policy.

Ramamurti, Ravi (1986). "Public Entrepreneurs: Who They Are and How They Operate," *California Management Review* 28: 142–158.

Rasmussen, Einar and Roger Sørheim (2012). "How Governments Seek to Bridge the Financing Gap for University Spin-Offs: Proof-of-Concept, Pre-Seed, and Seed Funding," *Technology Analysis and Strategic Management* 24: 663–678.

Roberts, Nancy C. (1992). "Public Entrepreneurship and Innovation," *Policy Studies Review* 11: 55–74.

Roberts, Nancy C. (1999). "Innovation by Legislative, Judicial, and Management Design: Three Arenas of Public Entrepreneurship," in *Public Management Reform and Innovation: Research, Theory, and Application*, edited by H. G. Frederickson and J. M. Johnston. Tuscaloosa, AL: University of Alabama Press, pp. 89–109.

Rosenberg, Nathan and Richard R. Nelson (1994). "American Universities and Technical Advance in Industry," *Research Policy* 23: 323–348.

Sadler, Robert J. (2000). "Corporate Entrepreneurship in the Public Sector: The Dance of the Chameleon," *Australian Journal of Public Administration* 59: 25–43.

Sahni, Nikhil R., Maxwell Wessel, and Clayton M. Christensen (2013). "Unleashing Breakthrough Innovation in Government," *Stanford Social Innovation Review* Summer: 27–31.

Samuelson, Paul A. (1954). "The Pure Theory of Public Expenditure," *Review of Economics and Statistics* 36: 387–389.

Schacht, Wendy H. (2009a). "The Bayh-Dole Act: Selected Issues in Patent Policy and the Commercialization of Technology," Washington, DC: Congressional Research Service.

Schacht, Wendy H. (2009b). "Technology Transfer: Use of Federally Funded Research and Development," Washington, DC: Congressional Research Service.

Schneider, Mark and Paul Teske (1992). "Toward a Theory of the Political Entrepreneur: Evidence from Local Government," *American Political Science Review* 86: 737–747.

Schneider, Mark, Paul Teske, and Michael Mintrom (1995). *Public Entrepreneurs: Agents for Change in American Government*, Princeton, NJ: Princeton University Press.

Schnellenbach, Jan (2007). "Public Entrepreneurship and the Economics of Reform," *Journal of Institutional Economics* 3: 183–202.

Schumpeter, Joseph A. (1928). "The Instability of Capitalism," *Economic Journal* 38: 361–386.

Schumpeter, Joseph A. (1934). *The Theory of Economic Development*, translated by R. Opie from the 2nd German edition [1926], Cambridge: Harvard University Press.

Schumpeter, Joseph A. (1939). *Business Cycles*, New York: McGraw-Hill.

Schumpeter, Joseph A. (1950). *Capitalism, Socialism and Democracy*, 3rd edition New York: Harper and Row.

Shackle, G. L. S. (1979). *Imagination and the Nature of Choice*. Edinburgh: Edinburgh University Press.

Shalley, Christina E. and Jill E. Perry-Smith (2008). "The Emergence of Team Creative Cognition: The Role of Diverse Outside Ties, Sociocognitive Network Centrality, and Team Evolution," *Strategic Entrepreneurship Journal* 2: 23–41.

Shane, Scott (2003). *A General Theory of Entrepreneurship: The Individual-Opportunity Nexus*. Cheltenham, UK: Edward Elgar.

Shockley, Gordon E., Roger R. Stough, Kingsely E. Haynes, and Peter M. Frank (2006). "Toward a Theory of Public Sector Entrepreneurship," *International Journal of Entrepreneurship and Innovation Management* 6: 205–223.

Siegel, Donald, David Waldman, and Albert N. Link (1999). "Assessing the Impact of Organizational Practices on the Productivity of University Technology Transfer Offices: An Exploratory Study," NBER Working Paper No. 7256.

Siegel, Robin (1979). "Why Has Productivity Slowed Down?" *Data Resources U.S. Review* 1: 59–65.

Smith, Adam ([1776] 1976), *An Inquiry into the Nature and Causes of the Wealth of Nations*, edited by A. Campbell and A. S. Skinner. Oxford: Oxford University Press.

Stevens, Ashley J. (2004). "The Enactment of Bayh-Dole," *Journal of Technology Transfer* 29: 93–99.

Stewart, Luke A., Jacek Warda, and Robert D. Atkinson (2012). "We're #27!: The United States Lags Far Behind in R&D Tax Incentive Generosity," Information Technology and Innovation Foundation report, July.

Streitfeld, David (2012). "As Boom Lures App Creators, Tough Part Is Making a Living," *New York Times* <http://www.nytimes.com/2012/11/18/business/as-boom-lures-app-creators-to ugh-part-is-making-a-living.html>.

Stuart, Toby E., Salih Zeki Ozdemir, and Waverly W. Ding (2007). "Vertical Alliance Networks: The Case of University-Biotechnology-Pharmaceutical Alliance Chains," *Research Policy* 36: 477–498.

Sullivan, Michael Ann (2010). "Establishment of Sandia National Laboratory, 1945," New Mexico Office of the State Historian, <http://www.newmexicohistory.org/filedetails. php?fileID=458>.

Tassey, Gregory (1992). *Technology Infrastructure and Competitive Position*, Norwell, MA: Kluwer Academic Publishers.

Tassey, Gregory (1997). *The Economics of R&D Policy*, Westport, CN: Quorum Books.

Tassey, Gregory (2003). "Methods for Assessing the Economic Impacts of Government R&D," NIST Planning Report #03-01, Gaithersburg, MD: National Institute of Standards and Technology.

Tassey, Gregory (2005), "Underinvestment in Public Good Technologies," *Journal of Technology Transfer* 30: 89–113.

Tassey, Gregory (2007a). "Tax Incentives for Innovation: Time to Restructure the R&E Tax Credit," *Journal of Technology Transfer* 32: 605–615.

Tassey, Gregory (2007b). *The Technology Imperative*, Northampton, MA: Edward Elgar.

Technology Administration (1990). *Emerging Technologies: A Survey of Technical and Economic Opportunities*, Washington, DC: Department of Commerce.

Terry, Larry D. (1993). "Why We Should Abandon the Misconceived Quest to Reconcile Public Entrepreneurship with Democracy: A Response to Bellone and Goerl's 'Reconciling Public Entrepreneurship and Democracy," *Public Administration Review* 53: 393–395.

The Economist (2002). "Innovation's Golden Goose," December 14, p. 3.

Thünen, Johann. H. von (1960). *The Isolated State in Relation to Agriculture and Political Economy*, vol. 2, translated by B. W. Dempsey, Chicago: Loyola University Press.

Ullrich, Rebecca (1999). "A History of Building 828, Sandia National Laboratories," Albuquerque: Sandia Report SAND99-1941.

U.S. Department of Justice (1980). *Antitrust Guide Concerning Research Joint Ventures*, Washington, DC: Department of Justice.

U. S. Constitution. art. I, §8, cl. 8.

van Atta, Richard and Marko M.G. Slusarczuk (2012). "The Tunnel at the End of the Light: The Future of the U.S. Semiconductor Industry," *ISSUES in Science and Technology* Spring: 53–60.

van de Ven, Andrew H. (1993). "A Community Perspective on the Emergence of Innovations," *Journal of Engineering Technology Management* 10: 23–51.

Wagner, Richard E. (1966). "Pressure Groups and Political Entrepreneurs: A Review Article," *Public Choice* 1: 161–170.

Walterscheid, Edward C. (1990). "The Need for a Uniform Government Patent Policy: The DOE Example," *Harvard Journal of Law and Technology* 3: 103–166.

Ward, Thomas B., Steven M. Smith, and Ronald A. Finke (1999). "Creative Cognition," in *Handbook of Creativity*, edited by J. Sternberg. New York: Cambridge University Press, pp. 189–212.

Weber, Max ([1904–1905] 1930). *The Protestant Ethic and the Spirit of Capitalism*, translated by T. Parsons, New York: Scribner's.

Welter, Friederike (2011) Contextualizing Entrepreneurship: Conceptual Challenges and Ways Forward. *Entrepreneurship Theory and Practice*, 35: 165–178.

Westwick, Peter J. (2003). *The National Labs: Science in an American System, 1947-1974*, Cambridge, MA: Harvard University Press.

Wright, Christopher O.B. (1986). "The National Cooperative Research Act of 1984: A New Antitrust Regime for Joint Research and Development Ventures," *High Technology Law Journal* 1: 134–193.

Zahra, Shaker A. and Mike Wright (2011). "Entrepreneurship's Next Act," *Academy of Management Perspectives* 25: 67–83.

Zampetakis, L. A., and Moustakis, V. S. (2010). "An Exploratory Research on the Factors Stimulating Corporate Entrepreneurship in the Greek Public Sector." *International Journal of Manpower.* 31(8), 871–887. DOI: 10.1108/01437721011088557

Zeckhauser, Richard (1996). "The Challenge of Contracting for Technological Information," *Proceedings of the National Academy of Science* 93: 12,743–12,748.

Zerbinati, Stefania and Vangelis Souitaris (2005). "Entrepreneurship in the Public Sector: A Framework of Analysis in European Local Governments," *Entrepreneurship and Regional Development: An International Journal* 17: 43–64. DOI:10.1080/0898562042000310723

Zrinyi, Joseph (1962). "Entrepreneurial Behavior in Economic Theory: An Historical and Analytical Approach," Ph.D. dissertation, Georgetown University.

Zucker, Lynne G., Michael Darby, and Jeff Armstrong (1994). "Intellectual Capital and the Firm: The Technology of Geographically Localized Knowledge Spillovers," NBER Working Paper No. 4946.

Zucker, Lynne G. and Michael R. Darby (2001). "Capturing Technological Opportunity via Japan's Star Scientists: Evidence from Japanese Firms' Biotech Patents and Products," *Journal of Technology Transfer* 26: 37–58.

INDEX

Page numbers followed by *f* or *t* indicate figures or tables, respectively. Numbers followed by n indicate notes.

Public Law 106-554. *see* Small Business
Reauthorization Act of 2000
Public Law 108-237. *see* Standards
Development Organization Advancement
Act (SDOAA) of 2004
Public Law 108-311. *see* Working Families
Tax Relief Act of 2004
Public Law 109-58. *see* Energy Policy Act of
2005
Public Law 109-432. *see* Tax Relief and
Health Care Act of 2006
Public Law 110-10, 143
Public Law 110-69. *see* America COMPETES
Act of 2007; America Creating
Opportunities to Meaningfully Promote
Excellence in Technology, Education, and
Science (COMPETES) Act of 2007
Public Law 110-235, 143
Public Law 110-343. *see* Emergency
Economic Stabilization Act of 2008
Public Law 111-312. *see* Tax Relief
Unemployment Compensation
Reauthorization, and Job Creation Act of
2010
Public Law 111-358. *see* America COMPETES
Reauthorization Act of 2010
Public Law 112-81. *see* National Defense
Authorization Act of 2012
Public Law 112-240. *see* American Taxpayer
Relief Act of 2012
public policy, 52–53; economic growth
policy, 21–24; Energy Policy Act of 2005
(Public Law 109-58), 132*t*; examples,
75–190; historical background, 193–201;
innovation policy, 3, 65*t*, 66, 196*t*–200*t*,
201, 203, 204*t*, 213n16; technology policy,
2–3, 15, 65*t*, 66
public sector entrepreneurship, 62–71,
202; definition of, 1, 5–6, 7*t*–11*t*, 13–14,
27–71, 209n7, 213n16; as direct, 7*t*–11*t*,
12; economic objective, 16; as indirect,
7*t*–11*t*, 12–13; intellectual history of,
3–13, 7*t*–11*t*; as never-ending, 122–126;
perspective of, 193–207; policies that
represent, 203, 204*t*; policy examples,
75–190; theory of, 43–61
public spending: R&D expenditures,
122–123, 123*f*, 129, 129*f*, 218n1; R&E
expenditures, 218n1
public-private partnerships, 15–17,
16*f*–17*f*
Puget Sound Regional Council, 97*t*

QED Proof of Concept Program, 92*t*–93*t*
Quesnay, François, 4, 28*t*, 211n4

Ramamurti, Ravi, 6–12, 10*t*, 12, 231
Randazzese, Lucien, 225
Rasmussen, Einar, 215n14, 231
rates of return, expected, 145–146, 146*f*,
219n3
Ray, George F., 50, 230
R&E Tax Credit of 1981 (Economic Recovery
Tax Act, ERTA), 65*t*, 69–70, 127–139,
136*t*, 214n4, 218n2; economics of,
130–134, 133*f*; impact on technology and
innovation, 66, 66*t*; intended economic
impact of, 20*t*; legislative background,
127–130, 131*t*–132*t*; public sector
entrepreneurship characteristics of, 203,
204*t*; relationship to *Science—the Endless
Frontier* (Bush), 198*t*
Reagan, Ronald, 127, 164
recession (2008-2009), 18
Rees, Daniel I., 169, 174*t*, 175, 225
Rees, John, 228
Renault, Marie, 229
research. *see also* cooperative
research: applied, 157, 218n6; basic, 157,
218n6; definition of, 156–157
research and development (R&D), 157, 171,
206–207. *see also* cooperative research and
development (cooperative R&D); expenditures on, 122–123, 123*f*, 129, 129*f*, 218n1;
tax credits, 134, 135*t*
research and experimentation (R&E),
127–128; expenditures, 218n1; tax credits, 134, 135*t*, 137–139
research collaborations: examples, 161–165;
university-industry partnerships,
168–181, 173*t*, 174*t*
research joint ventures (RJVs), 154–155,
159–160, 164–165, 181; *Antitrust Guide
Concerning Research Joint Ventures* (U.S.
Department of Justice), 152–153; High
Technology Research and Development
Joint Ventures Act of 1983 (H. R. 3393),
64–65, 153; membership sizes, 165, 167*t*;
trends and patterns, 165, 166*f*, 167*t*; university participation in, 171, 174*t*
Research Triangle Committee, Inc., 57–58,
60
Research Triangle Development Committee,
57
Research Triangle Foundation, 60
Research Triangle Institute, 60
Research Triangle Park (North Carolina), 53,
55*f*, 221n21; case study, 54–61; development of, 58, 213n23; fundraising for, 58,
59*f*, 60
resource constraints, 49–50